POLISH WAR VETERANS IN ALBERTA

POLISH WAR VETERANS IN ALBERTA

The Last Four Stories

Aldona Jaworska

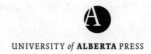

UNIVERSITY *of* **ALBERTA** PRESS

Published by
THE UNIVERSITY OF ALBERTA PRESS
Ring House 2
Edmonton, Alberta, Canada T6G 2E1
www.uap.ualberta.ca

LIBRARY AND ARCHIVES CANADA CATALOGUING IN PUBLICATION

Jaworska, Aldona, author
    Polish war veterans in Alberta : the last four stories / Aldona Jaworska.

Includes bibliographical references and index.
Issued in print and electronic formats.
ISBN 978-1-77212-373-9 (softcover). —ISBN 978-1-77212-430-9 (EPUB).
ISBN 978-1-77212-431-6 (Kindle). —ISBN 978-1-77212-432-3 (PDF)

    1. Polish people—Alberta—History—20th century. 2. Veterans—Alberta—
History—20th century. 3. Polish people—Alberta—Social conditions—20th century.
4. Veterans—Alberta—Social conditions—20th century. 5. Polish people—Alberta—
Social life and customs—20th century. 6. Veterans—Alberta—Social life and
customs—20th century. 7. Immigrants—Alberta. I. Title.

FC3700.P7J39 2018   971.3'0049185   C2018-904108-0
                                              C2018-904109-9

First edition, first printing, 2019.
First printed and bound in Canada by Houghton Boston Printers, Saskatoon, Saskatchewan.
Copyediting by Joan Dixon.
Proofreading by Meaghan Craven.
Indexing by Stephen Ullstrom.

University of Alberta Press is committed to protecting our natural environment. As part of our
efforts, this book is printed on Enviro Paper: it contains 100% post-consumer recycled fibres and is
acid- and chlorine-free.

University of Alberta Press gratefully acknowledges the support received for its publishing
program from the Government of Canada, the Canada Council for the Arts, and the Government
of Alberta through the Alberta Media Fund.

Canadä

Contents

Preface

MY INTEREST IN THE STORIES of Polish World War II veterans
living in Calgary started when I organized an exhibit commemorating the sixty-fifth anniversary of the formation of the Polish
Combatants' Association in Canada, Branch No. 18.[1] This Calgary
branch was formed on November 11, 1947, by Polish Army Corps
ex-servicemen[2] who moved to the city after completing their two-
year labour contracts on Alberta farms. The Canadian chapter had
been formed on October 3, 1946 by II Polish Army Corps soldiers
then stationed in the Falconara camp in Italy before their departure
to Canada.

The exhibit featuring their stories took place on December 4,
2011, in the Polish Canadian Cultural Centre and was open to
the members of the Polish Combatants' Association, guests of the
Polish Canadian Cultural Centre, and the public. For the first time,
the stories of combatants—II Polish Army Corps veterans among
them—were presented in English, allowing a wider community to
learn about their experiences. All interviews with the combatants

had been conducted in Polish, and that gave me (fluent in Polish and English) unique access.[3]

The exhibit was inspired by an interview I conducted on October 5, 2011, with Władysław Niewiński, a ninety-three-year-old II Polish Army Corps combatant who fought in the 1944 Battle of Monte Cassino, during which he was wounded twice. When I learned that he came to Canada as part of the Polish Resettlement Corps to work on a farm, I asked why he had chosen to immigrate to Canada after the war.

"Before the war, when I was still in Poland, I saw sacks filled with high-quality wheat flour. These bags had stamps indicating that they came from Canada," Niewiński said with nostalgia, and as if by way of explanation.

Niewiński went on to talk about the challenges of his life as a detainee in the Soviet Gulag, his experience as a soldier in the Anders Army (II Polish Army Corps), as well as his involvement in building the Polish community in Calgary. He talked in detail about a close-knit group of Polish veterans and combatants actively involved in the work of the association from the time of its inception. After hearing Niewiński's story, I decided to look for other veterans, learn about their experiences, and create an exhibit to share their stories with the larger community. Information about this project was shared on the association's website, in the Polish church's weekly bulletin, during the Polish weekly television program in Calgary, and in a short promotional video clip on the Polish gossip website, *Ploty*. The Polish community responded with enthusiasm and interest. However, the challenge was that not many World War II (WWII) Polish veterans were still able to share their stories. I heard comments such as, "This project should have been done decades ago. Now, almost all WWII Polish veterans have died."

However, not discouraged, I kept looking for Polish war veterans living in Calgary and willing to share their stories. I found four such veterans, or members of their family, to participate. During the research phase, I had a unique opportunity to access artifacts from the time of war that the Polish veterans had in their possession. I saw pieces of a liturgical garment found in the obliterated monastery of Monte Cassino after the famous battle. I touched military uniforms worn by II Polish Army Corps soldiers in combat on the Italian Front. I was offered views of original military documents, personal military artifacts, pamphlets printed in Great Britain for Anders Army soldiers, and medals awarded for service and sacrifices. I also was given access to photographs, some of them taken while serving during the war. Examining these artifacts of historical significance also had a significant impact on me. I am a descendant of the postwar generation, and had first-hand experience living behind the Iron Curtain. I was educated in the postwar Polish People's Republic governed by a pro-Soviet government.[4] I came to Canada as a refugee in 1990, having left Poland in 1988. Years later, I graduated from the University of Calgary with a Bachelor of Arts in Canadian Studies and a Master's of Arts in Communication and Culture. Despite the generation gap separating me from the veterans who I met and interviewed, as well as the different, polarized political systems in which we were born, raised and educated, being born a Pole created a connection that allowed me to research and create this project. I feel indebted to the Polish ex-servicemen/veterans/combatants who shared their stories with me.

While conducting the interviews, I observed how the events of war influenced not only the lives of the WWII Polish veterans who immigrated to Canada, and their families, but also how they had long-lasting, inter- and multi-generational implications that could still be felt by the members of the Polish community in Calgary. While researching the events surrounding the men's stories, I was also able to analyze how the media of the time portrayed the veterans and the circumstances that led them to Canada, and how that reporting helped shape their identity in their new home. The urgency of this work lies in the fact that many of these veterans have passed away and few are still alive who can share their stories. I believe it is important to collect and research war veterans' first-hand accounts to preserve their stories for future generations. Our experiences become part of our personal and collective heritage, and we have to explore and maintain our relationship with the past to move forward.

Acknowledgements

THIS BOOK IS DEDICATED to all the Polish combatants who
served in the II Polish Army Corps and came to Alberta to work on
farms as part of the 1947 Polish Resettlement Act.

My grateful thanks are extended to the interview participants
for graciously sharing their life stories with me. I am truly privileged
to have had the opportunity to hear the stories of individuals who
participated in significant world events, such as the Battle for Monte
Cassino that took place over seventy years ago, January 17, 1944–
May 18, 1944.

I would like to thank Professor George Melnyk for his encouragement and support, invaluable in creating this book, and my entire
family in Canada and in Europe (in particular my husband Wiesław
Jaworski, and my children, Adam Jaworski, Michał Jaworski and
Natalia Jaworska for their unwavering encouragement).

I

POLISH
WORLD WAR II
VETERANS

1

From Citizens to Prisoners

WORLD WAR II BEGAN WHEN the German battleship *Schleswig-Holstein* attacked a Polish ammunition depot located on the territory of the Free City of Danzig on September 1, 1939.[1] The shots fired from the battleship were a signal for the other German armed forces to start a military assault on Poland. The attacks came from the air, land and sea, and via northern, western, and southern borders that Germany shared with Poland. After taking over the Polish borders, on their way to the capital city of Warsaw in central Poland, Nazi armies synchronized their military attacks not only on significant Polish military and industrial centres but also on large concentrations of the civilian population. The Third German Army moved toward Warsaw from the south, after taking several major cities on its way. The Fourth German Army, after attacking the Polish corridor leading to the Free City of Danzig, also proceeded toward Warsaw. Another German army (Group South) crossed the Polish–German southwestern border, while a Slovakian military unit crossed the nearby Polish–Slovakian border in support of the

German aggressors. The Eighth German Army proceeded toward Łódź, a major industrial city.

The German armies were not only much larger and better prepared than the Polish armed forces, with double Poland's 950,000 troops, they were also armed with more advanced military equipment. Ultimately, the German armies swiftly crushed the troops trying to defend not only Poland's borders but its entire territory. After the attacks by German forces, lasting from September 8 to 27, 1939, Warsaw was no longer able to defend itself.

The second extensive military assault on Poland started on September 17, 1939, when the Soviet Union's Red Army invaded Poland from the east and annexed its eastern territory. After undergoing several weeks of intense military operations repelling the massive German attacks from the north, west and south, as well as the Red Army's unexpected attacks from the east, Poland could no longer defend its territory. And Poland's hopes for military assistance had not materialized.[2]

The news of the military aggression in Europe reached Canada immediately on September 1. The fast-developing events required that at least one Canadian paper, the *Montreal Gazette,* print a second *Extra* that announced in a front-page banner: "Reich Invades Poland, Warsaw Raided: Gdynia Blockaded; Free City Annexed; France Decrees General Mobilization." The news report from London was headlined, "U.K. House Called; War on Vast Front," and provided details on the extent of the German offensive, including the names of Polish cities raided by the German air force. The reaction of Great Britain to the events was considered serious enough that the "Privy Council was summoned by the King to meet."

On September 1, 1939, German Chancellor Adolf Hitler's speech in the Reichstag was broadcast by radio all over the world. The *Montreal Gazette* included a summary of Hitler's territorial grievances toward Poland, claiming that Danzig (Gdańsk) was a German city, as was the corridor leading to it from Germany. He claimed that the area had been separated from Germany based on "the 1918 Versailles Diktat" of the previous war and that these "territories owe their cultural development exclusively to the German people." Hitler declared that Germany had exhausted the peaceful methods of settling the territorial revisions since Poland had rejected all of his proposals. Hitler argued that German minorities living in Danzig had suffered for a long time because of the territorial dispute.

The *Montreal Gazette* printed Hitler's declaration to the German people, that he would take "Danzig and Pomorze and halt Polish attacks on Germans or die fighting," and his message, "I am putting on the uniform, and I shall take it off only in victory or death." Even though Hitler never declared war explicitly, he confirmed the German army's aggression on Poland but also alluded to Polish "attacks," falsely claiming that "this night for the first time Polish regular soldiers fired on our territory." As a result, he said, he gave orders to his army to use "force against force."

As for the world's reaction to this military aggression, the *Gazette* informed readers of the news as sourced from London: "Britain Mobilizes Fleet, All Army Reserve Called to the Colours." The *Gazette* also reprinted a special cable from Moscow sent to *The New York Times* that said ominously, "Soviets Ratify Tie with Reich." The news from Berlin in the same newspaper documented the ferocity and fast pace of the attack on Poland as it announced that Hitler declared the Free City of Danzig part of the Reich, turning his threats into fact.

The ripples of the swiftly progressing military conflict in Europe caused by German aggression toward Poland were inevitably felt in Canada and reflected in newspaper articles as Canadians took special note of the reaction of the mother country, Great Britain. The build-up of tension also showed its economic impact in Canadian news, with a report from the Winnipeg Grain Exchange about the price of wheat both sliding and rising on the same day, illustrating the market's reaction to the uncertain situation in Europe. In addition, the *Montreal Gazette* reported that an armed policeman was monitoring the water intake facilities on the St. Lawrence River. News articles like this one brought the sense of insecurity closer to home, hinting at the possibility of war on Canadian soil.

The *Montreal Gazette* also reported on seventy bomber planes being built in the United States (US) for Britain and France, alluding to a military preparedness and perhaps bolstering a feeling of control. Due to the supposed secrecy, however, the newspaper could not reveal technical details of those planes and instead offered specifics on the numbers, the scheduled shipment dates and the names of the ships carrying those planes to Europe. In the early days of the war, the media had apparently not yet grasped that German U-boats and bombers were targeting the trans-Atlantic ships bringing military supplies to Europe.

The impact of the developing war was spreading beyond Europe and the Americas, as indicated in the news from Cairo reporting that the remains of King Tutankhamen had been packed and hidden in bombproof underground storage because of destruction threatened by the military aggression.

The *Montreal Gazette's* reports about the war seemed to refer mostly to the global and economic influences of this fast-moving military conflict and to the level of military preparedness of countries that might get involved (including Canada, then still considered a dominion of Great Britain).

In contrast, in Alberta, *The Calgary Herald's* coverage of the war in Poland was much more localized in approach. The front page reported how Calgary's population reacted to the war. And when reporting on the events in Europe, unlike Montreal's *Gazette* or Ottawa's *Citizen,* Calgary's *Herald* relied to a large extent on news sources from Berlin and later from Moscow, and to a lesser extent on the news from London.

On September 1, *The Calgary Herald* printed a large headline across its front page, sourced to Warsaw: "Nazis Bomb Warsaw Child Asylum; Britain and France Send Ultimatum; Canada Mobilises to Help Britain." The first line on the front page reported that "A large hospital for feeble-minded Jewish children was said to have been hit by the German air raiders." Thus, the first and predominant news of Germany's aggression on Poland brought to Calgary readers was focused on the welfare of vulnerable children, which naturally evoked emotions and sensationalized war events. The political news appears in smaller print among a series of articles on the front page:

> Poland's president, Ignace Mozciki [sic], proclaimed a state of war after Nazis bombed Warsaw and other Polish cities, and troops smashed across the border. He reiterated, however, that a state of war did not mean a declaration of war.[3]

This distinction might have caused confusion for some Canadian newsreaders. The German army's attack had been swift and relentless while Great Britain and France were sending only diplomatic warnings demanding the withdrawal of German troops. Hitler's actions had clearly disregarded international laws. He had not informed neutral powers about waging war and firing on the 209 Polish defenders of the garrison near Danzig. The German battleship had supposedly been on a courtesy visit before it launched the first shot that started the war. But these international laws and agreements, The Hague Conventions, were not mentioned in the newspaper.

Instead, the *Herald* reported how air sirens had been heard in Berlin, indicating a possible Polish air force bombing, only to finish with a comment that the alarm had simply been a rehearsal. Through its reporting on this important event, the newspaper chose a speculative approach, which either created or added to Calgary readers' misunderstanding of the complicated situation overseas. Perhaps its distance from the major urban centres in Canada and Europe had an impact on how *The Calgary Herald* received and formulated the news it printed, but the choice of sources that this newspaper relied on also inevitably shaped the way its news was expressed and delivered to readers. When sourced to Canadian Press (CP) in Ottawa or London, the news came with a disclaimer that it had been passed by a British censor and therefore could be expected to be more informative and accurate, in comparison with news of unverified origins.

The *Herald* reported first on the tension in Calgary caused by the military aggression in Europe. One of the newsboys delivering the newspapers and extras in the early morning hours on September 1 said that "he had never seen so many women in tears." This localized approach again exploited emotions rather than delivering useful news. The newspaper's *Extra,* published later that day, offered in large headlines, "Germany Launches War Against Poles" and "Bombs Dropped on Warsaw; First Casualties Reported." The article pointed out that the German attack on Poland "began shortly after midnight, Calgary time," putting the events of Europe into the readers' timeframe and perspective. While the newspaper did bring the news closer to its readers in this way, it also emphasized the physical distance between Poland and Calgary. Telegraphs and telephones were required to send information overseas, and delays caused by the time difference demonstrated how far removed Calgary was from the events in Europe.

Yet the fear of Hitler's aggression was growing. A headline on page two announced the dictatorial power with which Hitler might strike and govern: "Defence Council Gives Hitler Power for Instant

Action." This was followed by several editorials on the same page discussing the force of the aggressor and highlighting the gravity of the situation and how such power could be reinforced. Furthermore, the headline, "Evacuation of London, Other Key Cities Ordered," sounded an alarm to indicate that even places located far away from the war events in Poland could be affected and highlighted the uncertainty the war might bring to the world.

The aggression inflicted by the German armies on Poland was only the beginning of problems for this already severely battered country. A couple of weeks later, it again led the war news, but this time the newspapers reported on the Soviet invasion of Poland. The headline in the September 18, 1939, edition of the *Montreal Gazette* read: "Red Invaders Strike Deep into Poland; Polish Resistance to Germans Crumbles as Army, Government Flee to Romania." The reports from Moscow brought news of the Soviet army crossing the five-hundred-mile long Polish border fifty miles into Poland's territory, positioning itself just forty-eight miles away from the German army. "Soviet Russia's great Red Army marching on orders to 'liberate' their 'brothers' in Poland, moved to that embattled country today along the entire frontier, from Latvia to Romania." Only with quotation marks indicating irony, did the newspaper express its doubts about the USSR showing good faith toward Poland. It suggested instead that the Soviet Union, following in the footsteps of Hitler who had claimed German minorities in Poland were being mistreated, had jumped into the country's partitioning, claiming the mistreatment of eleven million Ukrainian and White Russian minorities living in Poland. The Montreal newspaper stated that the Polish troops fought fiercely against the Soviet invasion, but also that the Red Army crossed Poland's border in some places without facing resistance (which merely illustrated the fragmented or dismantled Polish defence system). By attacking Poland under the pretext of defending minorities without declaring war, the Soviet

Union also disregarded international laws agreed upon at the Hague Conventions.

Furthermore, the *Gazette* reported that Foreign Affairs Minister Vyacheslav Molotov's reason for invading Poland was to implement preventive measures because "Poland has become a fertile field for any accidental and unexpected contingency which may create a menace to the Soviet Union." Molotov's explanation contradicted or muddled the initial claim of protecting the Ukrainian and White Russian minorities in Poland. Moreover, the newspaper reported that the Red Army received assistance from the German air force, which conducted air raids on the railway centre in Baranovichi, while Soviet troops marched into Poland, suggesting collaboration between the two aggressors. It also reported that the Soviet army took cities along the Polish–USSR state border, including Lwów, Tarnopol, Przemyśl, Kolomea, and Równo, illustrating how swiftly the Soviet attack on Poland was executed.

The *Montreal Gazette* also published an article about Canada's political stance, entitled "Ottawa Weighs Russian Move." Although King George VI had issued a proclamation of war against Germany, Canada entered the war only after the proclamation was adopted by the Canadian Parliament. "Canada entered the war on the side of Great Britain...she did so voluntarily and an exercise of her right as a free nation, and not because of any pledge." Canada was taking steps as an independent country, making its own political decisions and not just acting as a dominion of the British Empire. The article stressed that Prime Minister Mackenzie King and his colleagues were monitoring the European situation caused by the Soviet invasion of Poland and were considering refreshing the proclamation of war with the USSR if that country was to side with Germany. Yet, at the same time, the newspaper reported from London that the Soviet Union had declared its neutrality to Great Britain. The Soviet declaration was likely a pre-emptive move since its aggression on

Poland had not been unexpected in Europe. Examining this new, confusing German–Soviet alliance and their invasions of Poland, the British government reportedly had to carefully re-examine its strategy. Measures taken by Great Britain and Canada against the Soviet Union after its invasion of Poland could potentially differ, the *Gazette* stressed, reinforcing the fact that Canada was considering, and making, its own geopolitical decisions.

The next day, in Canada's capital, Ottawa's *Evening Citizen* brought confirmation of the Soviet invasion, stating that "Russian Army Continues Swift Drive across Poland." The news from Romania illustrated the desperate situation with "Battered Remnants of Retreating Polish Army Barely Able to Escape," and the paper informed readers that the president of Poland, Ignacy Mościcki, and the members of the government had fled to Romania.

The unfortunate predicament of Poland was ominously pre-dicted by the newspapers even before Warsaw had capitulated. *The Evening Citizen* offered an analysis of why Poland's defence failed so fast under the pressure of the German invasion: the advancement of the German military technology used in the sudden assault; the strength of the German intelligence system that detected the where-abouts of the key Polish political figures; and subsequent, precise air assaults at their positions. Weather conditions had supposedly helped too. The article pointed to the inefficiency and failure of the Polish communication system that prevented the Polish army of one and a half million soldiers from communicating with their com-mand centres and defending their territory. The German air attacks that targeted Polish military equipment were impossible for the Polish army to deal with and that added to the "Impossible Task" of defending Poland. Finally, the paper reported, "Warsaw is still fighting gallantly, and individual armies scattered over Poland are making heroic stands. But Poland has lost the war." By describing the futile effort of the Polish army to defend their homeland from the massive German attacks, the newspaper report also built up fear of what might happen next in a destabilized Europe. With the possibility of Hitler taking total control of the territory of central Europe, giving Germany access to vast resources, the article predicted an enormous challenge for the British Empire and France, and conveyed fears that these two countries would face German attacks from the air.

On the same day the capitulation of Warsaw took place, September 28, 1939, representatives of Germany and the Soviet Union, Joachim von Ribbentrop and Vyacheslav Molotov, discussed the German–Soviet Boundary and Friendship Treaty that was to take effect immediately. The two sides agreed ("after the collapse of the former Polish state" and "to re-establish peace and order in these territories") on the location of the new German–Soviet border on the territory of Poland, even though battles defending Poland were still taking place in some areas. The new border was crafted along the Pisa, Narew, Sun, and Bug Rivers, dividing the entire territory of Poland between Germany and the Soviet Union. This partition was based on a plan that had been amended as a secret clause to the original Molotov–Ribbentrop Pact of non-aggression the month previous, which divided not only Poland but all of Europe between Germany and the Soviet Union.

In the war news of September 19, *The Calgary Herald's* front-page headline was "Sub Sinks British Plane Carrier 'Courageous'," but beside this article was the news sourced via London (CP), "Russia Plans to Divide Poland with Germany." This offered a grim illustration of how the events of war were moving swiftly through the far ends of Europe, extending beyond the territory of Poland, and targeting Great Britain's ships on patrol. The location of the sunk aircraft carrier was not disclosed, possibly to avoid alarming the public about enemy submarines in the so-called Western Approaches southwest of Ireland. The news instead reported on how, although 519 men lost their lives, the brave survivors were in the water for more than an hour singing and cheering, demonstrating their unwavering heroism.

On the same front page, the Calgary newspaper cited a joint communiqué from Moscow and Berlin in "Two Invading Forces Meet, Soviet Policy Still Neutral Toward Britain and France" as providing the reason for the Soviet invasion of Poland: "The mission of the troops is to bring order and peace to Poland," and added that the armistice might soon take place "as soon as Poland's fate is determined." Furthermore, the newspaper quoted a communiqué from Berlin: "The Nazi swastika and the Bolshevik hammer and sickle met today in the fallen Polish city of Brest-Litovsk, where Russian revolutionists and Germans signed their separate peace in the last war. Russian and German leaders shook hands, it was said." It added that "the Russian occupation was being carried out by 2,000,000 Red Army troops." The article took substantive space, was placed on the left side of the page, and spanned two pages, thus drawing the primary attention of a reader. However, it delivered the news from war-battered Poland in such an unclear and confusing manner that readers would potentially not grasp whether the German and Soviet leaders were meeting in person in Brest-Litovsk or whether it was referring to their meeting decades ago during World War I. Only later was it announced that the German and the Soviet armies had been sixty-eight miles from each other.

Besides this extensive article sourced to Moscow and Berlin, there was a square inch and a few lines of communiqué from the British government in London under the headline, "'Lightning War' Against Poland Seen Near End. Cavalry Endlessly Machine-Gunned From Air. Government Collapse." It stated that the attack "upon Poland could not be justified by the arguments put forward by the Soviet government" and expressed disapproval of the military aggression. However, the difference in size between these two

articles and their placement most likely favoured the news from
Moscow and Berlin for influencing readers' opinion on the situation
in Europe.

By publishing the news of Poland's invasion on its front page,
referring to the sources from Moscow and Berlin, and putting the
news from Great Britain further along in the newspaper, the *Herald*
potentially skewed the perception of the events for its audience.
Undoubtedly, what was happening in Europe was being followed
closely by readers of *The Calgary Herald*, evidenced by paperboys
distributing *Extras*. At that time, besides the radio, newspapers
were the only other source of information available to the public. Therefore it was certainly possible for the newspaper to create
an unclear and biased interpretation of the events and a prejudicial discourse that could be carried into the later years of war and
aftermath.

Still on September 18, but well back on page three of *The
Calgary Herald*, an article sourced to London (CP) and headlined
"British Press Calls Soviet Move 'Betrayal' of Poland," stated that
the British government was "[more] than ever determined to fight
Germany to a finish despite the new situation created by Soviet
Russia's invasion of Poland." The later placement of the article
criticizing the Soviet Union's attack on Poland indicated less
importance, and that, too, could have indirectly influenced read-
ers' opinion. Additionally, when *The Calgary Herald* referred to the
"British Press," not to the British government's reaction, it possibly
splintered the public's perception of the war news. The headline,
"Further Aid for Germany Thought Likely to Follow: The Balkan
States Threatened," was ambiguous, suggesting that Germany
might receive help, making it look more like a victim than an aggressor. In the article that followed, *The Calgary Herald* quoted United
Press sources from several locations in the world, stating ambiguously, "German casualties in Poland to date total 100,000 killed and

wounded." Were these casualties of the Polish population or of the invading German armies? Similarly the choice of words and the use of quotation marks when reporting that a German submarine was "accidentally" captured a few yards from a British destroyer not only illustrated how the war events were unfolding beyond Poland, but also how the newspaper was favouring sources that were more sympathetic toward the Germans and the Soviets.

In contrast, other Canadian newspapers such as the *Montreal Gazette* and Ottawa's *Evening Citizen* reported on the events of war using in many instances the Associated Press sources from London, New York, or Paris, and with a more factual tone, thus avoiding the ambiguity and sensationalization of the news from the war front.

By comparison, it was not uncommon to see in *The Calgary Herald* a vague headline and one even contradictory to the content of the article, such as the presentation of the German aggressor as possible victim not warmonger. As one of the very few sources of information available to Calgarians, *The Calgary Herald* was shaping the perception its readers were building about the war by muddling and confusing their readers' understanding of the events overseas and consequently their opinion about Poles and how they had or had not defended their country. There were no stories about Polish soldiers defending their country from two aggressors, no information on the casualties and no explanation for why presenting such information was not possible, such as the severity of the attacks. All these elements contributed to presenting the news in a blurred and obfuscated way, projecting an unclear if not incorrect picture of the war in Europe to readers. Access to the daily news was important, especially at the outbreak of war. The way *The Calgary Herald* presented the news prejudicially impacted and even shaped public opinion.

2

From Prisoners to Soldiers

THE STORIES OF THE WORLD WAR II Polish veterans who came
to Alberta after the war were of course intertwined with the world
events that affected millions, but, as already shown in the analysis
of the early days coverage in the newspapers, only some of the context and not many details reached Canadians. For instance, during
the invasions of Poland, between 95,000 and 97,000[1] Polish soldiers were killed by German and Soviet armies and 130,000 were
wounded. Canadian newspapers did not report these Polish casualties, nor the immense refugee crisis that followed.

Before this war, the territory of the Second Republic of Poland
was the sixth largest country in Europe and comprised many nationalities: more than 68 per cent Poles, but also approximately 15 per
cent Ukrainians and 3 per cent each, Belarusians and Germans.[2]
The majority of Poles were Catholic but 8.5 per cent were Jewish.
Poles constituted approximately 60 per cent of the total number
of peasants, almost 80 per cent of the workers, 80 per cent of the

intelligentsia, 40 per cent of the bourgeoisie, half of the entrepreneurs, and the majority of landowners.

German military attacks affected the entire territory and population of Poland and sent hundreds of thousands of civilians in search of safer places. Escaping on foot or using all forms of transportation, they carried with them their hastily collected possessions, even their livestock. Countless lifeless bodies of children, women and men, as well as of domestic animals, lay along the major roads. German bombers and other aircraft flying low above the ground meant more terror and death to the helpless and defenceless refugees.

Anybody fleeing from the west toward the eastern part of Poland had also faced the attacks of the Red Army, which had crossed the Polish–Soviet eastern border to invade the already severely weakened country. With military assaults coming from two directions, the casualties among the retreating or repositioning Polish troops, as well as among the civilians fleeing bombarded Polish cities, towns and villages, multiplied. Soviet troops obliterated whole villages and small towns en route. This new type of warfare—aimed at the vulnerable civilian population—brought great destruction, disorientation and further loss of human life.

Inside war-torn Poland, chaos had not only resulted from the military assaults but also by the breaks in communication that contributed to improper distribution and implementation of the frequently changing military orders. Not much information was available to either the armies or to the civilians. So any news about the rapidly developing situation in Poland travelled out of the country very slowly. Several major Polish cities, such as Vilno, Tarnopol, Stanisławów, and a large part of the country, had already been overtaken by the Soviet army advancing on the eastern territory of Poland, when three days afterward, in Britain's House of Commons, Prime Minister Neville Chamberlain announced, "On the morning of 17th September Russian troops crossed the Polish frontier at points along its whole length and advanced into Poland." The Soviet offensive was not entirely unexpected, despite a non-aggression pact between the two countries that had been signed in 1932. The Soviet Union had been amassing troops along their shared border for some time. Chamberlain said that the Soviets claimed that their military action was a result of Poland's inability to defend itself and that the collapse of the government in Poland had thus created a hazard for the Soviet Union. Despite some pockets of resistance from Polish troops fighting under enormous pressure on many fronts, the whole country disintegrated quickly.

A quick evacuation of the Polish government added to the chaos. American diplomats in Europe, watching the developing situation closely, reported that, on the same day the Soviet army invaded Poland, September 17, the Polish government left by airplane via Romania, heading to France with intent to carry on all its duties. By then, Poland had been severely weakened by the German army's offensive that resulted not only in death but capture of 587,300 Polish prisoners of war (POWS) of whom 420,000 were sent to POW camps in Germany (where 10,000 died from wounds). During the Soviet invasion, the Red Army detained 452,500 Polish POWs, and sent 200,000 of them to forced labour camps in Siberia or other camps in the remote territory of the Soviet Union. (Some 120,000 Polish POWs of German nationality were later released from German captivity, and 17,420 of Ukraine and Belarus nationality released to the Soviet Union.)

Most of the first detainees were reserve officers and soldiers from the Polish armed forces mobilized by the Polish government at the beginning of the war to defend the country from Nazi military aggression on the western border and the central part of Poland. However, to protect the Polish–Soviet border from the almost simultaneous invasion of the Red Army, Polish soldiers had also been transferred to the eastern part of the country. During the Soviet offensive on Poland, thousands of Polish troops were captured in the central and eastern areas of the country and imprisoned in the transition camp in Szepietówka. Later, the war captives were moved to the Równe–Lwów camp, where the Polish POWs were forced to work on the reconstruction of the road (Nowogród Wołyński–Równe–Dubno–Lwów) to connect Ukraine with the Polish territory annexed by the Soviets. Stefan Koselak, whose story is part of this book, was one of the 22,000 Polish POWs detained in this camp after being arrested on September 25, 1939.

Many detention camps for POWs were set up in complete isolation near the Arctic Circle, where the Polish detainees worked in gold or other precious metals mines. Polish POWs suffered from severe malnutrition, worked in extremely harsh weather environments, and lived in housing so severely inadequate to shelter them from the elements that it impacted their life expectancy. The Soviets calculated that the Polish POWs would survive for one season only. Some lived there for a year or a maximum of two years.

Furthermore, young men like Władysław Niewiński, who lived in the territory of Poland annexed by the Soviet army and refused to abide by the Soviet rule, were sent to labour camps. Thousands of young men of military age were forcefully enlisted into the Red Army under the premise that they were no longer Poles but had become Soviet citizens after the 1939 annexation of Poland. Those who refused military service or Soviet citizenship were imprisoned and sent to labour camps, where the temperature dropped to –60° C during the winter. Many of them died of exhaustion, illnesses, or starvation. They lived in isolation from the external world.

Another large group of Poles forcefully relocated to remote places were civilian deportees, including Anatol Nieumierzycki, who was deported with his family to Siberia, and Zbigniew Rogowski, who was deported with his family to Kazakhstan. Soon after the Soviet attack on Poland, the Union of Soviet Socialist Republics government started deportations of the Polish population living in the eastern territory of Poland. All communities were affected by these systemic arrests. The deportees, whose names had been placed on lists prepared by the Soviet authorities in advance of the invasion,[3] belonged to all levels of society and were involved in the political, economic, social and community life in Poland. In each district, one or two hundred of the leading anti-communist members of the so-called "capitalistic groups" were executed, and the leading members of the population believed to be unsympathetic to the Soviet Union were rounded up for deportation. Among those on the lists were high- and low-ranking officers of the local police and their families, including Zbigniew Rogowski, whose father Henryk Rogowski was a police officer and arrested soon after the war started. The Rogowski family was deported in late 1939, while the father was still held in jail.

Other deportees in this group were Polish settlers who had moved to this eastern territory when the Bolshevik army moved out, after Poland regained its independence in 1918, following 123 years and three consecutive partitions of its territory between Prussian, Austrian, and Russian empires. The peace negotiations after World War I (WWI) specified an "independent Polish state should be erected which should include the territories inhabited by indisputably Polish populations, which should be assured a free and secure access to the sea, and whose political and economic independence and territorial integrity should be guaranteed by international covenant." The Second Polish Republic was thus formed, and Danzig became a Free City when Germany ratified the Treaty of Versailles.

Border conflicts between Poland and Russia had nevertheless continued after WWI. In 1919, the Bolsheviks, believing their October Revolution was the beginning of a world-wide revolution, won the civil war in Russia and began to prepare for assaults on Poland. Many military conflicts, uprisings and plebiscites took place over the access to the disputed territories involving the eastern and western borders of Poland. After the 1920 Polish–Russian war fought over the territory of Ukraine and White Russia, the 1921 Treaty of Riga stipulated the borders of Poland to include cities Vilno (Wilno, Vilnius),[4] Grodno, Novogrod (Nowogródek), Baranowicze, Brest-Litovsk (Brześć Litewski/Brześć nad Bugiem), Pinsk (Pińsk), Kovel (Kowel), Lutsk (Łuck), Rivne (Równe), Tarnopol, and Stanisławów. To prepare for these border changes, the Bolsheviks ordered an evacuation, and Poles living on Soviet territory moved in.

The territorial conflicts between Russia and Poland affecting civilians, and resulting in deportations as punishment for differing political views and affiliations, date back to the sixteenth century. The settlement of people in a different place, however, is distinct from deportation, which removes a foreigner from a country; understanding this distinction is critical to understanding the situation of the Polish people.

In the several attempts to calculate the number of Poles deported starting in 1939, sources once estimated a total as high as a million; however, after the archives opened in the Soviet Union,[5] and more recent (2009) research, the numbers were revised to 320,000. The first systemic and massive deportation that took place on February 10, 1940, involved 140,000 ethnic Poles. The majority of this group comprised families of military settlers, middle and lower civil servants, forest-service workers and railroad employees. Entire families were forcefully deported and resettled in remote locations in the Soviet Union without exception, regardless of age or physical condition. On February 10, 1940, Anatol Nieumierzycki and his family were among those deported to a no-longer-used settlement that had been built by previous deportees to Siberia several decades earlier. Many other families from his village spent several weeks in crowded cargo wagons, and many died of exhaustion, hunger and illnesses during this time.

The second wave of forced deportations by the Soviet government started on April 13, 1940, when 61,000 people were exiled to remote places in the USSR. The third phase took place in June 1940, when 79,000 Poles were deported, and the fourth major wave of deportations was conducted in June 1941, when 40,000 more Poles were deported. In total, the estimated number of the deported and resettled Poles was 320,000 (or a third of the original estimate). However, it is possible that the original number of a million included an estimated 500,000 Poles from the eastern territory of Poland who died or were killed between 1939 and 1945 and an estimated 200,000 Polish citizens of various nationalities who had also been drafted into the Soviet army (according to data revised in 1993 and 1994).

This massive deportation of the Polish population was not reported by the European or the Canadian press. The rest of the world could not know what was happening in the newly annexed territory of Poland or about the struggles faced by the many deported. The Soviet *Pravda* newspaper reported on its front page on February 11, 1940, only that all was quiet "In the Small City of Sokolke." Sokolke (Sokółka) is a town in Podlaskie Voivodeship in northeastern Poland, halfway between Białystok and Grodno. The paper does not mention the mass deportations that had taken place there the day before.

In the meantime, the global military conflict marched on, and it complicated Poland's situation. On June 22, 1941, acting on its expansionist ideology and disregarding the terms of the Molotov–Ribbentrop Pact, Nazi Germany invaded the Soviet Union. The military operation named Barbarossa took place less than two years after their signing of the non-aggression pact. As a result, the Soviet government now had to look for allies against Nazi aggression and therefore sought normalization of its relationship with Poland. On July 30, 1941, the representatives of the Soviet government and the Polish government-in-exile signed the Sikorski–Mayski Agreement in London. The signatories were General Władysław Sikorski, then prime minister of Poland and the first prime minister of the government-in-exile, and Ivan Mayski who was the Soviet ambassador to Great Britain. It stated that the "two governments mutually agree to render one to another aid and support of all kinds in the present war against Hitlerite Germany." This international agreement was of critical importance and relevance for the entire population of Poles imprisoned in the POW camps and forced labour camps, and for those sent to work in *kolkhozes* (collective farms) in Siberia and Kazakhstan, including the four featured later in this book. Significantly, the Soviet Union expressed its consent to:

> the formation on territory of the U.S.S.R. of a Polish Army under a commander appointed by the Polish Government in agreement with the Soviet Government, the Polish Army on territory of the U.S.S.R. being subordinated in an operational sense to the Supreme Command of the U.S.S.R., in which the Polish Army will be represented.[6]

Diplomatic relations between Poland and the Soviet Union were to resume, and amnesty declared for the hundreds of thousands of Polish soldiers and citizens who had been taken captive during the Soviet army's invasion and annexation of the eastern territory of Poland.

Despite Soviet reluctance, an important revision implemented on August 14, 1941, stated that the Polish armed forces in the USSR would instead "become part of the Armed Forces of the Sovereign Polish Republic," with Polish soldiers "subject to Polish military laws and regulations." This agreement offered the important prospect of sovereignty and self-governance for both the Polish government-in-exile and its proposed new army. General Władysław Anders was put in charge of the new army. He had been injured and captured during the invasion of Poland, and then detained in Moscow's infamous Lubyanka prison, where he was being held when given the command. The headquarters of the army was set up in Buzuluk, Orenburg Oblast, Russia; the 5th Division was placed in Tatishchevo, Russia; and the 6th Division and the Reserve Regiment were set up at Totskoye, Russia. The Soviet authorities allowed Polish officers to visit three Polish POW camps to seek army recruits.

The diplomatic documents that flowed between the Polish government-in-exile, the Polish, US and British ambassadors to the Soviet Union, and the Soviet government, offer telling behind-the-scene glimpses of these 1941 events. General Anders informed the US ambassador that the Polish prisoners being released from the Soviet detention camps were of high spirits and willing to fight against the Germans. Even though the authorities had not clearly stated the number of Polish POWs detained, Anders hoped for 60,000 to join the army. Brigadier General Zygmunt Bohusz-Szyszko, chief of the Polish Military Mission in Moscow, believed four or five divisions of Polish troops would be created, one of them motorized, and hoped that some weapons and ammunition confiscated by the Red Army during the invasion of Poland would be recovered and returned to the Polish army. On behalf of the Allies, the British government would help equip these units with uniforms and some arms and ammunition, supplemented by the US.

The Polish army in the Soviet Union grew quickly, and by August 1941, 40,000 Polish troops were expected during the early phase of its formation. After learning that the Soviet government was not able to provide adequate warm clothing, General Sikorski asked that either the British or US governments assist with supplies under the terms of the Lend-Lease Act. (On July 1, 1942, the Polish government had signed the agreement, which allowed the United States to lend or lease war supplies under the condition that they were "Vital to the defence of the United States.") Due to logistical challenges, however, Great Britain had to supply the necessary uniforms and non-military equipment for 60,000 troops. The Polish ambassador inquired about finding a method that would provide American equipment to three military divisions. In September 1941, General Sikorski asked for the assistance in arming as many as 100,000 Poles. The Polish army had already formed two divisions, and their participation in the war depended on how quickly they were supplied. Since the battle for Moscow was tying up the Soviet Union's massive human and military resources, Molotov said they would not be able to provide food supplies, nor more arms or equipment, for the Polish army beyond the 44,000 troops already registered.

Ever since Anders announced the Polish autonomous armed forces in the USSR and called on all Polish citizens to do their duty and join the army, many had felt a renewed hope for a free Poland. Poles rushed to join the new Polish army via all sorts of transportation. Such was the case of all four men featured in this book. Anatol Nieumierzycki recalled the great response to Anders' call, resulting in thousands of Poles embarking on journeys to reach one of the locations where the army was being formed. Władysław Niewiński, after he was released from the Siberian labour camp, travelled in a cargo train with other Poles with whom he had been incarcerated. The call to join the army was also answered by the youth deported to Kazakhstan and Siberia where they worked in kolkhozes, as in the case of Zbigniew Rogowski and Anatol Nieumierzycki.

When Anders made his first visit and inspection of the camps at Totskoye, where the 6th Infantry Division was being formed, he found most of the 17,000 soldiers severely emaciated, with lesions on their skin indicating that they suffered from illnesses and prolonged malnutrition. Moreover, Anders recalled that most of them had no boots or shirts. Some of them wore remnants of their Polish military uniforms in which they fought in September 1939. Nonetheless, they showed great spirit, strength of character, and willingness to fight for the freedom of their homeland. Not only men but women also joined the army; Anders believed the Women's Auxiliary Services gave Polish women and girls imprisoned in the Soviet Union an important chance to fight for Poland's freedom.

The military record of Stefan Koselak, one of the soldiers featured, indicates he was in this Polish army camp on September 14, 1941, when Anders made an effort to look into the eyes of every soldier he passed during the review. In their eyes, he saw the expression of their "strong will and faith." Anders also visited the Tatishchevo camp, set up like the Totskoye recruitment camp in which soldiers were housed in tents in a forest.

Once again, the fast-growing unarmed army required more resources and drew the attention of the US president and British prime minister. Given the Soviet government could apparently not adequately equip, and consequently use, the Polish forces, the US president's special representative, W. Averell Harriman, suggested to Stalin that the reconditioned Polish troops fight as a national unit against the Nazi regime—as previously discussed with the Polish government. With agreement and assistance from the USSR government, they could be moved to Iran and more quickly reconditioned, uniformed and armed with help from the US and Great Britain. This would be done with the goal to return them to the Soviet Union front as a fighting force.

Sikorski, stating he wanted the Polish army formed in the USSR to be an asset to the Allied forces, offered his government-in-exile's full collaboration. Yet, despite the amnesty, a majority of Polish citizens imprisoned had still not been released, and those who tried to reach the Polish armed forces were denied assistance from the Soviet government. Moreover, the Soviet practices of using trained Polish soldier POWs for public and agricultural works was deemed inappropriate and unacceptable. The Polish government hoped to see an expression of goodwill from the Soviets, and on December 11, 1941, Stalin agreed to move 25,000 Polish troops, 9,000 to strengthen the British forces in North Africa, and 16,000 to Scotland. The transfer was possible based on the 1940 Allied Forces Act passed by the British government, permitting the "[exile] governments in Britain to form, train and maintain military units in action under their own offices, their own flags and their own military law." Moreover, it stated that in "matters of strategy these units are under the command of the British High Command" and this act applied to the "Belgian, Czech, Dutch, Norwegian and Polish governments in exile." Later, the Polish government-in-exile passed a law "[legalizing] the service of Polish citizens in other than Polish military formations." Introduction of this law was important for the Poles who wanted to join the army or had already been drafted, because in 1920, Poland had implemented the Polish Citizenship Act which stated that entering military service in a foreign country could result in the loss of Polish citizenship.

In the exchange of diplomatic correspondence, Stalin was quoted as not being open to allowing all Polish troops to leave the USSR as he would become the "laughing stock of the world." He not only set a limit on the size of the Polish army to 40,000 recruits but would not allow more Poles to join. Stalin did allow General Sikorski, however, to take more soldiers from the group of 40,000 who were already in the army and move them to Iran. To deal with the still growing number wanting to join, Stalin ordered an area in Turkmenistan prepared for a new Polish army, limited only by the number of Poles available, to fight instead on the side of the Soviet Union on the Eastern Front.

Fighting the German invader obviously involved human, military, economic and strategic resources and the efforts of many countries, but US diplomats to the USSR noted in their diplomatic correspondence how Stalin didn't mention that the Soviet Union was receiving assistance and financial support from the US and Britain. Neither did he admit how the Allies were supporting the Soviet Union in fighting the Nazis. In contrast to these notable omissions, Stalin instead complained how Germany was receiving support from Italy, Romania, and Finland, and stated, "Not far off is the day" of the Red Army giving a powerful blow to the enemy when "the Soviet flags will again wave victoriously over all Soviet soil," as if he was going to single-handedly liberate Russia and other nations from the German invasion. In the meantime, the Polish government-in-exile had to sign an agreement on January 23, 1942, to borrow 300 million roubles from the Soviet Union for the upkeep of the Polish army on Soviet territory.

The issue of supplies kept coming up for the army of now 66,000 soldiers. Every day a thousand to fifteen hundred men arrived in the military camps to enlist. The Polish army continued to face food resources challenges, due to starvation in the destroyed area recovered from the Germans and significant shortages in a grain shipment promised from the US. Anders raised the issue of Polish women and children, hoping they also could be evacuated with the troops to Iran where they could find help from the American Red Cross. Stalin allowed Anders to evacuate only the number of soldiers that exceeded the new number of food rations.

The evacuation was in process on March 30, 1942, when the US ambassador to the Polish government reported that 40,000 Polish troops began evacuating to Iran, alongside the 10,000 Polish women and children permitted by Stalin. More Poles rushed to enlist in the army, but unprepared for this sudden move, the British government cited lack of food and shelter at the destination. The Polish government argued that the resources in the Middle East would still be much greater than in the USSR. This massive evacuation allowed the troops and civilians to move first to the Soviet port in Krasnovodsk and then by boat to Pahlavi, Persia, in the Soviet zone of occupation. Those who reached Pahlavi suffered from malnutrition, and many were ill but happy to leave the USSR. They were housed in the military and civilian camps, given medical care, and fed, but in the first month, a thousand died as a result of the circumstances in which they had lived while in the Soviet Union.

Throughout the summer of 1942, an estimated 115,000,[7] including children, women and men of all ages, reached the Polish armed forces' recruitment camps in the Soviet Union and were transferred to Persia and later to the Middle East. While stationed in tents in a camp set in the desert near Quizil Ribat in Iraq, the Polish troops faced new challenges brought about by the hot desert weather, the lack of water, and the outbreak of malaria. At night, scavenging hyenas frequented the central camp where the food was prepared, fighting for the food scraps with foxes, jackals and vultures.

In November 1942, military training of the Polish soldiers started, during which 20,000 drivers (including Stefan Koselak) were trained. The troops had been armed with equipment after General Maitland Wilson, the commander of all British forces in Iran and Iraq (PAI Force[8]), visited the previous month. During this period of military training, Anders was required to send 3,500 troops (including Władysław Niewiński, before his injury sidelined him) to Great Britain to reinforce the Polish air force in the Battle of Britain.

The Polish government-in-exile saw its strained relationship with the USSR turn into a crisis, escalated by a note the Soviet representative handed to the Polish ambassador that stated that all Poles who were still on the territory of the Soviet Union but who had lived on the territory of Poland at the time of its Soviet annexation in

1939, would be considered Soviet subjects. This decision[9] affected detained or deported ethnic Poles from the eastern part of Poland. The Soviet government in its political communication informed the Polish government that its move was motivated by the unwillingness of the Polish government to accept that the territory of White Ruthenia (also known as White Russia) and western Ukraine belonged to the Soviet Union. These territories were located within the 1939 borders of Poland. The Polish government-in-exile saw the decision as completely disregarding the terms of the 1941 Sikorski–Mayski Agreement.

Polish–Soviet relations attracted continued close observation by Allied governments, which noted how Polish citizens were being conscripted into the Red Army, despite the protest of the Polish government-in-exile. Recognition of ethnic Poles as Soviet citizens had broader consequences, allowing the Bolshevik government to stop relief activities to the "former" Poles and prevent their evacuation as they were no longer eligible to receive help from the Polish government. For many Polish soldiers, who were already in the Middle East and had left their family members behind in the Soviet Union, the complete halt of evacuation efforts caused uneasiness.

Despite the growing tension, Sikorski told the US and the UK that his Polish government, in "close understanding with the British government," was ready to disregard the fact that the Soviet Union had only joined the fight against the Nazis two years prior and only after it was invaded. The Polish government stated it was ready "to disregard these wrongs in solidarity in the fight against the common enemy and being desirous to lay the foundations for friendly cooperation between the two countries after final victory." But in April 1943, the Polish government-in-exile sought the involvement of the US and the British governments to intervene with Stalin over the escalating issues: ethnic Poles in the Soviet Union forced to give up their Polish passports under the threat of torture, starvation and imprisonment; Soviet interference with the activities of and closing of the relief program for the Poles; the arrest of Polish aid workers, and confiscation of supplies provided by the US; Soviet refusal to allow the previously agreed-to evacuation of 30,000 people related to the Polish soldiers already in the Middle East and 60,000 Polish children, as well as the treatment of the Polish women and children left behind in the Soviet Union. The Soviet government had implemented its decision to create separate military units made up of Polish refugees under the premise that they were now Soviet citizens. The plans for this new army of 1.5 million troops involved active military duties after the war.

A more significant rift affecting the political relationship between the Soviet Union and Poland was yet to come. The Germans claimed that they had found a mass grave with the bodies of thousands of Polish officers in Katyn (Katyń), near Smolensk, an area they had occupied only from October 1941 until March 1943, and so did not want to take responsibility. Based on the evidence, including military uniforms, documents, and memoirs found in proximity to the bodies, these Polish officers had most likely been killed in the spring of 1940. Poland appealed for a Red Cross investigation.

According to General Anders, Poland had reasons to believe the information because Polish representatives in the Soviet Union had been unable to locate a large number of the high-ranking Polish officers captured during the Soviet invasion. When Anders visited detention camps after the amnesty, he had not been able to trace their whereabouts, either, except for a small group of Polish officers from one of the three Buzuluk camps. Most Poles joining the Polish forces in the Soviet Union had been either civilians or low-ranking soldiers. When General Sikorski handed Stalin a total of 4,645 names collected from testimonies of the former Polish prisoners who had been detained at the same time as the Polish officers, Stalin insisted that the Polish officers had been released.

However, according to the official newspaper of the Soviet Ministry of Defence, *Red Star*, which claimed 181,000 Polish POWs had been captured and detained, officers had been placed in three detention camps for army and police officers located in Kozielsk near Smolensk, Starobielsk near Kharkov, and Ostashkow near Kalinin. When the Soviets began liquidating those camps, the Polish minister of National Defence heard, every few days a group of Polish POWs had been transported toward Smolensk. It was also rumoured 8,300 officers had been executed by the Soviets in 1940.

The Soviet government nevertheless claimed Germany was just whitewashing its own war crimes, and a front page-editorial in *Pravda* accused Poles of being collaborators of Hitlerites. But the Polish government-in-exile also strongly condemned Germany for capitalizing on Soviet crimes and using them as a defence to conceal their own war crimes, such as conscripting 200,000 Poles from occupied territory and killing the families of any who fled or hid.

The US ambassador to the UK indicated suspicion about Germany's timing of the fuss and suggested that the Polish government had made a mistake to believe the propaganda and ask for Red Cross assistance, knowing how the allegation of mass murder would cause strong anti-Polish feelings in the Soviet Union and anti-Soviet feelings among the Poles.

The Polish government-in-exile continued to adamantly assert that "the Polish nation is prepared to live on good neighbourly terms with the Soviets provided the Soviets recognise without reservation Poland's pre-1939 Eastern Frontiers, as defined in the Riga Treaty, and do not interfere in Poland's internal affairs." But the approximately 100,000 Polish troops in the Middle East, former

POWs of Soviet detention camps, were "becoming increasingly dissatisfied" with the situation of Polish civilians left behind in the
Soviet Union.

The Soviet government broke off relations with the Polish
government-in-exile on April 25, 1943, with Stalin complaining to
Roosevelt of a relationship "absolutely abnormal and contrary to all
rules and standards." Stalin saw General Sikorski's position as an act
of disloyalty and concluded that "the present government of Poland,
having fallen into the path of collusion with the Hitler government,
has actually discontinued relations of alliance with the U.S.S.R.
and assumed a hostile attitude toward the Soviet Union." Despite
Churchill's attempts to convince him otherwise, Stalin argued that
"the ingratitude and treachery of the Polish government" toward the
people of the Soviet Union demanded such action. Churchill nevertheless asked Stalin to "consider allowing more Poles and Polish
dependents to go into Persia" to "allay the rising discontent of the
Polish Army formed there" as it would enable him "to influence the
Polish Government to act in conformity with our common interests
and against the common foe."

Roosevelt for his part, showed concern about the potential
adverse reaction from the millions of Poles in the US, since many of
them served in the US army and navy and these Soviet allegations
would not help them fight the Nazis. Roosevelt also asked Stalin to
allow more Poles to leave and offered to provide support. Sikorski
offered a compromise, in which the Polish press would scale down
their comments on the issue of missing Polish officers, and he would
not seek the further assistance of the International Red Cross.
Sikorski then turned to Roosevelt, seeking help to move out the tens
of thousands of Polish soldiers' families, and thousands of Polish
orphans, from the USSR.

The lengthy diplomatic correspondence about the issue suggested a sense among the British diplomats that the Soviets'

breaking of the relationship took place "primarily because they were trying to cover up their guilt in connection with the Smolensk affair." Despite the efforts of his government, Roosevelt had no opportunity to read and react to the Soviet Union's unilateral decision which Poland refused to accept. Any hope of reconciliation between Poland and the USSR faded after the Soviet newspaper *Izvestia* published an article written by the chairman of the Union of Polish Patriots (who was allegedly married to the newly appointed vice-commissar of Foreign Affairs in the Soviet government). The anti-Polish article, "The Polish Patriots are against the Government of General Sikorski," presented the Polish government-in-exile as defeated in 1939 and thus not a legal representative of the Polish people. General Anders was described as anti-Semitic, anti-Soviet and a coward because he pressured for the evacuation of the Polish armed forces to the Middle East. The Polish government-in-exile, controlled by "Hitlerite elements," was accused of stealing from the Polish exiles in the Soviet Union, collaborating with the Nazis, and expressing an imperialistic intention toward Soviet territory. According to the article, the Union of Polish Patriots had requested Polish military units be created on the territory of the Soviet Union that, unlike Anders Army, "would proceed to the front to fight shoulder to shoulder with the Red Army." The article's author predicted that a "Free Polish Government," tied to the Soviets, would be created on the territory of the Soviet Union, to be recognized as the only representative of the Poles under the German occupation. The rhetoric introducing such a government forecasted the shift in the makeup of Europe in which other Slavic states would have their nucleus created in the Soviet Union, to serve as buffers separating it from the West.

Soviet pressure continued demanding changes in personnel in the Polish government, as well as more control over the Polish press and the anti-Soviet attitude among the Polish armed forces in the

Middle East. The evacuation of the Polish diplomatic mission in the Soviet Union especially concerned soldiers with family members left behind in the Soviet Union. Two categories of Poles remained: the families of the Polish troops in the Middle East, and the Poles whom Soviet law had made Soviet citizens. Moreover, Polish *matériel* in the Soviet Union still required attention, since 35 per cent of the supplies and 90 per cent of the clothing had been provided by the US. After extensive backroom negotiations, the Australian minister of External Affairs eventually and quietly agreed to take over the diplomatic representation of Polish interests in the USSR.

More serious political changes were afoot. A newly formed Polish Legion affiliated with the Union of Polish Patriots, and not supportive of the Sikorski government, was made up of Poles who were recognized by the Soviets as their citizens. The new Polish military units included Polish nationals who had been living in the western territory of Ukraine and White Russia and were considered Soviet citizens. Molotov saw nothing inappropriate in "a distinction between nationality and citizenship": these soldiers were Polish by nationality, yet because they lived in western Ukraine and White Russia, they were, in fact, Soviet citizens. Even though Molotov saw the issue of the Union of the Polish Patriots as internal policy of Poland, and not Soviet foreign policy, this organization's stature was rising. In a message to the Presidium of the Congress of Polish Patriots in Moscow, Stalin stated, "I warmly greet you and the Union of Polish Patriots in the U.S.S.R., who have begun the successful work of uniting your forces and strengthening the friendship between the peoples of Poland and the Soviet Union."

Some rumblings about Poland's evolving political situation did reach Canada's capital at this time. In an *Evening Citizen* editorial entitled "Fascist Polish Intrigue" on April 30, 1943, Prime Minister Sikorski was praised as a great statesman representing "the spirit of the Polish people," and the Polish soldiers who fought against the German army "have won the respect of comrades in arms" and "have gone valiantly into action on every fighting front," thus earning their high regard in the United Kingdom. The editorial, however, then turned on unnamed exiles holding positions in the government-in-exile who opposed re-establishing relations between Poland and the Soviet Union. It accused them of being supportive of the Fascist movement, and of considering the USSR "a discredited nation of a slave people ruled by a ruthless dictator." This, the editorial claimed, would prevent Western countries from forming a good relationship with the Soviet Union. It labelled the Polish officials reactionary while blaming the opposition to the Soviet Union on hostile propaganda doing a grave disservice to Poland. Even though this issue was not widely discussed around the world, the Soviet Union was certainly paying attention.

Other similar-in-tone articles published in Canada also insinuated Fascist sentiments in certain Polish officials. On May 4, 1943, *The Evening Citizen* in Ottawa published an editorial by Edmund Stevens,[10] entitled "Polish Fascist Politics," which named Polish–Soviet borders the underlying cause of the strain in the relationship. The author claimed that the matter was politically motivated and initiated by those in Polish political circles described as old-school, ultra-nationalistic and "far more Anti-Soviet than Anti-Nazi in sentiment." This article was written in a convoluted and enigmatic way, attempting to address several issues only to insufficiently describe complex political problems that involved Polish refugees and the Polish military in the Middle East. However, while the article was not clear in its description of the political background, it brought the reader's attention to possible pro-Nazi sentiments brewing among Poles. It suggested that some Polish officers or former Polish government officials who had been transferred from the USSR to Iran were anti-Soviet and anti-Semitic. The article even referred to some Poles who, while still in Soviet camps, had wanted to overtake their Soviet guards and appeal for liberation from the advancing German troops. The appeals for food for the starving were presented as political propaganda, spread by "self-seeking Polish officials to get a large shipment of food consigned to them ostensibly for distribution to the Poles still in Russia." Moreover, Stevens quoted Polish refugees transferred to Tehran who said that while in the Soviet Union, they were not treated any worse than the local population. No names were specified, yet the substantial allegations of Poles siding with Fascists threatened long-term political implications.

When describing the Soviets, in contrast, the author praised the Red Army's achievements without referring to any particular battle or land taken from the Germans. Not much information ever came out of the USSR, and so Stevens' article might have planted some doubts in the minds of the readers about the loyalties of Poles. He referenced two Polish Red Cross delegates, reportedly expelled from the USSR in 1942, who he said were looking for secret military information under the guise of humanitarian work. Articles like this one could easily create a different perception of the Poles detained in the Soviet Union as well as those evacuated to the Middle East.

Nevertheless, on May 27, 1943, when Sikorski visited the Polish Army Corps in Iraq he reported their spirit still "of most ardent patriotism," and devoted to fighting for the Polish cause. Sikorski reassured them that the Polish government was continuing to address the outstanding issues: the evacuation of Polish orphans still in the USSR, Poland's borders, and the issue of citizenship of Poles still in the USSR. Discussions about reorganizing the Polish troops in the Middle East with General Henry Pownall (commander-in-chief of Persia) resulted in Anders being appointed the acting commander of all Polish forces in the Middle East. General Pownall stated that once training was finished, the forces would be ready to be part of a larger military operation. General Anders thought that the Allies' offensive would have to come from the south, through

Italy, which he saw as the best solution from both military and political perspectives.

General Anders still insisted that General Sikorski should take overall command, but a most unexpected change to Poland's situation came on July 4, 1943. While visiting Gibraltar on the way back to London, Sikorski sent a telegram to President Roosevelt on the occasion of American Independence Day, expressing his belief that the United States' leadership and close collaboration with Great Britain would bring victory to the United Nations over the Nazi enemy. Soon after takeoff, the plane carrying Sikorski crashed. An estimated sixteen people on board died, including Sikorski's daughter and his chief of staff; the pilot was the only survivor. The sudden death of Sikorski reportedly caused "depression bordering on despair among the Polish people" since the entire nation recognized Sikorski as their military and political leader. Count Raczyński, minister of Foreign Affairs, immediately requested Roosevelt's support to raise Poland's spirit and faith to continue their "united and unbroken resistance in their struggle to regain Poland's independence."

In the meantime, preparations of the Allied armed forces for battles with the German enemy were under way. The Polish Corps had already taken part in preparatory military manoeuvres in the Middle East to be ready for action by January 1, 1944. After observing the exercises, and the support offered by the new Polish commander-in-chief, General Kazimierz Sosnkowski, British General Henry Maitland Wilson reported to the War Office that the Polish forces were "fully prepared for battle, in excellent fighting spirit, and an asset that should not be wasted by delaying their departure to the front." Although Anders knew he had limited recruitment options to replace losses on the battlefield, he reassured Wilson that he planned on recruiting any Poles who had been forcefully conscripted into the German army. Anders reasoned that as soon as they learned about the Polish army, they would cross the line and join the Polish troops. Later on, special camps for POWs were created where Poles in the German army who'd defected or surrendered were sent for "screening" to ensure suitability for the 7th Reserve Division in the Middle East. The II Polish Army Corps would eventually become the fourth-largest Allied army.

In charge of the Italian Campaign's Cassino sector was the British Eighth Army, which was to include the 1st Canadian Division and 5th Division (Armoured) of the I Canadian Corps. The II Polish Army Corps would join it as an independent component, beginning in December 1943. All Allied army forces in Italy were under the command of General Wilson, Supreme Allied Commander of the Central Mediterranean Forces, who made a note of his pleasure at having the Polish Army Corps involved. For the Italian Campaign, the Polish and Canadian armies unified under the command of British General Harold Alexander. The merger of forces of various nationalities supporting the Allied troops would later be described by historian Edgar McInnis as "a single coherent fighting machine."

The first attack on Monte Cassino was part of the landing of Allied troops in Italy in an operation intended to capture Rome. The Monte Cassino stronghold was considered the "Gate of Rome" because the only way to Rome was through the Liri Valley. The valley was strategically defended by German troops who were well fortified in the monastery, a massive building towering on top of Monte Cassino, a rocky hill that rose 1,700 feet above the town. This battle between January 20, and February 14, 1944, involved two Allied armies, the American Fifth Army and the British Eighth Army (including the I Canadian Corps) against fourteen large, highly trained and carefully selected German military units. The II American Army Corps, part of the Fifth Army, crossed the Rapido River to take advantage of progress previously made by the French

Corps, but heavy casualties under German fire caused them to withdraw. These troops were replaced by the New Zealand Army Corps.

When at the beginning of February, General Anders landed in Italy to take charge of the 50,000-strong II Polish Army Corps ready for the Italian Front, the Polish division consisted of only two brigades instead of the usual three because of the shortage of recruits. Nonetheless, Anders' soldiers were ready for battle, to face their German adversary.

Meanwhile, on the Russian Front, the Red Army had been making advancements toward Wilno and Lwów, while claiming in Soviet media that this Polish territory annexed during the September 1939 invasion belonged to the USSR. Furthermore, the first of the World War II strategy conferences in Tehran at the end of 1943 had already discussed a postwar Soviet–Polish border to be set on the Curzon Line (the same border on which the Molotov–Ribbentrop Pact had divided Poland) instead of where it was before the 1939 invasions. This development meant the Soviet government was still planning to apportion the territory of Poland, but unilaterally, and it caused serious concern among the Polish troops in Italy as they perceived a deal between the Allies had been reached at the cost of giving Poland's eastern territory to the Soviet Union. Soldiers' concerns grew, when on February 22, 1944, Churchill stated in a House of Commons speech, "We did not approve the Polish occupation of Vilna in 1920. The British view in 1919 stands expressed in the so-called Curzon Line." Churchill thereby lent his approval and conveyed a sense of fairness about the demands of the Soviet Union for the annexed eastern territory of Poland. Through that public statement, Poles were made aware that they could lose the part of Poland where they had been born and grew up. They had joined the Polish army to fight for freedom of their homeland, and this development confirmed the worst, not only for Poles from the eastern territory of Poland, but for all Poles.

If the Poles in Italy had any hope that their government would be part of the discussions about the postwar eastern border with the Soviet Union, Churchill's statement took that away when he said, "Marshal Stalin and I also spoke and agreed upon the need for Poland to obtain compensation at the expense of Germany, both in the North and in the West." Churchill gave this speech around the time when the II Polish Army Corps was being sent to the front line in the heavily fortified Monte Cassino sector to fight German troops. Not only were Churchill's words deeply depressing to the soldiers worried about Poland's uncertain future but they also shook their confidence in Great Britain. However, to keep their hope alive for a free Poland, they had to continue fighting.

At the beginning of February, the weather had been rainy and cold, and snowfall obstructed mountain roads already destroyed by previous military operations. Even the heavy tanks became trapped in mud. The second stage of the Battle of Monte Cassino took place between February 15 and March 24, 1944, and involved the American Fifth Army and the New Zealand Army Corps. The heavily fortified monastery was intensively bombarded by Allied air troops, and although some temporary gains of terrain were made by the British-Indian division, they did not defeat German forces dug inside the concrete bunkers. The bombardment of Cassino on March 15 resulted in further territorial gains by the Gurkhas who took Hangman's Hill, and the New Zealanders, who took nearly the entire Cassino town. However, these small, often temporary advances, in which a lot of military effort and time was invested, were not enough to take Monte Cassino and ultimately open the road to Rome. The American Fifth Army was then replaced by the British Eighth Army. By then, Monte Cassino had been attacked by the Americans, British, French, New Zealanders and Indians, and even though much of their blood was shed on the battlefield, the Germans in the monastery had not been defeated.

By that time, preparations for the involvement of the II Polish Army Corps were under way, as General Sir Oliver Leese of the British Eighth Army informed General Anders. On March 3, 1944, as Polish troops prepared to fight side-by-side with British, American and French soldiers against the Germans, General Anders gave a radio broadcast that was also transmitted in Poland. His speech was filled with words to renew soldiers' courage and remind them of the great sacrifices many of them had already made before joining the Polish Army Corps:

> Amongst us are soldiers from Tobruk and Gazala, soldiers from Narvik and from the fields of France, and the great majority have been through prisons and concentration camps in the far north. Went through the field and deserted spaces and were decimated by frost, epidemics and our enemies.

The II Polish Army Corps was assigned to maintain the communication between the Eighth and the Fifth Armies on the front line. Polish troops were also assigned to defend the mountain in the area from Monte Curvale to Colle Lettica and to protect both sides of the Isernia–Alfedena road. The presence of the Polish troops on the battlefield increased German propaganda calling for the Poles to desert.

The Canadian army newspaper, *The Maple Leaf*, reported on March 6, 1944, that General Leese was impressed with the Polish soldiers' confidence and determination, saying "we are proud to welcome the Polish Corps to fight beside us in our drive toward Germany and victory." Shortly afterward, General Leese proposed to General Anders that the II Polish Army Corps take on the most challenging task of capturing the unconquered Monte Cassino and taking Piedemonte as part of the Eighth Army's operation to break through the Gustav and Hitler Lines. General Anders agreed, even though he anticipated heavy casualties. He realized how important it was for the Polish soldiers in Italy to participate in this offensive, providing proof of their desire to fight the German enemy with the eyes of the world on them. Seeing Polish troops victorious, the battle could help boost the resistance movement in Poland, especially against the notorious German stronghold that had already caused so many Allied casualties.

The preparations started with studying the intricacy of the challenging terrain that required soldiers to fight the enemy on the stretch of hillside eight kilometres long and up to six kilometres wide under deadly fire from above. Before the battle, the soldiers amassed supplies, first brought by trucks to the bottom of the hill. Where the vehicles, and then mules, could no longer scramble up the mountain, the soldiers carried the supplies to their positions on the hill under cover of total darkness. Despite these precautions, there was a substantial loss of life, as the Germans conducted systematic attacks along the routes used by the Poles. This strategy of working through the nights stocking up on supplies was made possible by the telephone communication manned by the Polish units. Moreover, during this phase, the troops were trained in rock climbing, fighting in mountainous topography, and using the newly acquired flame-throwers. During the day, the hill was under constant surveillance of the German snipers, so activities had to quiet down so as not to give away preparations.

General Sosnkowski, the commander-in-chief of the Polish armed forces in the West, was to inspect his troops on March 27, 1944, near Monte Cassino, where the artillery was locked in a struggle after twelve days of the heaviest fighting. Relentless fire from the enemy positions came on Colli-Atina Road, about eleven miles from the villages of Cassino and Cairo. *The Maple Leaf* reported that day, "After a week isolated on Hangman's Hill, where the Allied troops were positioned 200 meters from the German positions, the soldiers had to be withdrawn under the Red Cross flag."

That same day, *The Maple Leaf* relayed Churchill's radio statement expressing satisfaction in the overall progress of the Allies'
fight against the enemy—except for the Italian Campaign, which
was not moving ahead as rapidly as hoped. For comparison, the
newspaper reported progress in other parts of Europe that day: the
bombardment of the German cities of Berlin, Kiel, Frankfurt, and
Schweinfurt. A thousand bombers from the Royal Air Force and
US Army Air Forces dropped 2,500 tonnes of bombs, explosives,
and incendiaries over the city's industrial area during "the greatest 60 hours of the concentrated bombing of the whole war." These
were not the only gains on the front line, since "Russian troops
swept over the collapsing German armies from the Odessa basin to
the Rumania borders in monumental weekend victories," and just
a few days earlier, *The Maple Leaf* had reported that the Red Army
was about forty miles from Polish cities. The tenor of Churchill's
reported speech put great pressure on everyone involved in the
Italian Campaign since the route through Italy was described as one
of "Avenues to Victory."

The storming of Monte Cassino and its abbey was set for May 11,
1944, with the Eighth Army's objectives still breaking "through the
enemy lines in the Liri valley and driving on to Rome." The II Polish
Army Corps was to take Monte Cassino. The I Canadian Corps
would enter the Liri Valley, followed by the XIII British Army Corp.
The X British Army Corps was put in charge of the Monte Cairo
sector, and the Fifth Army and the French Corps, as well as the
II Polish Army Corps, were also to be involved.

On the eve of the battle, the commander-in-chief of Allied armies
in Italy, the commander of the British Eighth Army, and General
Anders all issued orders of the day. General Alexander said that
the Allies' navy, air, and infantry troops were assembling to bring
destruction to the Nazis and long-awaited peace for all: "to us in
Italy have been given the honour of striking the first blow. We are

going to destroy the German Armies in Italy." He expected the battle would be "hard, bitter, and perhaps long," but was confident the Allies would be victorious. General Leese singled out divisions fighting for the first time as part of the Eighth Army, saying "our special greeting to the Polish Army Corps which fights now at our side for the liberation of its beloved country." General Anders specifically addressed his II Polish Army Corps: "Soldiers! The moment for the battle has come...Shoulder to shoulder with us will fight British, American, Canadian, New Zealand divisions as well as the French, Italian, and Indian troops." Anders then drew the soldiers' attention to the future when he said, "the task assigned to us will cover with glory the name of the Polish soldier all over the world." He appealed to their patriotism and sense of responsibility toward the Polish nation still under the Nazi regime and said, "at this moment the thoughts and the hearts of our whole nation will be with us." Finally, he asked the troops to keep the words sacred to all Poles, "God, Honour, Fatherland," in their hearts when they advanced on the battlefield.

At 11:00 p.m. the offensive began on the entire front line from coast to coast. The Allied artillery bombarded German positions in an intense assault that lasted forty minutes. Polish gunners started firing at the German infantry positions. At 1:00 a.m. two Polish divisions began attacking the enemy stronghold under the cover of night that was made darker by smoke coming from artillery shells. The soldiers engaged in intense and challenging close-range fighting while negotiating the rocky terrain under German gunfire. Polish officers on the hill were killed one after another. As they died their responsibilities were taken on by soldiers of the next highest rank. The battle lasted into the afternoon. The German troops defended their position, hiding behind the walls of the concrete bunkers and shooting from above, under cover of their artillery. The Polish forces could not use their artillery because the lines of communication between the observers on the front line and the main command unit had been broken.

General Anders described the battle as "a collection of small epics, many of which can never be told, for their heroes took to their graves the secret of their exploit." High casualties were suffered by the Polish troops, and Germans often retook places taken. When the Allied artillery fire could not reach the German positions located on the other side of the hill and inflict losses among their infantry, General Anders ordered the Polish brigades to move back to the lines where they had been when the battle started. Some of the units managed to withdraw, but others had to stay in position on the slopes for another day or longer. The Polish troops' attacks on the German positions engaged several enemy artillery units, and reinforcements had to be drawn from other places. This allowed the XIII Army Corps to attack the Liri Valley and cross the river.

General Leese ordered the second attack on the monastery on Monte Cassino to take place on May 17, at 7:00 a.m. The two divisions involved were positioned right behind the Allied artillery line shooting at the enemy. The II Polish Army Corps not only had to advance against the barrage of enemy fire but also deal with mines and traps set on the hill. They were successful in taking several positions such as Phantom Ridge, Sant'Angelo, and Hill 593. The next day, despite their having experienced high losses, the units used during the first phase of the attack had to be brought back to the battle. The Polish Commandos and part of the 15th Poznań Lancers were also transferred into the fight. Both sides engaged in fierce fighting and to complete exhaustion. On the morning of May 18, another attack by the 3rd Carpathian Rifle Division, part of the II Polish Army Corps, took place, but under cover of night, the Germans had already pulled out from the monastery, leaving only some detachments behind. On May 18, 1944, at 10:20 a.m., the Polish flag was hoisted above the ruins of Monte Cassino by the soldiers from the 12th Lancers.

The battlefield was covered with ammunition, unused mines and broken tanks. The bodies of soldiers from Allied and German units covered the ground. The air was filled with the stench of rotting corpses, many of which had been lying on the ground in the intense heat for many days. The monastery was utterly ruined; mangled and burned tree stumps were the only reminder of the oak groves that used to stand on the hillside. In places where there had been less artillery shelling, blooming red poppies covered the ground.

On May 19, 1944, *The Maple Leaf* reported that the Polish troops "led the onslaught that sealed the doom of Cassino." The soldiers "stormed the 2,000-foot hill north of Cassino, known as Hill 593, where the Hitler Line joins the old Gustav Line." In the battle fought hand-to-hand, the Poles drove out the Germans and "the victory was complete by Thursday morning." That the Germans had to withdraw from the monastery in a hurry was apparently signified by the amount of German horse-pulled artillery (enough to equip two divisions) left strewn on the battlefield. General Anders reported the II Polish Army Corps had lost 281 Polish officers, while 3,503 soldiers had been killed or wounded, or were missing. The fight caused 55,000 Allied casualties and became known as the longest battle of the WWII Italian Campaign.

However, despite the territorial advances made by the Polish and Allied troops, the road to Rome was not yet open. The XIII British Army Corps and the I Canadian Corps continued to fight the enemy defending its stronghold in Piedemonte, where the Gustav and Hitler Lines met. Despite its losses during the Battle of Monte Cassino, the II Polish Army Corps was sent to assist, and on May 25, Piedemonte was finally taken. On June 4, 1944, the road to Rome was open, and Allied troops entered the Holy See. The next day in his order, General Leese congratulated the Fifth and the Eighth Armies on the great achievement of breaking through the Gustav Line, capturing Cassino and Monastery Hill, breaking the Hitler Line and crushing several German divisions, thus impacting the enemy's ability to fight.

The 11 Polish Army Corps also participated in the Battle of Ancona (June 16–18, 1944) that resulted in Allied victory. Later, in August 1944, the Canadian and the Polish armies were involved in joint military operations on the Gothic Line. There, the 11 Polish Army Corps was designated to push the enemy over the Metauro River, and to prepare positions for the 1 Canadian Corps and the v British Army Corps for a further attack. The three armies involved in the assault on the Gothic Line included the 11 Polish Army Corps, positioned next to the sea; the 1 Canadian Corps, placed in the middle; and the v British Army Corps on the left (western) flank. The task assigned to the 11 Polish Army Corps was to reach the line of the Foglia River in the sector between the Canadian Corps and the sea. The joint efforts and skills of the Canadian and the Polish armies allowed the Canadian army to make a significant advancement through a minefield, reach and circle the enemy positions, and eventually link with the posts of the 11 Polish Army Corps. The battle for the Gothic Line ended on September 1, 1944, with British General Leese stating that the 11 Polish Army Corps had made "a notable contribution to the common cause on the battlefields of Italy."

Moreover, as part of the Italian offensive, the Polish troops also fought in the Battle of Loreto, and in the Battle of Bologna when the 3rd Carpathian Rifle Division entered the city on April 21, 1945. After the war was over, the 11 Polish Army Corps stayed in Italy until 1946.

3

From Soldiers to Stateless Immigrants

OF THE ESTIMATED 112,000 II Polish Army Corps soldiers stationed in Italy at war's end, many wanted to return home. However,
many also felt that they had no home to go back to because the
places where the majority of the Polish troops came from were no
longer part of Poland. The status of the II Polish Army Corps was
also becoming less clear.

After the Anders Army had evacuated, starting in the summer
of 1943, a new unit of a Polish infantry division in the Soviet Union
had been organized to participate in the Red Army's fight against the
Germans. This Polish military formation, the 1 Polish Corps, grew
into the much larger 1 Polish Army by mid-March 1944, and became
known as the Berling Army, under Lieutenant General Zygmunt
Berling. Similar to the II Polish Army Corps led by General Anders,
the 1 Polish Army was also made of Poles taken prisoner during the
Soviet Union's 1939 invasion of Poland, as well as of Poles who had
been forcefully deported to labour camps or kolkhozes in remote
locations in Siberia or Kazakhstan. However, Poles now considered

Soviet citizens were forced to join the Red Army in this division
under General Berling. Polish authorities in the West who managed
to make contact with Polish underground forces learned that Poles
who refused were executed by Soviet authorities as a warning that
"forced the others to join the Red forces."

The US was taking note of the development of these military and
political changes in the USSR. The ambassador to the Soviet Union,
W. Averell Harriman, reported on a March 21, 1944, conference that
General Berling organized in his Moscow apartment to address members of the pro-Communist Union of Polish Patriots and the Polish
army. He spoke of "the rapidity of military developments in the south,
where Polish troops were active." Most likely, General Berling was
referring to the 11 Polish Army Corps' successful involvement in the
Italian Campaign and fears that those military troops might soon
reach Poland still under German occupation and liberate the country. Such an outcome would adversely impact the political situation
and the post-war makeup of Europe—at least from the perspective
of a pro-Soviet Polish government and the Soviet Union. General
Berling stated that the time had come to "consider the formation of
'organs' which should be prepared to take over the administration
of Polish territory." Berling emphasized that this would have to be
a "national government," meaning the government of "the people
and the Army." However, clear from the US report was that "for the
present it [was] proposed to set up administrative organs which will
function as such in Polish areas west of the Curzon Line as they are
liberated from Germans." This implied that the Polish–Soviet border
was predetermined to territorially favour the Soviet Union and that
the new Polish government, which was in the process of being established, would not question Soviet expansionist aggression on eastern
Poland. Ambassador Harriman noted that the new Polish army fighting alongside the Red Army was also to include members of "the
guerrillas in the western Ukraine," and that the inclusion of those

military units was seen as satisfactory by sources close to General Berling, despite being former enemies. Significantly, the US ambassador cited the Soviet newspaper *Pravda* for information on the Third Polish Division, part of the 1 Polish Army, which not only included a large number of recruits from the western part of Ukraine that had been liberated from German domination but also Poles defined as former participants in "the illegal organisations created by the emigrant Polish Government in London." In this diplomatic communication, the US ambassador seemed to be condoning the characterization of Polish organizations supporting the Polish government-in-exile as illegal and now renegade, opposing Soviet doctrine.

On the Eastern Front, the 1 Polish Army had participated alongside the Red Army in the October 1943 Battle of Lenino near Smolensk, USSR. However, the newly formed and undertrained Polish military units paid a hefty price, often running out of ammunition and lacking the support of artillery, losing a quarter of their soldiers during this two-day battle. But in the summer of 1944, the Red Army and the 1 Polish Army had liberated the eastern part of Poland. At that time, the Soviets put new demands on the Polish government, requiring Polish underground forces—which were effectively fighting the German occupant in Poland—to "disband and enter the forces of either the Soviet Army or the forces of General Berling," the Polish general who was commanding a Polish contingent within the Red Army. Such was the case in the battle for the city of Lvov (Lwów), with the 3,000-strong Polish detachment of the underground. After its commander disclosed himself to the Soviet commander, he was told to surrender and disband the group within two hours and join the Red or Berling Army since the Polish underground units were considered to be operating on Soviet territory.

US Ambassador Harriman commented that even though the Soviet government refrained from including in the Soviet Union the

countries it had liberated but that were not part of its 1941 frontier expansionist politics, occupation translated as a wide range
of forms and practices. These included: "occupation troops, secret
police, local communist parties, labour unions, sympathetic leftist
organisations, sponsored cultural societies, and economic pressure."
The use of such forms of control would "assure the establishment
of regimes which, while maintaining an outward appearance of
independence and broad popular support, actually depend for their
existence on groups responsive to all suggestions emanating from
the Kremlin." This description previewed the future for those countries under new forms of occupation.

Under such circumstances, it was not surprising that Joseph
Stalin supported the newly formed Polish Provisional Government
of National Unity established on June 28, 1945, in Lublin on the territory of Poland liberated by the Red Army and the 1 Polish (Berling)
Army. At the Yalta (Crimea) Conference, the Three Powers had
jointly declared that a "new situation has been created in Poland as a
result of her complete liberation by the Red Army. This calls for the
establishment of a Polish Provisional Government." The new government already functioning in Poland should "be reorganized on
a broader democratic basis with the inclusion of democratic leaders
from Poland itself and from Poles abroad" (meaning the government-in-exile) and then, the governments of the United Kingdom,
the US, and the USSR agreed, they would "exchange Ambassadors."
They also stated that this Polish Provisional Government of National
Unity "shall be pledged to the holding of free and unfettered
elections."

During the same conference, however, the Big Three concurred
that "the eastern frontier of Poland should follow the Curzon Line"
and that "Poland must receive substantial accessions in the territory in the north and west...and that the opinion of the new Polish
Provisional Government of National Unity should be sought in due

course of the extent of these accessions and that the final delimitation of the western frontier of Poland should thereafter await the peace conference."

Not involving the government-in-exile[1] in a decision that related to the sovereign country was "a violation of the spirit of the Atlantic Charter and the right of every nation to defend its interests," complained the prime minister of Poland's government in London to Roosevelt, and furthermore stated that "the decisions...were received by all Poles as a new partition of Poland leaving her under Soviet protectorate."

The final Big Three conference took place at Potsdam between July 17 and August 2, 1945, with the US now represented by its new president, Harry S. Truman. The conference delegates established "diplomatic relations with the Polish Provisional Government of National Unity...resulting in the withdrawal of their recognition of the former Polish Government in London."[2] And the Potsdam Declaration addressed the issue of Poles who had served with the British army, saying that "the Three Powers are anxious to assist the Polish Provisional Government of National Unity in facilitating the return to Poland as soon as practicable of all Poles abroad who wish to go, including members of the Polish Armed Forces and the Merchant Marine."

The Polish soldiers from the Anders Army saw the results of those conferences adding yet another reason to be unwilling to return to Poland. The Polish–Soviet borders had been discussed and drawn without the involvement of representatives of Poland during the 1943 Tehran Conference, and later during the 1945 Yalta Conference, which further influenced and solidified the distribution of political power in Europe. During the 1945 Potsdam Conference, once again the location of the western border of postwar Poland was discussed, and for the first time, representatives of Poland were consulted, namely members of the provisional government.

However, the location of the eastern border between Poland and the Soviet Union was not part of the declaration. The territory of Poland annexed by the Soviets in 1939, as well as Ukraine and Belarus—that were part of the pre-1939 territory of the Second Polish Republic, based on the 1921 Treaty of Riga—became part of the Soviet Union.

General Anders recalled how, in 1940, Churchill had given General Sikorski, then prime minister of Poland, reassurance that Poland and Great Britain were "bound together in this war for life or death." This attitude had clearly changed under pressure from the Soviet Union, and as Anders commented, "the Polish Government in London, and the Polish forces, who fought so long at the side of Great Britain and the United States, were discarded." Taking into consideration the battles the Polish fought alongside Allied troops, the families left behind in the USSR, and the deprivation of the rights to free speech for those opposed to the pro-Soviet government installed in Poland, Anders recognized how the return to Poland became impossible. He went on to say that the six years of suffering under the German and Soviet occupations and the blood sacrifices of the Poles had been made in vain, in light of the Big Three decisions affecting Poland.

However, not wanting to influence individual Poles' decisions, General Anders conveyed to General Alexander and, later on, directly to the soldiers that Polish troops who wanted to return to Poland would have complete freedom to make such a choice, despite their country being under Soviet domination. To ensure that the soldiers could exercise free will in where they would want to reside after the war, General Anders asked that after demobilization, such Poles be transferred to repatriation camps under British or Allied control. According to General Anders, out of 112,000 Polish soldiers, only seven officers and 14,200 men applied for repatriation to Poland. Among those who asked were 310 soldiers who had joined the Polish army while still in the USSR. As a result, a special camp in southern Italy was set up, and every soldier who wanted to return to Poland was sent there before departure. However, a considerable number of servicemen who were repatriated to Poland found their way back to Italy and offered eye-witness accounts. The other source of information came from letters sent from Poland to Italy, which also painted a grim picture.

Concerns among the Anders soldiers in Italy grew stronger. They believed that the repatriated would have to report to the authorities in the location of their last residence. In most cases, these places had become part of the Soviet Union after the war. The soldiers feared that they would need to undergo "rehabilitation" and that might mean being sent to the same forced labour camps in remote areas of the Soviet Union in which they had been imprisoned during the war. Facing the new political circumstances in Poland under the influence of the Soviet Union, the vast majority of servicemen decided to stay in exile rather than return to Poland.

At the same time, thousands of Polish refugees were escaping Poland, or coming from Germany and France, to the II Polish Corps in southern Italy, where a special camp was set up. Vocational training was organized to help many of them get primary education and/or learn a trade, but many also attended the universities at Padua, Bologna and in Rome.

In March 1946, General Anders was called to London where he learned that the British government and Poland's Provisional Government of National Unity in Warsaw had devised a draft plan to return troops to Poland with details of the treatment they would receive, including "reprisals and punishments inflicted on certain categories of them." The agreement to organize the resettlement of as many soldiers as possible back to Poland disappointed the Polish troops. Yet, the Polish armed forces had to be demobilized after the war, and those who wanted to stay in Italy faced the prospect of living in exile for the rest of their lives.

On March 20, 1946, British Foreign Secretary Ernest Bevin announced that he "hoped shortly to be in a position to make a statement on the problem of the Polish Armed Forces under British command." At this point, in agreement with the Polish provisional government, "every individual member of the Polish Armed Forces" would receive "a document in Polish explaining the policy of His Majesty's Government in regard to the future of the Polish Armed Forces and of the men themselves." Bevin stated he was not going to force these soldiers to return to Poland, yet, in his opinion, they ought to go back to help rebuild their country. Bevin also stated that "we cannot relieve ourselves of responsibility for those who feel in their conscience that they cannot go back," especially since "these men fought in the common cause." A few days later, a decision was made by the British government to create the Polish Resettlement Corps based on the 1947 Polish Resettlement Act, designed to deal with the 250,000 Polish veterans and women who remained in Great Britain or Italy. This act also included the British dominions. The first step of this process was to bring the Polish forces from Italy to Great Britain and begin demobilization before they could join the Polish Resettlement Corps. Membership in the Polish Resettlement Corps was available only to the specified Polish forces who had served in the armed forces of the Crown during the war. The act did not allow other nationalities to join it. The assistance board created by this act dealt with the issue of displaced persons and former prisoners of war who refused to go back to Poland.

The Resettlement Act focused on providing assistance with accommodations in camps or other institutions, health and education services, and financial aid with emigration. The British House of Commons heard that "the net cost of the pay, allowances and maintenance of the Polish Land Forces under British command and the Polish Resettlement Corps during the financial year 1946–1947 [was] estimated at about £33 million." This amount did not include the approximate cost of transport from Italy estimated as £250,000 and "the estimated extra cost involved in providing accommodation for the Resettlement Corps in this country...about £200,000."

Eligible soldiers from the II Polish Army Corps were considered displaced persons, for whom the British government needed to find civilian work "either in Great Britain or in suitable openings overseas as soon as possible," reported *The Times* in London, on October 10, 1946. Canada as a British dominion, accepted 4,527 Polish Resettlement Corps members from 1946 until 1948, under the condition they work on farms for two years before being granted landed-immigrant status. (Canadian citizenship was not automatically granted; they would then have to go through the usual application process that required a five-year waiting period.) According to data from the Department of Labour, Alberta accepted 750 Polish vets from that group.

During the recruitment process to immigrate to Canada, over 7,000 men applied to participate in this program, and the strict selection process excluded those who were married and those who did not have agricultural experience. Those accepted had to be single, in good health, and able to perform heavy labour. Based on the Canadian–British agreement, the selection process was handled by a Canadian interdepartmental commission, which reviewed all applications and denied participation based on three reasons: medical grounds (23 per cent), security reasons (31 per cent), or failure of a brief test of agricultural knowledge (46 per cent). Only after meeting the criteria set by the program, were the veterans accepted as "qualified agriculturalists" and granted landed-immigrant status. On the day of their departure to Canada, the servicemen received their military discharge documents, indicating that their military service with the Polish forces had taken place under British command.

By joining the Polish Resettlement Corps, which was designed to help find employment or provide further training, soldiers of the

II Polish Corps risked being considered still involved in the military service of a foreign country. And according to *The Times* on September 4, 1946, Polish soldiers who elected to join the Polish Resettlement Corps would have their citizenship revoked by the Polish government in power based on 1920 Polish citizenship law, which read, "Polish citizenship is lost by the acceptance of a public office or through entering into the military service of a foreign country without the consent of the Polish Government." Poland's Provisional Government of National Unity considered all Polish soldiers who joined the Polish Resettlement Corps renegades. The article in *The Times* described the situation of the Polish soldiers discharged from the Anders Army and stationed in Great Britain as complicated because in order to train them for civilian duties they had to be placed under military law in order to effectively deal with large number of Polish solders affected. (The legal situation was even more complex for those who refused to return to Poland and refused to join the Polish Corps.)

So, in addition to an uncertain future, those veterans who refused to return to Poland had to deal with the prospect of losing Polish citizenship. The II Polish Army Corps of General Anders had comprised thousands of Poles who refused to be drafted into the Red Army by force, and who had been imprisoned in Soviet gulags or labour camps as a result. Thus, the idea of revoking their Polish citizenship caused bitter feelings and was seen as a blow to their military honour, as is reflected in an inscription at the cemetery at Monte Cassino:

> We Polish soldiers
> For our freedom and yours
> Have given our souls to God
> Our bodies to the soil of Italy
> And our hearts to Poland

The situation of the Polish veterans was truly complex. It included finding a country where they could start a new life after becoming stateless because of their decision to join the Polish Resettlement Corps. Unfortunately this background was not presented to the Canadian public by the Canadian media; it was written about only in newspapers in Great Britain. According to Ernest Bevin, the British foreign secretary involved in the creation of the Polish Resettlement Corps, "the corps was essentially designed to facilitate the transition from military to civil life," referring not only to the II Polish Army Corps but to the entire Polish armed forces in the West. Articles published in *The Times* in London, based on information from a diplomatic correspondent in Poland, noted how "the Polish Government expressed its anxiety over the military guise which the Resettlement Corps threatens to assume." The Polish government reasoned that not stripping Polish citizenship from those who would not return to Poland would be "prejudicial to the development of friendly Polish–British relations."

The recruitment for the Polish Resettlement Corps scheduled to start on September 11, 1946, at first sent a hopeful message to the distressed members of the Polish armed forces in the West who felt they had no country. The British government distributed hastily prepared and error-laden leaflets printed in Polish to Polish soldiers serving under British command. Foreign Secretary Bevin's message in these pamphlets came out of several months of negotiations between the British government and the provisional Government of National Unity, the authority allowed to speak on behalf of Poland. These talks had tried to find a way for all Polish soldiers—including infantry soldiers, marines, and air-force pilots—to return to Poland. The British government declared that it was satisfied with the outcome of those negotiations and with the declaration by the Polish government on how these Poles would be treated upon their return to Poland. Furthermore, Bevin stated that the British government did not intend to allow Polish armed forces to stay outside of Poland as an independent military unit under British command. Instead, the British government announced demobilization of the Polish troops in the West, not intending to guarantee all soldiers would be allowed to settle in Great Britain or its dominions. The British government seemed convinced nothing stood in the way of the soldiers' return to Poland. Moreover, Bevin encouraged the Polish armed forces to help with the rebuilding of a liberated Poland and emphasized this was the only way to serve their country. Bevin said, however, that Polish soldiers who did not see returning to Poland as viable would be treated by the British government in a way worthy of their merits. However, the level of help would be limited by sources available. The messages conveyed by Bevin did not convince many Poles serving in the Polish armed forces in the West to return to Poland; they felt Britain had sided with the pro-Soviet Polish government, and even with the Soviets themselves, as confirmed by the Polish veterans interviewed. But Bevin asked they consider the alternatives and their situation conscientiously, arguing that such an opportunity might not be available to them again. For many, this came as a warning of a possible change in the relationship between the Polish government and its citizens remaining in the West.

The Polish government followed through on its threatening words, and the situation of the Polish servicemen was further complicated when an article titled "Training of Poles as Civilians. An Unhelpful Speech" was printed in *The Times* on September 14, 1946, confirming fears that an individual who voluntarily elected to join the Polish Resettlement Corps "would lose not only his rank and Polish decorations, but his citizenship too" as stated by Marshal of Poland Michał Rola-Żymierski. During the interviews conducted, the veterans recalled that they were given a one-week deadline to return to Poland where they would be given "a chance to rehabilitate." Niewiński and Nieumierzycki believed they had to go back to the place of their birth, which for them and others meant territory of the Soviet Union. On September 30, 1946, *The Times* reported that seventy-five senior Polish officers, including General Anders, in charge of the II Polish Army Corps, and General Kopański, commander of the Carpathian Brigade, and four other generals, would lose Polish citizenship because, by joining the Polish Resettlement Corps, they had committed the crime of treason. *The Times* correspondent in Warsaw pointed out that the list of the military personnel losing their Polish citizenship would expand further, adding to the feelings of uncertainty. Under such circumstances, the majority of the soldiers from the II Polish Army Corps, fearing persecution and imprisonment, opted to stay in exile and joined the Polish Resettlement Corps. As a result, the Polish veterans had their Polish citizenship taken away.

The Canadian media, however, did not present any of these complex issues to the Canadian public, which might have facilitated understanding and compassion for them. Instead, the veterans had no one to turn to for help or advice. They had no contact with family left behind in the war-divested Europe. All they had were their friends and comrades from the battlefields of Europe, who came together to a new country to start a new life in an unfamiliar environment and culture where they had to blaze new trails as stateless people. They had no fatherland, no home and no family to go back to.

In addition to the first-hand stories shared by the WWII Polish veterans, how the Canadian press portrayed those soldiers and veterans during the WWII and postwar periods sheds more light on the challenges they faced. On February 16, 1945, the *Toronto Daily Star* printed an article titled "Pole Boys in Italy Veto Big 3 Ruling" that quoted General Anders in his opposition to the outcome of the Yalta Conference, and his criticism of the practices that he described as undemocratic. General Anders lent his unwavering support to the Polish government-in-exile in London that had been derecognized by the governments led by Churchill, Stalin and Roosevelt, their successors and, consequently, by the entire world. Even though this article reported some details of General Anders' official statement in a straightforward manner, the headline framed his position differently, as immature and soon to be dismissed. The media portrayal also used the headline to frame the Polish troops negatively by referring to them as "Pole Boys in Italy." His protest, interpreted as reactionary and trivial, could be considered evidence that Anders and the Polish troops in the West under his command would become problematic.

This article and other similar-in-tone articles about the Polish troops published in Canada in 1945 represented a change of the discourse about the Polish soldiers in the West. The words used to describe the Polish troops affected their image. In this reformulated discourse, the Polish soldiers were presented as disgruntled renegades, unwilling to accept the new postwar world order, and most likely influenced how they were perceived upon their arrival in Canada. Because the article "Pole Boys in Italy Veto Big 3 Ruling" did not elaborate on the Polish troops' involvement in the Italian military campaign, fighting alongside Canadian soldiers during one of the most challenging and lengthy battles, they were not seen as Allied soldiers who fought for freedom. Instead, the Polish troops in the West were portrayed as "refusing to recognize the Big Three's solution to Polish Problem," and suggested their disapproval of the new political order might pose a problem in the future.

Later on, newspaper articles published in Canada concentrated on the issue of the Polish soldiers who were to come to Canada to work on farms but the trend toward a less favourable description of Polish veterans in Canadian media continued. Anticipating the group of 4,527 who were scheduled to arrive in Canada as part of the Polish Resettlement Corps, an article titled "Plan Make Poles

Good Canadians" was published on November 13, 1946, in the *Edmonton Journal*. The author H.R. Hardy discussed the plans in place for "the handling in Canada of the Polish soldiers who are coming to take over jobs on Canadian farms." Hardy reported that three hundred of the "so-called 'London Poles'" were scheduled to arrive in Lethbridge, Alberta, that week, and the plan was to "make them into Canadians in the quickest possible time." Referring to the II Polish Army Corps veterans as the "London Poles" recalled General Anders' protesting the Yalta Conference outcome and the derecognition of the Polish government-in-exile. The Polish soldiers were again portrayed as troublemakers and seen as opposing the new postwar order in Europe. Hardy's article not only criticized the Polish veterans but also managed to trivialize their protests.

Moreover, author Hardy drew potentially negative attention to the Polish vets, stating:

> Some propaganda has been spread among the so-called London Poles, indicating they are to be the nucleus of an army to fight the Russians in a couple of years, and therefore this is the only place for the army to wait, in the meantime. The Canadian government intends to knock that theory into a cocked hat. The Poles are coming here to become good Canadians.

The comment carried a serious allegation—that of the Polish veterans wanting to start a new international military conflict in the near future and suggesting their intentions were to use their time in Canada to prepare for it. With the war just finished, and considering the damage it produced around the world, no one in Canada was interested in taking part in another military conflict. Hence, the portrayal of the Polish veterans as potential warmongers and troublemakers had a serious impact on their treatment and reception in Canada.[3] This opinion about the veterans presented by Canadian media could have been sufficient to justify putting them on farms where they had limited access to Polish organisations and to other Poles who had immigrated to Canada earlier.

Since the media is the public sphere where discourses are formed, comments such as Hardy's carried power and his words were influential. Moreover, the article used ambiguous language that could cause misunderstanding and lead readers to form an inaccurate and skewed image of the Polish soldiers coming to work on Lethbridge farms. By saying that the Poles had fought "with the Canadians," the author could be interpreted as indicating they fought either in support of, or against, the Canadian troops. Some readers might have concluded that the Polish veterans had been siding with the German aggressor during the war. Words used ambiguously can produce long-lasting consequences.

Moreover, author Mark Bourrie in his book, *The Fog of War: Censorship of Canada's Media in World War Two*, noted a trend where most censors wanted bad news included in newspapers to keep the population in a state of controlled fear. Both the Polish veterans and the Canadian public were subjected to this practice, which put them on opposite sides.

Another statement in Hardy's article illustrates the power vested in words and how they could have contributed to the formation of discourse describing this group: "Plans have been completed for the handling in Canada of the Polish soldiers who are coming to take over jobs on Canadian farms." This suggests that the Polish soldiers were brought to Canada to take over jobs performed by others, who would then become jobless. There was a shortage of agricultural labourers in Canada during the later years of the war, because farm work had been performed by German POWs. Once again, because of the ambiguous presentation of the labour situation on Canadian farms, the Polish veterans were portrayed as being part of a problem, rather than the solution. By implying that the veterans would be taking

jobs that others needed, Hardy showed a lack of trust and acceptance, and built distance between Canadians and the Polish soldiers.

At that time, Canada was not yet a mosaic and any newcomers
who did not speak English or French were seen as "others," further
emphasizing the immigrants as outsiders as described by Ivana
Caccia in her study of wartime citizenship policy. The war highlighted "otherness" and put boundaries between "us," the dominant
majority, and "them," the ethnic minorities. Caccia argued that
diversity in Canada was attributed not only to the language spoken
by an ethnic group but to other cultural differences such as religion,
folklore, dress, food, and traditional practices, thus extending the
perception of "otherness." Through that extension, an imbalanced
power relationship formed between these groups.

Hardy's article, and others like it, illustrate how the dominant
majority in Canada might have viewed the Polish veterans as problematic "others" and how their "otherness" was further exacerbated
by events of the war. The Polish veterans thereby became an unwit-
ting part of this uneven status between the majority (those already
established in Canada) and the minority of "others" (newcomers to
the country). Discursive practices contribute to such power relationships in societies where there are distinct relations of dominance
based on class, gender, or belonging to a cultural group. How media
presented the issue of Polish veterans as "others" contributed to
the formation of the discourse of Polish veterans as undeserving
of being viewed as veterans but rather as posing a potential danger to the public. Thus, it was implied that their case needed to
be dealt with—and swiftly. The term "handling" suggests that the
Polish soldiers were viewed as objects and not as people; it implies
an impersonal approach and illustrates a sense of separation by
removing their human characteristics. Hence, this suggests the pre-
existence of a distance between the dominant majority and people
of ethnic background and shows how the soldiers were treated as

"others" even before they reached Canada. In this case, they were to be seen and identified only as farm labourers and not as war veterans, potentially blurring the sense of their achievements. The media portrayal determined their position in Canadian society even before their arrival and thus formulated the discourse of Polish veterans as farm help.

Hardy's article also addressed plans on how to integrate the soldiers into Canadian society: 1) Teach them English; 2) Offer education facilities; 3) Provide entertainment; 4) Encourage them to mix with Canadians; 5) Go slow in forming Polish societies. If the main point of this plan was to teach them English to help with their integration, sending them to work on farms, with limited contact with others, was an ineffective way. During the interviews, the veterans commented on their feelings of isolation from society when working on farms for an extended time. In some cases, they were left alone for months to look after the farm when the farmers went away to work as hired hands on farms in the US, leaving them in charge.

Moreover, suggesting entertainment as the only form of counselling that was required for the soldiers so they would not "brood or espouse nationalistic causes in company with other Poles," underestimates or denies the stress they might have been experiencing after being exposed to the atrocities of war. Some of the surviving veterans reported how challenging it was to deal with past events, and were likely suffering from what is now recognized as post-traumatic stress disorder (PTSD). Some stated that they experienced suicidal thoughts related to isolation, feelings of powerlessness, and difficulties dealing with the stress after they were put into an unfamiliar and unfriendly environment with no contact with others like them.

The last point Hardy listed, "go slow in forming Polish societies," reflected society's approach to assimilation through obligatory separation from one's ethnic roots, which did not allow the soldiers to offer their own ideas. They were expected to assimilate quickly and take on the values and beliefs of Canadian society. Hardy added that based on the experience with other ethnic groups, "block segregation" was needed because:

> In the past, authorities say it has been found that among Canadians of foreign birth much of the trouble develops when not understanding English, and having no place to go, they crowd into Polish halls and Polish societies. Such societies are considered all right if the Poles have been in Canada some time and have developed a sense of balance.

Hardy cited an unnamed official who explained a need to prevent potential future problems the Polish veterans might experience by encouraging them not to think about such issues: "we do not want these newcomers brooding over Poland's troubles, we want them to become Canadians and to forget all European's troubles." The tradition of assimilation of immigrants into Canadian society through the acceptance and incorporation of practices of dissemination of power in society was apparently the proven method to deal with the Polish veterans. In the first step of assimilation, they were expected to fit into the pre-existing structure in society without analyzing their needs as survivors of war. Then, the Poles should undergo further assimilation geared toward aligning their behaviours with those of the dominant Canadian culture. The Canadian authorities had taken such steps to deal with assimilation of immigrants in the past, according to the article.

If the desired result was for labourers to stay on farms beyond their two-year contracts and forget about their homeland, this process of assimilation by separation did not work, as some of them reported during the interviews. Examining the program from the perspective of benefits for Canada, Dr. Martin Thornton saw the program as a failure, considering that "when the farm contracts were completed, 97 per cent of the Polish vets moved to the towns and cities." Not satisfied with their working conditions and their treatment on the farms, many wanted to change their jobs or be assigned to work for another farmer. However, they had to work on farms for two years before being allowed to take different jobs, and changing farms was not something the Canadian government wanted them to do.

4

The Immigrant as Ethnic

THE LIVES AND STORIES of the Polish veterans who came
to Canada after the war to work on farms were set in a unique
socio-historical setting when concepts of ethnicity were changing.
The evolution of ethnic consciousness and definition in Canada
in the post-WWII period had a direct impact on the Polish veterans who were brought to this country as part of the 1947 Polish
Resettlement Corps.

According to the accepted definition at the time of WWII, an
ethnic group was a distinct group sharing a historical identity and
traditions of its own.[1] Persons identified as "ethnic" were considered
outsiders to the dominant national identity, and their ethnicity was
the primary focus of their identity. Members of an ethnic group usually shared common and distinct characteristics acquired at birth.
Cultural factors such as language, religion, national origin and history, played a role in forming cultural and ethnic groups, within
which members formed ties of solidarity and loyalties. Hence,

ethnicity bound together and formed an exclusive, transgenerational group, because an individual had to be born into it.

At the same time, ethnicity was perceived differently in the Anglo-American and the European traditions. The Anglo-American tradition of the time called minority groups within a larger society of the nation-state "ethnic." In European culture, however, ethnicity was understood from the perspective of nationhood defined historically by ancestry or territory. An ethnic group could share roots, customs, memories and possibly physical traits, though not necessarily blood ties.[2]

An ethnic group could also exist or be formed via a political or social trigger, as in the case of the Polish veterans in this book.[3] When an ethnic group shares (and teaches the next generation) cultural practices and beliefs, they help to form a status group with others who share their roots. Belonging to such a status group allows members to benefit and feel a sense of dignity, as with the Polish veterans when they were able to join a Polish army or community.

But in a situation where the dominant group in society maintains social, political and economic dominance over the status group, that group could also be deprived of benefits, especially in cases of limited resources. The life stories in this book show how this was experienced by the Polish veterans both in the USSR and in Canada. The dominant group exploited its position over the ethnic group of the Polish veterans who came to Canada as potential immigrants.

"Ethnicity" as a term has always carried with it a sense of subordination and inequality and, as a sociological term, has lost favour in the postmodern period. The term "diaspora" has come to replace it because it conveys a sense of neutrality and equality. Until the 1970s, the meaning of diaspora referred more to religious groups who were physically scattered, but political scientist William Safran notes that this has changed: a "diaspora community" includes "expatriates, expellees, political refugees, alien residents, immigrants, and ethnic and racial minorities." Immigration produces diasporic communities in which ethnic identity has to be negotiated within the group and with the broader community.[4] Those who had to flee Poland during the years of WWII "could be considered members of a genuine diaspora." As shown in earlier chapters, the veterans who came to Canada were identified as the "Polish problem" and seen within the media and Canadian society as replacements for German POW farm labourers, and less welcome as potential immigrants. They were primarily seen by Canadian society not as war veterans but as members of an ethnic group.

During and after WWII, Canadian immigration policies were not welcoming and disallowed the admittance of a substantial number of potential citizens.[5] At the outbreak of war, Canadian immigration offices closed in Germany and Poland and, by 1941, also in Paris, Antwerp, and Rotterdam. Later, the closures also affected the Canadian immigration offices in Great Britain, which handled all Canadian immigration issues in Europe, and therefore had a significant impact on the number of admissions.

In the postwar years, Statistics Canada figures indicated some increase in the number of immigrants: from almost the lowest number on record, 7,576 in 1942, to 71,719 in 1946. (The highest number between 1852 and 1946 was 400,870 in 1913.) The reasons for this decline in the 1940s included applicants not being able to meet the financial requirements after losing their property and source of income due to war, travel restrictions and the closure of the Canadian immigration offices in Europe.

The complexity of the restrictive immigration process, and even the cost of a visa, were also factors, as seen in the case of Ewa (née Kulawska), the wife of Stefan Koselak. She received a permit in her temporary travel document allowing for a single journey to Canada from a displaced persons (DP) camp. Her immigration visa was valid for only six months, yet she had to twice undergo a health examination by the Department of National Health and Welfare. The fee for the visa was twenty German marks.[6] After surviving the Soviet takeover, being captured by the German invader and being sent to a forced labour camp, Ewa Koselak spent several years working as unpaid domestic help in Germany. After the war, while still in Germany, she worked for the International Red Cross, saving money to immigrate to Canada because she was told by relatives not to return to her pre-war residence in Poland since it was already part of the Soviet Union.

Of course, war events also significantly affected the situation and civil liberties of other groups of immigrants already settled in Canada. Some 22,000 Japanese Canadians in British Columbia were sent to internment camps and their properties confiscated; thousands of German and Italian descent were also imprisoned, as was anyone who displayed any Fascist, Communist, or radical labour sympathy. Jewish refugees were not allowed to come to Canada. This all took place with the widespread support of the Canadian public, corroborating a belief that ancestry contributed to the forming of allegiance among ethnic group members, thus not only legitimizing the actions of the Canadian government but also exhibiting the distrust of Canadians toward members of ethnic communities, especially those considered "enemies" at the time. The years between 1930 and 1945 were described by immigration researchers Kelley and Trebilcock as the "blackest cloud in Canadian immigration history" when Canada earned the "worst record of any democracy in providing assistance to the persecuted Jews of Europe." The humanitarian values for which Canadian soldiers fought abroad were apparently not practised at home at that time. Even the occasional sign or words to the contrary offered only empty gestures, since they did not provide assistance for refugees.

In 1943, when concentration camps were set up and fully operational in Europe, the Canadian prime minister was quoted in the House claiming the majority of refugees were on territory controlled by the Axis powers and few had been able to escape. For the rest, "there is nothing the allied governments can do for those hapless people," Mackenzie King said, "except to win the war as quickly as and as completely as possible." King saw European refugees as an international issue requiring an international solution and indicated that when such an international solution was found, the number of refugees accepted to Canada would depend on the availability of employment, transportation to Canada and, later, their repatriation to Europe after the war. He also expressed concern for Canada's domestic security, namely preventing the immigration of spies and secret agents.

The official position on restricting entry to Canada was the uncertain postwar economy. However, internal government documents and memoranda indicated that restrictions were kept in place "to ensure that the country did not become a haven for the displaced and mainly Jewish refugees from Nazi aggression." A few members of Parliament, the Jewish community, various church groups, humanitarian organizations and some members of the press voiced support for introducing a more humanitarian policy for refugees. But that was not enough to relax the immigration policies as public opinion polls indicated that Canadians would not support this, in addition to a widely held belief that European Jews would not adapt to Canada. Throughout Canada, those of Jewish background experienced limited access to professions such as teaching and nursing, were prohibited from purchasing certain land and houses, and were ineligible for membership in private clubs. This approach to immigration resulted in an increase in only British and American nationals admitted, from 57 per cent in 1940 to 98 per cent in the five years that followed, and then mostly to reunite the families of Canadian residents.

In 1940, in response to a plea from the Polish government-in-exile requesting that Canada accept two thousand Polish refugees, Canada agreed to admit, temporarily, only one thousand of them. The Polish government was to cover the cost of their transportation and their repatriation after the war, and it had to adhere to a rule limiting the number of Jews in this group. The Canadian government accepted seventy-nine Polish Jews who fled from eastern Poland to Japan as part of this program.

To the Canadian government making the decisions, the skills of those refugees seemed as important as the refugees' need for finding a safe place to live. Such was the case for a group of seventy Polish engineers and technicians who escaped to France from war-torn Poland, and for whom the Polish government-in-exile requested assistance from the Canadian government in September 1941. The process of accepting them took several weeks, and the cost of their arrival was to be covered by the industries interested in employing them. These highly skilled Poles were to repay the expenses related to their transportation to Canada through deductions from their future wages. The Polish government promised financial support for those engineers and technicians unable to find jobs within the first four weeks. However, war events and rules implemented by the French government in January 1942 disallowed those under the age of forty-five to leave France, so the Polish engineers and technicians were unable to immigrate to Canada. Instead, the Canadian government allowed "several hundred Polish scientists and engineers" who were staying temporarily in Great Britain to come to Canada under the same rules.

The pre-WWII Canadian immigration policies did not change and the restrictive approach to immigration stayed in effect for approximately two years after the war. In the years following, however, Canada's economy adjusted to the postwar production requirements of industry and changed how Canada viewed refugees and displaced persons in Europe. At that time, the Canadian government became more involved in supporting international organizations bringing relief to countries affected by the war. Canada became an active participant in the United Nations' Relief and Rehabilitation Administration program to help countries affected by the war.

As the Canadian economy improved, Canadian immigration policies introduced from 1946 until 1962 were meant to accommodate the growing needs for labour. In 1947, Prime Minister Mackenzie King stated, "admission was a privilege, [and] immigrants were to be viewed in terms of their potential contribution to the economy; and immigration was not to change the fundamental demographic character of the community." The prime minister's ideas of privilege and of maintaining a static demographic character to Canadian identity thus had a negative impact on the Polish veterans regarding job opportunities, self-image and social status in Canada. The immigrant was viewed as un-Canadian, suggesting a contradiction between fostering assimilation and focusing on differences.

Such selective admission to Canada was criticized by the Senate Standing Committee on Immigration and Labour, which recommended revising the Immigration Act and policies to deal with the postwar problems of displaced persons in Europe, as well as bring to Canada a qualified labour force that could be employed in agriculture and industry. In addition to this internal pressure to change Canadian immigration policy, the British government requested Canada assist resettling a group of Polish veterans from the II Polish Army Corps who refused to be repatriated to a Poland that was under the Soviet Union's influence. In July 1946, Mackenzie King responded to the request and initially "rejected the idea of accepting Polish soldiers as immigrants." However, anticipating a shortage of agricultural workers, the Canadian government allowed for an admission of more than three thousand Polish veterans under the condition they work on farms. Under this agreement, the British government was to organize and pay for their transportation and in July 1946, the Canadian government passed an order-in-council approving the admission of some three thousand Poles to work on farms.

Thus, in 1947, Canada accepted 4,527 Polish veterans from Britain and Italy under a contract labour scheme, an agreement to work on a farm for two years, even though some of the Canadian farmers protested they wanted to guarantee employment for only one year. Under this agreement, Polish veterans accepted as qualified agriculturalists were to be granted landed-immigrant status.[7] Before their departure from Europe, they underwent health screening conducted by the Departments of Justice, Health and Welfare. Nevertheless, after some of them arrived and were screened in Canada, several showed signs of tuberculosis so could not work.

The arrival of Polish veterans took place in several phases. On September 23, 1946, *The Calgary Herald* reported, "Alberta's share of the 4,000 former Polish soldiers will be 450. All men have farm experience, are single and under 35 years of age." The *Herald* article further stated that their wages would be no less than $45 per month. Their wages were significantly lower than those paid to other farm workers; according to Statistics Canada, average wages of male farm help in Alberta was $60.25 per month with board, and $86.01 without board.[8] Moreover, since the Polish veterans were offered approximately the same wages as the German POWs previously employed on Canadian farms, the Polish veterans felt offended.

Work clothing caused further offence and assimilation problems, not only when the Polish veterans were required to return their good British army greatcoats in exchange for a clothing allowance of $41.25, but also when the Canadian authorities provided agricultural clothes intended for German prisoners or, in some cases, used by them. The misunderstanding caused was unsurprising; when

Canadians saw Poles wearing the provided uniforms, they often confused them with the German POWs. Taking into consideration conditions under which these veterans participated in the two-year farm service, it was no wonder that they felt more like prisoners of war than immigrants.

In 1947, the Canadian Citizenship Act replaced the old British subject category with Canadian citizenship and in 1952, a new Immigration Act outlined requirements for candidates. Until 1962 Canada focused on bringing immigrants from western European and some Commonwealth countries. An applicant's country of origin played a role in acceptance or rejection, especially if they were suspected of Communist sympathies, given the sensitive issue of national security during the Cold War. After that year, the focus was put on skills, education and training, and these became the primary selection criteria. During the drafting phase of the new Immigration Act, many organizations were consulted; notable was a new reaction to the matter of increased immigration from the labour movement in Canada. Until 1946, labour unions had opposed the growing number of immigrants out of fear that it would affect the number of available jobs in Canada, increase unemployment, and therefore cause lower wages. However, organized labour approved of postwar immigration as a way of raising the international position of Canada. Also, Canadian business pushed for increased immigration because of the shortage of skilled labour.

In May 1947, under pressure to deal with the issue of displaced persons in Europe, the government introduced changes that allowed for an increase in the number of new immigrants, dependant on an "absorptive capacity" that was not specified. Under this amendment to immigration policies, new immigrants were meant to alleviate labour shortages, and as Mackenzie King stressed, "the racial and national balance of immigration would be regulated so as not to alter the fundamental character of the Canadian population."

Canada's new approach to the issue of refugee and displaced persons and recognition of its moral obligation to deal with the postwar crisis was, according to political historian Valerie Knowles, the first step in relaxing immigration policies and introducing new categories, such as sponsored and non-sponsored, which resulted in more immigrants to Canada. In 1947, the Department of Labour sent teams of immigration officers to Europe to the camps of displaced persons to help with selection. The preferences were for "able-bodied refugees," which John Holmes, a postwar undersecretary of state for Canada's Department of External Affairs, described "like good beef cattle, with a preference for strong young men who could do manual labour and would not be encumbered by ageing relatives." During the selection process, the immigration officers screened the immigrants, assessing them on how useful they would be for the Canadian economy. The Canadian officials also looked at ethnic background as a central criterion in the selection process, and routinely rejected Jewish applicants. Preference was given to those whose political views did not support communist ideology, which was also deemed "undesirable."

In 1950, the Canadian government created the Department of Citizenship and Immigration. As a result, a higher number of immigrants were accepted to Canada under the following conditions: "any European who could 'satisfy the Minister that he is suitable, having regard to the climatic, social, educational, labour and other conditions or requirements of Canada.'"[9] In 1952, the *Immigration Act* came into force and simplified the process of bringing new immigrants to Canada. However, the significant difference of this *Act* was that categories such as nationality, ethnicity, occupation, or lifestyle were not allowed as criteria for exclusion. Moreover, to help immigrants come to Canada, a system of loans was established to assist with the cost of transportation.

Many of the WWII Polish veterans who arrived in Canada had obtained education when serving in the Polish Resettlement Corps in Great Britain and Italy as part of the Polish Resettlement Act. Polish veterans serving in the Anders Army also received vocational training in shoemaking, tailoring and carpentry, and learned new skills such as driving and operating heavy equipment, machinery and trucks or setting up telecommunication lines and operating complex telecom equipment. Hundreds of the men attended Italian universities. Had the Polish veterans been given the opportunity to work in their professions or trades, they might have been more valuable and productive workers in Canada and adapted to the Canadian culture much faster, but they were put into isolation on Canadian farms removed from mainstream society. It needs to be noted that many of them, after fulfilling the two-year contract of working on farms, went on to work in their acquired professions or trades.

Regarding the issue of power relationships between ethnic groups and society, Canadian sociologist John Porter pointed out how immigrants were expected to fit into the social structure already in place. Furthermore, the socio-economic status of immigrants was determined by the social and economic position of the corresponding ethnic group that already resided in Canada. Between 1946 and 1951 almost half of the immigrants who came to Canada worked in agriculture, reflecting Canada's long-lasting preference for immigrants to take on farm jobs. Porter referred to the notion of "entrance status," when, over a more extended period, a less desirable ethnic group was fitted into a lower level of social and economic position. The expectation was that these immigrants would take on lower-level occupations and be subjected to assimilation rules set up by the dominant group in Canadian society. Furthermore, Porter argued that the socio-economic position and opportunities for upward social mobility of members of these ethnic

THE IMMIGRANT AS ETHNIC   81

groups affected not only the first generation but also the second and third generations born in Canada. Groups affected included Ukrainians, Poles, Finns and Czechoslovaks. There was a difference between behavioural assimilation, which Porter defined as the level of engagement of the ethnic group in the culture of the society, and structural assimilation, which he described as a process in place that defines and implements the position of immigrants in society. Over time, structural assimilation is followed by behavioural assimilation.

The issue of ethnic groups in Canada had become more complicated at the start of World War II; its political implications created allies and enemies in Canada. In 1939, Deputy Minister of Justice J.F. MacNeill communicated his concerns to the prime minister that those residing in Canada with a background other than British or French potentially posed a threat to Canada's security if the adaptation process to Canadian life and society was left unregulated. Furthermore, MacNeill pointed out that immigrants relied on their ethnic newspapers as a source of information, indicating their lack of knowledge of English or French, and accentuating their position as outsiders or "others." The "otherness" that was further highlighted by military conflicts put boundaries between the dominant majority and the ethnic minorities. Being seen as an outsider in Canada was not only attributed to the language spoken but also to other cultural differences such as religion, folklore, dress, food, and traditional practices.

When articles written by immigrants or about immigrants were published in Canadian newspapers, their names were sometimes Anglicized to disguise their ethnic roots because such names were seen as alien and impossible to pronounce; this practice also influenced the situation of the immigrants in Canada. For instance, the shortage of skilled labour often led qualified workers from Alberta to seek jobs in other provinces, but when their names suggested Slavic descent, they were not hired in Ontario. Stories about the

WWII Polish veterans that changed Władysław to Walter, Anatol to Tony, Czesław to Chester, Eugeniusz to Eugene, Karol to Carl, and even adjusted the spelling of last names to the English version are common. The negative implication of this practice greeted the Polish veterans when they came to Canada.

Upon their arrival in Canada, the Polish veterans were seen as members of a distinct ethnic group. Their national origin was not only a characteristic in common but influenced their actions in this new setting, affected how the Canadian institutions treated them before and after their arrival, and influenced how the rest of Canadian society related to them. The notions of solidarity and loyalty to each other and their nation of origin is obvious in the veterans' narratives when they describe themselves as the survivors of deportation to Siberia and Kazakhstan, and as soldiers of the II Polish Army Corps who fought for Monte Cassino. The cultural factors such as common language, common national origins and common religion prove that the group of the Polish veterans saw themselves as a distinct community.

The role of the Canadian media in further fostering an ethnic identity is evident in an article, "Poles Here Are Asked to Register," published November 21, 1946, in *The Windsor Daily Star*. Referring to the Polish soldiers as "Poles" stressed that they shared common characteristics and belonged to a larger group of Poles, including those already in Canada. In the article, the group of WWII Polish veterans was defined as a group of Polish nationals destined to work on farms. By highlighting that they belonged to an ethnic group, and as non-Canadians were required to register with authorities, the article stressed how they differed from Canadian society as a whole.

Upon their arrival in Canada, the Polish veterans could not rely on access to Polish language newspapers: only three weekly papers existed in 1946 with 15,157 copies in circulation, most likely unavailable except in the major urban centres in eastern Canada. Thus, the majority of information about the Polish veterans was printed in English-language newspapers, to which the Poles had limited access because of the language barrier and unavailability in rural settings.

A small group of Polish soldiers who came to Alberta to work on farms was introduced to the public for the first time on November 26, 1946, when *The Calgary Herald* published an article titled, "Polish Soldiers Happy to Start New Life on Canadian Farms." It reported on their arrival while emphasizing their non-Canadian nationality as the focus of their identity. The headline framed their role as farm workers in Canada, further highlighting how they differed from the dominant majority. On their way from Lethbridge to Calgary, they were "escorted" by a representative of the provincial government Department of Agriculture. Another ethnic frame was applied when the soldiers' names were Anglicized, even though a police court interpreter and a representative of the Polish Canadian Alliance was there to interpret for them.

According to the newspaper article, the Polish soldiers arrived in Calgary to start "a new life in a new country," and their new jobs would "eventually lead them to Canadian citizenship." By pointing to the group's solidarity and their loyalties that brought them to Canada, the news further highlighted their ethnicity, as they expressed gratitude to everyone for everything, as they drank coffee and ate sandwiches prepared by the Red Cross. The article then referred to how the Polish soldiers' solidarity had deeper roots in their shared "experience in Russian concentration camps and under Russian rule at the beginning of the war before they were released to serve in General Anders' Polish army." The ties and loyalty among the Polish veterans were described as forged by the common suffering they experienced in the labour camps in the Soviet Union and during fighting alongside the Allies in the military campaign in Italy. Presenting this background information, intentionally or not, accentuated the Polish war veterans being seen as "others" by mainstream Canadian society. The newspaper article pointed out the issue of the language barrier causing difficulties in communication between the employers (members of the provincial government's Department of Agriculture) and the soldiers–employees, with their need for an interpreter. The social interaction between the soldiers and those greeting them in Calgary centred on their plans for the future when the Polish soldiers "used universal sign language" to answer the question, "Do [they] hope to marry a Canadian girl and stay in Canada?" When asked about their war experience, they were not willing to talk about the internment camps in the Soviet Union. Their military involvement on the battlefields in Europe was only described through the presence of "campaign ribbons" affixed to their military uniforms.

Many of the Polish immigrants had kept their uniforms, or at least parts of them, such as hats, identification tags ("dog tags"), documents and, most important, medals. In the stories they shared later, they used metaphors related to their military uniforms that were instrumental in creating mental associations with the positioning of themselves as soldiers. The way they talked about their uniforms invoked compelling images of their attitudes as soldiers fighting for freedom. Therefore, when they had to wear their military uniforms while performing farm duties, they had to find a way to explain this change to themselves and others. The interviews shared later in this book allowed the veterans to tell their stories, describe their lives as soldiers, veterans and farm workers, and, ultimately, illustrate how they positioned themselves within the events of WWII and how they constructed their identities differently from how the Canadian media portrayed them in their stories of the period.

However, the identity of the Polish veterans as presented to Calgarians kept deteriorating. On December 14, 1946, there were two examples in *The Calgary Herald*: one headline read "Polish Vets Suffering T.B., Venereal Disease" and another article that seemed to favour the German POWs over the Polish veterans as farm workers. The differences in their constructed identities are a direct response to the way they were treated and/or perceived by the dominant society that kept affirming their "otherness."

Lacking access to mainstream venues to tell their stories, the Polish veterans felt they had no platform or voice, especially during the initial two years of their life in Canada. Many years, if not decades later, some did engage in writing autobiographies where they recorded their stories and how they positioned themselves within Canadian society: as soldiers who fought for freedom and as immigrants who undertook the challenges of starting a new life in a new country while building a community for themselves and their families. Now offered in the context of the story of a group of WWII Polish soldiers who came to Canada after the war, part of two of this book finally allows them to tell their stories directly.

5

Polish Veterans and Canadian Veterans

A Comparison

WITH THE UNITED KINGDOM looking to resettle as many as "228,000 Polish ex-servicemen (apart from other Polish civilians)" the Polish Resettlement Act was the British promise to assist a select group of Poles who wished to settle outside Poland, given the new geopolitical makeup of postwar Europe. The act was introduced in the British House of Commons in 1947 and "open only to members of the Polish armed forces under British command."

The primary purpose for accepting the Polish veterans, as Thornton has stated, was that Canada wanted to find replacements for German prisoners of war who had been working in the sugar beet fields of Ontario and other provinces. Thus, because of the need for farm workers, Canada accepted 4,527 Polish veterans: 2,876 veterans came from the II Polish Corps stationed in 1946 in Italy, and the remaining 1,651 came from Great Britain. Canada's response to the crisis was to get maximum economic gain by bringing people to

Canada rather than getting involved in the humanitarian response overseas. Under the agreement between the Polish veterans and the Canadian government, they were not classified as displaced persons, and only after fulfilling the requirements of working for two years on farms were the Polish veterans to be granted landed-immigrant status.

Canada's approach was "in a limited sense, an example of the functional theory of representation or 'functionalism' that has been attributed to Canadian foreign policy," according to Thornton.[1] Canadians believed that Canada should play a role in the international system only to the extent it could afford to, so the level of assistance for the II Polish Army Corps was aligned with that belief. Moreover, the assistance was considered "an argument for not doing more for the displaced persons problem in Europe, particularly with respect to Jews." Accepting alternative refugee groups such as displaced persons, Thornton noted, would have incurred considerably more cost. And he quoted this comment from the Polish government protesting the Canadian immigration practices related to Polish veterans: "Certain groups of Polish citizens who happen to be outside of Poland should not be regarded as a human reservoir upon which a foreign country could draw without the approval of the Polish Government."

Even though none of the four veterans interviewed for this book reported working directly for a farmer of German origin in Alberta, Ewa Koselak had been sent to work for a family of German descent in the Pincher Creek area where other Polish veterans were also sent. Although she reported a mostly positive experience, she obliged her employers' request that she speak German to the children in her charge.

A situation in Saskatchewan offered a different version of the Alberta experience and support. As reported by the *Winnipeg*

Free Press in an article on May 17, 1947, with the headline "Polish Veteran Assailant Jailed," a Saskatchewan farmer "was convicted of ill-treating a former Polish soldier and sentenced to serve two months with hard labor in the Regina jail and in addition, to pay a fine of $100 and costs." Not satisfied with the individual court action, the Saskatchewan government ordered a general investigation into the treatment of Poles that Arthur MacNamara, deputy minister of Labour, welcomed. The article claimed, "Reports as to a farmer's character, and the condition of his farm were obtained in every case before a Polish war veteran was placed on a Saskatchewan farm." A dominion–provincial farm labour committee also made "periodic investigations at farms where Polish veterans were placed to check on their progress and welfare, but in this particular case no investigation had been made because of severe winter conditions." The head of the committee did offer the defence that other Polish war veterans placed in the community "appeared to be quite happy living with German families." The case shows how differently the Polish veterans were looked after in Saskatchewan in comparison with Alberta; none of the four Polish veterans interviewed reported the existence of a similar program in Alberta.

News from Alberta did not help to foster positive relations between Canada and Poland, and might have lent some credence to the Polish foreign minister's comment in 1947 that the majority of the Polish agricultural workers who came to Canada under this scheme worked on "German farms and were treated as 'polnische Schweine' [Polish pigs]" and if they hadn't signed a contract, would return to Poland.[2] The case of Polish veterans sent to work on farms in Canada drew attention internationally because the Polish veterans embodied anti-Soviet sentiments. Assigning them to work on farms that belonged to the Canadians of German ancestry strained the relationship between Canada and Poland and the Soviet Union.

These two countries saw the Canadian policy "as endorsing a reset-tlement policy contrary to the interests of the Soviet Union" and antagonizing the Polish government, according to Thornton.

Canada seemed most interested in economic value; costs to bring in the Polish veterans amounted to $5.54 for clothing for each individual, $125,000 in transportation costs from Halifax for the first 2,876 Poles who came from Italy, in addition to $20,000 travel costs to their assigned farms. The provincial Departments of Agriculture shared these expenses with the federal Department of Labour. Based on the data from the Department of Labour in September 1948, almost two years after the 4,527 veterans' arrival in Canada, 4,081 were employed on farms, but 91 were counted miss-ing, 14 deceased, 18 hospitalized, 12 in mental institutions, and 16 in Brandon Sanatorium. The British government covered half of any hospitalization costs in Canada.

From the perspective of short-term and long-term economic benefits for Canada, the program can be pronounced a failure, con-sidering that 97 per cent of the Polish veterans moved to towns and cities after their contracts were over. The assimilation program did not work either, especially when some Canadians did not recog-nize the difference between the German uniforms and the uniforms worn by the Poles and mistook them for Germans or enemy aliens, adding to their sense of undeserved mistreatment.

In distinct comparison to the situation of Polish veterans, docu-mented earlier and through their own stories, Canadian veterans returning from the front after wwii were encouraged in many ways to resume their pre-war life and employment. Legislation for the reintegration of veterans into civilian life and the 1944 Veterans Charter had been introduced to avoid what Canadian veterans had experienced upon their return after wwi, when they had received insufficient support from the government. The charter dealt with two main issues that affected the Canadian veterans of wwii:

compensation and recognition for service. Several acts dealt with the principle of recognition, and legislation was put in place to establish entitlement and eligibility, and to deal with compensation, life insurance, physical rehabilitation (or situations when rehabilitation was not possible). The charter also provided $1.2 billion for re-establishing Canadian veterans upon their return from war. The veterans could claim $100 for civilian clothes, obtain a life insurance policy in $500 increments up to $10,000, and apply for a grant of $7.50 for every thirty days of service with additional compensation for service in Europe and Asia. Ian A. Mackenzie, minister of Veterans Affairs from 1944 until 1948, wrote that the Veterans Charter was created "in the same high spirit of service which inspired Canadians to fulfil their obligations to the crucible of war."

The government considered the Canadian veterans' return to civilian life of highest priority. Other acts that followed included such legislation as the Veterans Rehabilitation Act to provide Canadian veterans with the opportunity to gain an education based on free university tuition or vocational training. Furthermore, the Veterans' Land Act was introduced as well as the Veterans' Business and Professional Loans Act that was aimed at assisting Canadian WWII veterans in establishing themselves in business, trades and professions. Moreover, the Canadian government re-established the Civil Employment Acts that assisted veterans in re-establishing their employment by introducing "veteran preference" for civil service jobs. The Reinstatement of Civil Employment Act guaranteed veterans their jobs back upon their return, plus any promotion they might have received in their absence. These laws were put in place to assist Canadian veterans returning from war to reintegrate into civilian life, even start a new career if they wished. Canadian war veterans were treated in a humane and dignified manner with numerous possibilities for new careers and reintegration into Canadian society. In contrast, the Polish war veterans felt that were treated poorly, more like prisoners than Allies. They had no career choices for two years and were often treated inhumanely on farms. These differences influenced their identity formation in Canada. For Canadian war veterans, there was honour and help; for Polish war veterans, there was shame and humiliation.

In December 1946, *The Calgary Herald* published articles and information on the help and assistance available to Canadian WWII veterans, how to alleviate the shortage of housing for veterans, as well as about the future of veterans' families. This response illustrated the eagerness of Canadian society to provide help and support to its WWII veterans. On December 14, 1946, the newspaper printed an advertisement about the training organized by the joint efforts of the Department of Lands and Mines, the Department of Veterans Affairs, and Canadian Vocational Training for returning veterans. Single men aged twenty-one to twenty-eight were offered vocational training that provided employment as assistant forest rangers. The qualified veterans were to receive the "usual training allowance" while attending the program.

Veterans who attended colleges and universities were also offered allowances to continue their studies. The article, "DVA 'Hopes to Pay' Vets' Allowances," published December 12, 1946, informed veterans attending Alberta universities that the Department of Veterans Affairs would make every effort to have their cheques "made out for the full month of December" since some "worried that they might not receive their allowance for the holiday period." This small insight illustrates the level of assistance and care given to the Canadian veterans.

Another issue of obvious importance to the Canadian government was the case of several hundred brides that Canadian veterans wanted to bring home from overseas. On December 10, 1946, *The Calgary Herald* published an article "Gov't Turning Cupid and Santa for Vets" assuring the veterans:

> Giving a hand to Cupid, the Canadian immigration department is ironing
> out a few rough spots in the course of true love for several hundred
> overseas fighters of the Second Great War.

The article further stated that the government "may even play a role
of Santa Claus in bringing over European fiancées of the former
servicemen in time for Christmas season marriages." To deal with
bureaucracy and to facilitate this "virtually impossible" undertaking, special immigration offices in Holland and Belgium were set up
"where many Canadians found future wives while fighting through
those countries." The article assured the public that the new system
was expected to work quickly. Canadian visas for brides would be
issued immediately upon the women passing the civil and medical examination. The article cites one of the Canadian servicemen
saying "there must be around a thousand other fellows in the same
position...and this will certainly be good news for them." This
article illustrates that the Canadian veterans and their future wives
were given preferential treatment by Canadian immigration officers
to speed up the arrival of war brides, allowing them to start a new
family life after the war.

With thousands of new marriages expected to take place within
a short time, there was a pressing need for more housing. The new-
lywed couples were experiencing problems finding homes because
of a shortage of rental properties available, and construction of
new housing was often stalled by the lack of building materials.
On December 14, 1946, *The Calgary Herald* printed a one-page
Calgary construction industry advertisement, declaring how the
industry "unites to aid veterans' housing." Driven by a desire to
help Canadian veterans who could not finish the building of their
houses due to the shortage of construction materials, all branches
of Calgary's construction industry, the local house builders' association and a Priorities Advisory Committee formed in Calgary

unified their efforts. The committee was asked by the Department of Reconstruction and Supply to survey unfinished homes of veterans and submit results to Ottawa. All three levels of government further supported this initiative, which was intended to complete at least three hundred homes in Calgary.

These *Herald* articles illustrate the initiatives undertaken by the community, the involvement of different levels of government and private industry, to help Canadian veterans obtain an education, find suitable employment, build a house and start a family.

The support and recognition given to Canadian war veterans was well-deserved. Applying such high standards of integration to other Allied soldiers like the Poles would have resulted in an entirely different experience for the Polish war veterans. They would have been integrated more speedily and received the recognition they deserved for their sacrifices in the war. The evidence of an obvious double standard in their treatment compared to that of the Canadian veterans was a sign of the divisions perpetuated in Canadian society and the status of ethnic minorities.

II

POLISH WAR VETERANS' STORIES

6

Interviewing the Veterans

THE MOST ESSENTIAL INFORMATION for this book came from
the Calgary Polish war veterans and their survivors.[1] The selection criteria for interview subjects included: service in the II Polish
Army Corps, immigration to Canada via Britain's 1947 Polish
Resettlement Act, fulfillment of the mandatory two-year farm work
contract, and later residency in Calgary.

During interviews with the veterans (or, in one case, with the
surviving family) I was presented with memoirs and physical artifacts such as military uniforms, war medals and original military
and immigration documents. I was also given access to the photographs taken during and after the war. These source documents and
artifacts added information about the participants' experiences as
detainees, soldiers, stateless people, war veterans, farm workers and
immigrants. I learned of their emotions, opinions and interactions—
both with individuals from the same ethnic group and with other
ethnic and mainstream groups involved in the integration process
after their arrival in Canada. In addition to their life stories, I was

able to learn about their motivations and expectations as individuals and members of an ethnic group.

Being born and educated in Poland helped me establish and maintain a rapport with the veterans throughout the research. My cultural awareness from living in Poland and in Canada—two culturally distinctive and different countries—helped me understand the perspectives presented by the Polish veterans. Talking with the veterans allowed stories to surface and put faces to stories documented in history books and reported in newspaper articles. The interviews provided me with the opportunity to learn what these people thought about the events they lived through and allowed a rare opportunity to ask how they felt about the events that took place in the past and how they feel about these events now.

Anatol Nieumierzycki, Władysław Niewiński, Zbigniew Rogowski and Stefan Koselak were all Polish veterans who served in the II Polish Army Corps under Lieutenant General Władysław Anders. They participated in the Battle of Monte Cassino that took place from January 17 until May 18, 1944. They came to Canada after the war as part of the Polish Resettlement Corps to work on farms for two years.

They were able to give information such as the dates of their deportations, names of institutions and geographical places, as well as personal data such as the composition of their families and the professions of their parents. They also provided documents such as discharge papers, personal photographs, and memoirs that supported their accounts. Their stories reveal their participation in, and observations of, global processes taking place at the time of WWII.

After the Soviet Union annexed the Polish territory along their shared eastern border, including Zachodnia Białoruś (western Belarus) and western Ukraine in 1939, Polish citizens experienced purges and mass deportation.

The four men featured in this book all joined the newly formed Polish army on the territory of the Soviet Union and served in the II Polish Army Corps that supported the Allies during the war. Their stories provide first-hand details about the deportation, forced resettlement and/or imprisonment the Polish population was subjected to after the Red Army attacked and annexed the eastern territory of Poland. They reported travelling for several weeks in freight cars over long distances and being detained in labour camps located in Siberia and Kazakhstan. They all had to perform heavy work, and they and their families underwent severe hardship, hunger and deprivation of the necessities of life.

The initial phase of deportation from the territory of Poland annexed by the Soviet Union took place on February 10, 1940. The first people of Polish ancestry who were deported were military settlers (police officers and forest rangers) who had moved there following the 1920 Soviet–Polish war, but that group was soon expanded to include security guards, government officers and their families. Nieumierzycki, Niewiński, Rogowski and Koselak were ethnic Poles, and that was grounds for deportation to Siberia and Kazakhstan. The military conflict of 1939 brought to the fore the ethnic divisions in the area where many different groups lived side-by-side as a result of territorial changes that had taken place over centuries and further highlighted these differences in the annexed territory.

Retelling their traumatic stories of displacement brought back memories of painful experiences that included being woken up in the middle of the night and forced to pack belongings before being taken to the railroad station, or being drafted into the invader's military. While travelling for a long time by freight trains, they witnessed many people dying of exhaustion, starvation and illnesses, and bodies being disposed of by the railroad tracks or at railway stations. They also recalled hunger when, as children, they were forced to beg for food for their families to survive. These powerful memories illustrate the traumatic experiences caused by larger political changes affecting the entire world. However, Koselak's reluctance to share his stories also illustrates a higher level of trauma. Ewa Koselak recalled, "my husband said nothing about the past. People did not talk about it, because it was sad, they talked very little." This approach was not limited to Koselak but was common among all people who experienced the events of deportation and war.

In their stories, they presented themselves as survivors of these events and thus created a common identity shared by members of the group as Polish veterans deported to Siberia and later on as survivors of the deportation. They focused on their own and their families' survival of the Siberian labour camps and kolkhozes in Kazakhstan. The emphases in their stories of this period is on family ties, obligations and suffering. Despite the challenges, they adhered to their core values, constructing their identity as individuals with strong family values and morals.

Nieumierzycki, Niewiński, Rogowski and Koselak's stories highlight the importance of Polish patriotism in their lives. They talked about their unwavering faith that Poland would become a free and independent country, which helped them survive the difficulties and challenges of labour camps. The ethnic origin of Anatol Nieumierzycki, Władysław Niewiński, Zbigniew Rogowski and Stefan Koselak; their moral values; their relationship with their fathers who served in military or police, or were military settlers, were all factors that contributed to the patriotism among the Poles detained in Siberia and Kazakhstan. Their stories illustrate their participation in the greater social movement before and during the war, which reignited their patriotism. Moreover, the way Nieumierzycki, Niewiński, Rogowski, and the family of Stefan

Koselak presented their relationship to the military through ances-
tral roots indicates that their multigenerational identity contributed
to their desire to join the Polish army as soon as they learned about
the possibility of its creation.

Nieumierzycki, Niewiński, Rogowski and Koselak then recount
how they joined the Polish army. Different paths led them to the
11 Polish Army Corps, but they all displayed a strong resolve to do
so since they identified themselves as soldiers ready to take up arms
despite young age, ailing health and the challenges they had to overcome to reach the army recruitment offices. Their determination to
join the Polish army was not only rooted in their ethnic ties to their
homeland but the socio-political circumstances of their situation.
Those socio-political triggers were the invasion of Poland and the
deportation of the Polish population to Siberia or Kazakhstan. They
all joined the 11 Polish Corps, also called the Anders Army, volun-
teering to form the Polish army on the territory of the USSR that
was made possible by the 1941 Sikorski–Mayski agreement.

Joining the Anders Army transformed their identity, and soon
afterward they presented themselves as soldiers, using the discourse
of soldiers. In the case of Niewiński, he not only presented himself as a fighter for freedom but also as someone who assisted other
Poles to move out of the Soviet Union. Rogowski presented himself
as someone fighting for a greater cause. The socio-political triggers
they experienced contributed to their identity transformation, and
their narratives illustrate this. Their motivations led them to change
from a cadet to a soldier, or from a detainee to a soldier specializing
in telecommunications, as in the case of Nieumierzycki. Niewiński
experienced transformation from a prisoner in a heavy-labour camp
to a member of the military involved in international rescue operations, and from a detainee to a military tank operator.

As soldiers of the 11 Polish Army Corps, all of them participated in the Battle of Monte Cassino in 1944. In their accounts,

Nieumierzycki, Niewiński, Rogowski and Koselak presented themselves as soldiers who were directly involved in this battle and as loyal to an independent and democratic Poland. They survived challenging and dangerous times under direct attack of snipers and heavy artillery, and they faced the harsh conditions of a battlefield, ready to give their lives for the higher cause. They emphasized that they were honourably discharged from the army after they fulfilled their duties. All of them received several military medals for their service in the 11 Polish Army Corps under British command. Their stories are being shared with the Canadian and Polish public and the media in their entirety for the first time and clearly show how their portrayal in Canadian media when they arrived to work on farms was not based on their own accounts of their battlefield experiences, where they saw themselves as patriotic soldiers. The media portrayal of the Polish veterans, as outlined earlier in this book, differs significantly from their own accounts, which follow.

The stories of Nieumierzycki, Niewiński, Rogowski and Koselak provide accounts of what led them to join the Polish Resettlement Corps in Italy and Great Britain and their experiences while working on Alberta farms. The 11 Polish Army Corps, from its inception, reported to the official Polish government-in-exile in London. Thus, the political changes brought about by the 1943 Tehran and 1945 Yalta Conferences, when Stalin, Roosevelt and Churchill defined the eastern borders of Poland to be on the 1920 Curzon Line, and when, during the 1945 Potsdam Conference, the Polish government-in-exile was derecognized by the Big Three heads of government, directly affected the situation of the Polish troops. This complicated their national status and led them to become stateless.

Some of the soldiers from the 11 Polish Army Corps did not want to, or could not, return to a Poland under Soviet influence. This feeling was predominant among the members of the 11 Polish Army Corps stationed in Italy and in Great Britain. Many joined the Polish

Resettlement Corps and some then immigrated to Canada to work on farms. In the accounts published for the first time here, are the stories of how four men tried to rebuild their lives in Canada.

The Polish war veterans from the II Polish Army Corps were bound together—even if they had not met in person because of assignments to different farms—by their identity as stateless people of common ethnic origin sharing their experience of identity transformation from soldiers and war veterans to unskilled farm workers. Moreover, their new identity was created within the discourse of their ethnic identity, of the "Polish Problem." How they were seen by the Canadian media, public policy, and the public influenced the veterans' personal interactions with others and influenced their personal spheres.

7

Anatol (Tony) Nieumierzycki

(1923–2017)

Introducing Mr. Nieumierzycki

WHILE COLLECTING STORIES of Polish veterans to share with
the community and contribute to the sixty-fifth anniversary commemoration of the Polish Combatants' Association in Calgary, I
learned that Mr. Nieumierzycki had been a soldier in the II Polish
Army Corps. Initially, he was reluctant to be interviewed and
instead directed me to a book in Polish. It detailed Hitler's invasion of Poland, the deportation of Poland's population to labour
camps in Siberia and Kazakhstan, and the formation of the II Polish
Army Corps on the territory of the Soviet Union. Nieumierzycki
then emailed me a copy of a book printed in 1945 in Rome[1] that
contained photographs and general information about the Soviet
Union's invasion of Poland in 1939, the forced resettlement of the
Polish population, and the formation of the Polish Army after the
1941 Sikorski–Mayski agreement. Nieumierzycki added, "I signed
a confidentiality agreement before I was discharged from the army,

and documents relating to the II Polish Army Corps matters will be unsealed in 150 years from the time they were created." The oath meant he would never share confidential information about his duty and involvement in the military operations.

After I had explained that I would like to hear his personal story without the need to disclose any military secrets, Nieumierzycki agreed to meet. In his home office in front of a computer, he showed me videos prepared for Polish television in Calgary in which he talked about his earlier life and deportation to Siberia. These interviews were fascinating, and I wanted to learn more about his life during the war and upon arrival in Canada. We spent many hours examining the original documents, photographs, and military artifacts that he had in his possession. One of the original documents was a pamphlet issued by the government of Great Britain directed at all members of the Polish armed forces under British command. The paper on which it was printed was yellowed by the many years that had passed since read by the Polish soldiers while stationed in Italy. It had deep creases after being folded and unfolded countless time. It was marked by smudges after being kept in the pocket of a military uniform. The leaflet encouraged the Polish soldiers to return to Poland, governed then by the Provisional Government of National Unity, which Great Britain, alongside the Soviet Union and the United States, recognized as the official government and the only authority that could speak on behalf of Poland. But that was not the Poland that Anders Army soldiers like Nieumierzycki had fought for on the battlefields of the Italian Campaign supporting the Allied armies. This Poland was under the influence of the Soviet Union. The Anders Army was made of soldiers who had spent years in labour camps in Siberia and Kazakhstan, experiencing unimaginable hardship and starvation, and witnessing the deaths of their families, and countrymen. They could not reconcile with this new order.

Holding this document felt like holding a piece of newly discovered history. I had grown up in the Communist country where stories of the Anders soldiers were not known. As I read the handout and listened to Nieumierzycki's stories, I was learning a history of Poland that had been denied to me.

Anatol Nieumierzycki

Anatol Nieumierzycki was born on June 4, 1923, in Moczul, township Chorsk, County Stoliński, province Polesie. His father Michał Nieumierzycki had been a military settler, who moved to this region after World War I. From early childhood, Anatol Nieumierzycki was destined to be a soldier, and until 1939, just a few weeks before the war started, he attended a military school for youth in Lubawa where pupils trained to take up higher military positions after they graduated. The following material is a reconstruction of his story based on interviews, a memoir, personal documents and photographs.

> The history of Poland had a lot of moments to which the words of Adam Mickiewicz could be applied: "If I forget about them, O God in heaven forget about me."
>
> —Anatol Nieumierzycki

How can I forget February 10, 1940, when our deportation story began. Even though that day, it was minus −30° C outside, this did not stop my brother and me from visiting our maternal grandfather to partake in the so-called *wieczorynki*—a social event customarily held during the winter months on Saturday evenings—typically spent dancing and singing. These social events attracted the young women and men from the nearby villages and provided us with the opportunity to socialize.

On the night of February 10, we looked forward to an evening of dancing and singing. We eagerly harnessed horses to the sleigh and, in an hour, arrived at our grandfather's house, located ten kilometres from Dawidgródek, where we lived with our parents. After an evening of songs and dance, we stayed for an overnight visit to our grandfather's house. That night around three o'clock in the morning, two Red Army soldiers pounded on the door, awakening everyone inside, and ordered that my brother and I, the children of a Polish military colonist, report to an assembly point for a mandatory resettlement of the Polish population. Despite the protest of our grandfather and the cries of our aunts, both of us were loaded onto a waiting wagon to be taken away.

One of the Red Army soldiers who escorted us, looked to me as of Tatar origin. He told us that according to the instructions the soldiers received, people who were scheduled for the resettlement had to be taken to the assembly point from their home, but they should be allowed some time to pack personal belongings. Going to our home in Dawidgródek to gather our belongings required an extra four kilometres' travel from the assembly point. The local civilian at the sleigh's reins was prejudicial toward the Poles and was not willing and complained about the diversion from the road, reasoning that our family was already at the assembly point, so there was no need for my brother and me to go back. I recall that the Red Army soldier threatened the driver with a pistol, making him obey the order.

Then the soldier said, "Your mother is already at the assembly point. She had a complete nervous breakdown and didn't take anything with her, except the two younger children. She told me where you and your brother were, and this is why I came to take you. You are both grown-up boys, and I will show you how to do the packing."

Despite the barbaric indoctrination the Red Army soldiers were subjected to, the soldier I met had a good heart and wanted to help the persecuted Poles scheduled for resettlement to prepare for their hard and arduous journey to Siberia or Kazakhstan. Eventually we were

Anatol Nieumierzycki. [Courtesy of Anatol Nieumierzycki]

loaded onto the sleigh and, under military escort, taken to our parents' home where we found the door open, and inside a completely drunk local policeman lying on my bed, oblivious to anything that was happening. He was holding a bottle of vodka in his hand. The Red Army soldier, angry at what he saw, and swearing under his nose, pulled the drunken man from the bed onto the floor.

Because every family that was to be resettled was given half an hour to pack essential belongings, the Red Army soldier wanting to help us started giving us instructions on how to pack in the most efficient way. He told us to use the duvet covers to pack extra beddings like linens, clothes and other things our family might need during our journey. The people in Polesie kept supplies of food for the winter and stored it in pantries, so the soldier told us to use potato sacks to pack any food we found at home. With the help of my brother and following the instructions the Red Army soldier gave us, we were able to pack and prepare for the speedy resettlement. Everything that we managed to pack was loaded onto the sleigh, and we were taken to the assembly point where we were reunited with our mother. She was dressed in a light jacket only, completely unprepared for the hardship that awaited us. Since the deportation was a sudden and unexpected development, this caused a lot of uncertainty. I was particularly concerned about the well-being of my mother, who alone had to take care of her young children. My father was not with us. After the Soviet army had annexed the Polish territory on September 17, 1939, he had been arrested with numerous other military settlers like him and imprisoned in Pińsk, a town in Belarus [White Russia] in the Polesie region.

After all the military settlers and forest workers who worked for the Polish government and their families selected for the resettlement had been gathered at the assembly point, we and our belongings were loaded onto a countless number of sleighs pulled by horses. Then, under the watchful eye of a military convoy, we started the journey. We travelled for several days to the closest railroad station. The sleighs loaded with people, bundles filled with a lifetime of possessions and hay for horses, set off cross-country through the only available road over a frozen Horyń (Horyn) river toward the Łachwy town, located close to the former Polish–Soviet state border. Our journey lasted several days, and we stopped only to rest and feed the horses. Those who managed to pack food for this voyage ate a little at that time, and those who didn't take any food or ran out of it didn't eat for several days and were left to *podychaj* (die).

On the Soviet side of the border, there was a town Mikaszewicze—an important railroad junction and a strategic place where the railroad tracks from Europe and the Soviet Union met. Because there was a difference of four inches (ten centimetres) between the width of the European and Soviet railroad tracks, this required a change of wheels on the train wagons or the transfer of goods between the European and the Soviet freight railcars.

Right after we arrived at the railroad station in Mikaszewicze, we were loaded onto the Soviet freight wagons. Several families were put into a single cart equipped with wooden bunk beds. In the middle of the cargo carriage, there was a cut-out hole that served as a toilet. Beside it, there was a stove for heating the wagon, if there was anything suitable to be burned in it. We had no idea where they were taking us when, after a few days of waiting and loading more deportees, the train started moving towards an unknown.

When the train stopped at a railroad station for the first time, armed guards let a few people from each wagon go to the station and bring buckets of *kipiatok/wrzątek* (boiling water in Russian/Polish), while the guards also started distributing shares of bread that the Russians called *pajok chlieba*. This was a slice of bread four fingers thick, and that was a ration of food for one person for one day. After this, the train continued travelling for several days, sometimes stopping at different railroad stations, but we still had no idea where we were being taken. Every day of this hardship claimed someone's life, and many people died of exhaustion, starvation and illnesses. I noticed that more and more bunk beds were empty. The bodies of those who died were left behind and were either unloaded beside the railroad tracks or at stations. Some families wanted to take the bodies of their loved ones and bury them in the cemeteries at our destination, but the corpses were not allowed in the wagons. Trying to mitigate this they tied the dead bodies onto the wagon's buffers, but in a short time, the bodies landed on the railroad tracks or under the wheels of the train.

One morning, the train stopped near the Minsk railroad station, and for the first time, we had some information about where we were. We were travelling towards the northeast. As usual, I went to fetch buckets of wrzątek for the entire family. While lifting a huge ladle filled with hot water, I felt a tap on my back, and when I turned around, I saw my father who put his finger to his lips to give me a sign to stay quiet.

"Take one bucket of water, go ahead to the wagon, and tell Mother I am bringing the second bucket," my father whispered to me. When we got there, I observed the people in the wagon, and hoped that no one noticed the newcomer. I learned that my father had escaped from the prison in Pińsk along with eight others, and they went to Russia looking for their deported families. However, I did not find out much detail about my father's escape. After a long journey, our family and the entire transport arrived in Wołogodzka Oblaść from where we travelled on sleighs to an internment camp located in the thick Siberian tundra. It took us three days to go the distance of around 140 kilometres through deep snow and thick forest to a place called Wołogodzka Oblaść Wierchtolszmienskoj Lesnoj Punkt Uczastok Kolbasz. We were housed in barracks built in 1932 for and by the former detainees, who were members of some Ukrainian–German religious sects imprisoned there for their religious beliefs. I could imagine that at that time they had worse conditions than ours because they were brought into an uninhabited wilderness.

Soon, we received permission to build our own kolkhoz about forty kilometres from Kolbasz where the soil was more fertile. My family spent almost two years of hardship there, working in the surrounding forests, cutting down the trees and transporting them to the nearby river for log driving. When we heard the German army invaded the Soviet Union in June of 1941, we couldn't believe the information and thought that some-one was spreading fairy tales among us. However, we started trusting this news after we noticed that the NKVD[2] agents began treating us bet-ter and talking in a friendlier manner. Around that time, we also heard about the signing of a pact between governments of the Soviets, US and Great Britain. Moreover, we learned about the creation of the Polish government-in-exile. The signing of the treaty known as the Sikorski–Mayski agreement, which resulted in the signing of a military agreement between Poland and the USSR on August 14, 1941, brought back my faith that we would create a Polish army.

Each passing day brought better news and prompted increased activities among the detainees. First, we looked for ways to confirm the information about the formation of the Polish army, and for that, my father travelled to a nearby town where he found out that the Polish army was to form in the southern part of the Soviet Union. People in the kolkhoz started building sledges and began looking for supplies needed to embark on a journey. The sledges had to be big enough, not only to transport the supplies necessary for a long trek but also to carry the children and those adults unable to move on their own. Since we had no horses, those well enough had to pull the sledges, trekking through the vast, deserted and snow-covered land to the nearest railroad station.

My family started building sledges to go on a journey to the place of a promised headquarters of the Polish army. We, too, endured a long and arduous journey through the snow and deserted land to the closest rail-road station. After a few weeks of travel in empty cargo trains, we almost reached the city of Kirov, where my family, unable to continue, decided to stay in a nearby kolkhoz, hoping to find work there. Actually, I was not in my best shape, either. I needed a medical intervention to deal with severe inflammation. My father realized that he had to stay behind and take care of the sick family, but he urged me to find a medical doctor to deal with my illness first, and then go south and continue my journey in search of the Polish army. My father said, "Son, I can't leave the family, but, you have enough strength. Go south! However, know that the decision we made is between us. Don't tell your mother. Because she might not let you go." Until the time of my departure, we kept these plans secret from my mother, not wanting to stress her further.

I travelled for forty days and nights toward Kirov, and during this time, I met other Poles who were also going to a place where the Polish army was being formed. During my journey, I didn't have to look for a doctor. The doctor found me. That is right! The doctor found me. When I disembarked the train at one of the stations in search of food and hot water, a serious-looking middle-aged woman carrying a briefcase approached me, and with a tender voice, asked, "*To, chto s toboy, mal'chik?*" (Boy, what is the matter with you?) and she quickly proceeded to examine my swollen neck. Then she ordered, "*Pojdi za mnoj!*" (Follow me!) and started walking toward the hospital located close to the railroad station.

I was surprised, but I followed her, and when we reached the hospital, I noticed that the Soviet soldiers standing guard saluted the woman with respect. The Russian woman doctor took me into an examination room where she treated me with a quartz lamp as preparation for a surgical procedure that I needed. The next day, after the treatment, the doctor gave me necessary medical supplies to tend the wound, and then wished me success in finding the Polish army. The Soviet doctor who treated me was the second person in Russia I will never forget because of the compassion and kindness she expressed toward me during the difficult times I experienced. The first one was the *Krasnoarmiejec* (Red Army soldier) who helped me pack for the journey before we were forced to resettle in Siberia.

After the surgery, following the doctor's order, I took care of the wound for forty-one days while I travelled on wagon bumpers or in empty freight boxcars toward the Polish army headquarters. I enlisted in

Nieumierzycki fulfilled his duty to Poland by serving with the Polish armed forces during World War II. A document signed by General Władysław Anders. [Courtesy Anatol Nieumierzycki]

the Polish forces on May 22, 1942, and I passed the medical examination given to recruits. First, I was assigned to the Sixth Lvov Communications Division, then after about six months to the First Communications Regiment, and finally to the 11th Battalion, Communications Artillery Company. The changes in my assignment were caused by a fluctuating situation in the army and the military leadership of the II Polish Army Corps had to adjust the makeup of the military to the number of soldiers available to them. Later on, the troops were evacuated through Krasnovodsk—a seaport on the Caspian Sea to the Iranian port Pahlavi (Bandar-e Anzali). From there we were ordered to move to Iraq, Palestine, Egypt, and later, Italy.

I served in the Army Signal Corps from May 22, 1942, until November 20, 1946, when I immigrated to Canada. My soldier tag is 28/3 KAU 3. I was demobilized from the Polish forces abroad at the rank of lieutenant sergeant. The certificate of demobilization was issued in Predappio, Italy, on October 4, 1946, by Order of Polish General Staff No. 738/0. Rozm./45, dated December 5, 1945.

During the Italian Campaign, my communications company was assigned to the artillery with a duty to connect the artillery's headquarters with the regiments. Our task was to provide radio contact, which was a dangerous undertaking because of the higher possibility of the radio stations being detected by the enemy and destroyed. We also provided telephone contact for which we had to lay down phone lines and set up telephone stations. During the Italian Campaign, I also cooperated with American and Canadian troops, and I worked closely and communicated with the Canadian soldiers serving there.

I was awarded The Medal of Armed Forces, The 1939-1945 Star, The Italy Star, The Cross of Monte Cassino No. 41142. Moreover, I received a certificate of Polish Armed Forces, issued in London on November 11, 1945, for Lieutenant Sergeant Nieumierzycki Anatol, proving that I fulfilled my duty towards Poland by serving with the Polish armed forces during World War II. General Władysław Anders signed

POLSKIE SIŁY ZBROJNE
Polish Armed Forces
Les Forces Armées Polonaises
Fuerzas Armadas Polonesas

MIEJSCE WYDANIA Place of issue Lieu de la délivrance Lugar del establecimiento	*PREDAPPIO* *ITALIA – ITALY*	DATA Date Le Fecha *4. 10. 1946*

ZASWIADCZENIE DEMOBILIZACYJNE
Certificate of Demobilization
Certificat de Démobilisation
Certificado de Demobilización

1. NAZWISKO I IMIONA
Name and Christian Names
Nom et Prénoms
Nombre y apellidos *NIEUMIERZYCKI ANATOL*

2. RODZAJ SIŁ ZBROJNYCH I BRONI
Branch of Service *Wojsko – Łączność*
Arme *ARMY – SIGN.*
Gen. de armas

3. STOPIEN WOJSKOWY *plutonowy*
Rank *L/Sgt.*
Grade
Grado

4. KATEGORIA ZDROWIA *A*
Medical Category
Categorie de santé
Categoria de salud

5. NUMER OSOBISTY *30573/42*
Service personal No.
No. de Matricule
No. de Matricula

6. LICZBA KARTY EWID *28/III*
Pol. Record No
No. de la Matricule Pol.
No. de la Matricula Pol.

7. IMIONA RODZICÓW *MICHAŁ – JULIA*
Parents' Christian Names
Prénoms des parents

8. DATA I MIEJSCE URODZENIA *4.6.1923 MOCZUL, STOLIN, POLSKA*
Date and place of birth *POLAND*
Date et lieu de naissance
Fecha y lugar de nacimiento

9. STAN CYWILNY *kawaler*
State whether single, married or widower *SINGLE*
État civil /célibataire, marié, veuf, etc./
Estado civil /soltero, casado, viudo, etc./

10. NAZWISKO PANIENSKIE I IMIE ZONY
DATA I MIEJSCE JEJ URODZENIA
Maiden Name and Christian Name of Wife
Date and Place of Birth
Nom de jeune fille et prénom de l'épouse
Date et lieu de naissance
Nombre de soltera y apellido de la esposa
Fecha y lugar de nacimiento

11. IMIONA DZIECI
Children's Christian Names
Prénoms des enfants
Apellidos de niños

12. OBECNY ADRES ZONY
Wife's present residence
Lieu de résidence actuel de l'épouse
Lugar de la residencia actual de la esposa

13. ZAWÓD CYWILNY ORAZ ew. TYTUL NAUKOWY *rolnik*
Profession and/or Degree *FARMER*
Profession et s'il y a lieu titre ou diplôme
Profesion civil, asi como el grado cientifico eventual

14. ODZNACZENIA *N.Wojsk. R.M.C. G.W. 1939-45 e IT.*
Decorations *At Med. C. Monte Cas. THE 1939-45 STAR*
Décorations *IT. STAR*

15. POCHWALY
Mentions in dispatches
Citations

this document. The military medals awarded and the letter signed by General Anders were the highest forms of recognition for my involvement in the Italian military campaign. My participation in providing radio and telephone communication was an important and dangerous mission, and I was involved in significant military operations.

The war had ended, but we couldn't return to Poland because we already had our Polish citizenship taken away. We learned that if we returned, we would be taken back to Siberia where we would undergo a so-called rehabilitation because Russia was antagonistic toward the II Polish Army Corps. The Polish authorities informed the II Polish Army Corps that soldiers had one week to make a decision and report, and anyone who didn't do that would be stripped of Polish citizenship.

Ernest Bevin, who was the foreign secretary in Great Britain, presented the soldiers with two choices; one was to return to Poland, the other to immigrate to the United States, Canada, Brazil or Australia. Each of these countries agreed to accept 4,500 Polish vets. Alternatively, all of us could go to Great Britain. I didn't want to go back to Poland liberated by the joint efforts of the Red Army and 1 Polish (Berling) Army. Following in the footsteps of the other former soldiers from the II Polish Army Corps, I decided to join the 1947 Polish Resettlement program. Canada offered a two-year contract of work on farms. At that time, I read the 1935 travel book *Kanada Pachnąca Żywicą* by Arkady Fiedler, a Polish writer, journalist and adventurer, and this spurred my interest in Canada. I was curious about the life of the Native people described in this book.

Like others, I had to take a test to determine if I was qualified to participate in the program. As a test of my farm work knowledge, I was shown different types of grains. My father was a farmer, and drawing on the knowledge and the experience I'd had, I passed this test. Since I was single, and of good health, I was accepted into the Polish Resettlement program. I received my demobilization and identification documents containing my fingerprints. My identification number was assigned as 805. Equipped with the documents, I was entitled to board the *Sea Snipe*

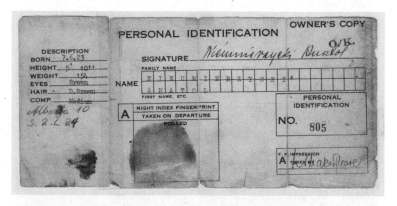

Nieumierzycki's identification document, also used to board the SS *Sea Snipe* and come to Canada. On its reverse is a stamp of Canadian Immigration, "Admitted Non Immigrant," dated November 24, 1946. [Courtesy of Anatol Nieumierzycki]

warship and come to Canada. At that time, many ships slated for decommissioning left Napoli for Halifax, where they were decommissioned from the military and dismantled. Our journey to Canada lasted about a month, and we slept below the ship's deck on hammocks hanging from the ceiling.

When we arrived in Canada, we came over here not as immigrants but to work on farms for two years based on a contract we signed and could not work anywhere else but on the farm to which we were sent. On November 24, 1946, I came from Napoli, Italy, to Halifax with other vets on board the *Sea Snipe* warship. Upon arrival in Halifax and after a brief assessment by the immigration officers, I boarded a CP Rail train to Lethbridge, Alberta. On the way to Lethbridge, the train stopped at several stations, and I witnessed some people protesting us coming to Canada. There were meetings with reporters, but for the most part, there were few friendly interviews. Some of those people even protested bringing soldiers to Canada. However, I did not pay attention to those protests. I had signed a two-year contract with the government, and I was going to fulfill it. I viewed the signing of the contract as part of my military service.

A PARTY OF POLISH WAR VETERANS who arrived in Calgary this morning is shown above. With them are J. R. Boon (left), of the Calgary office of the provincial department of agriculture; J. J. Smith, manager of the local office of the national employment office, and bending down, Jack Kilarski, police court interpreter.

Polish Soldiers Happy To Start New Life On Canadian Farms

The Calgary Herald, November 26, 1946.

Upon the arrival of our group of vets in Lethbridge, we were housed in quarters that used to house the German POWs during the war. There, I met some of the Germans who had stayed there, instead of going back to Europe. When I came to Canada, only then, I realized that by signing the farm-work contract, I was supposed to replace the German POWs.

Two days later, I met the owner of a farm to which I was assigned. He also had one more farm, and I was to work there too. The farmer had two sons. The Hambling's farm, on which I was to work for two years, was located fifteen kilometres south of Lethbridge. According to the contract, I was to earn $40 to $45 per month for tending the cattle and looking after the farm. However, the farmer didn't have $45 to pay me. Soon after my arrival at the farm, the farmer loaded his combine harvester on a truck and left me in charge of the farm. He was going to travel to the United States, where he could work as a hired farmhand harvesting and earning money.

On the farm, I tended the animals, fetched water for them and performed general farm duties. I had to cook for myself since there was no one else on the farm. I wore my military uniform as my work clothes because I did not have any other clothes to replace them. When we were discharged from the army, the servicemen were given some money, but that was not enough to buy new clothes.

I worked by myself on the farm with no access to newspapers or radio. I read the Polish books that I brought with me from Italy for my journey to Canada. My command of the English language allowed me to conduct military duty in Italy, but it was also limited. When I spoke Polish in public places, it was seen as unacceptable; I was chastised, and these comments had an aggressive undertone. Once when I was on a train in Calgary and talking with a friend in Polish, a man with a strong accent remarked aggressively, "Why the hell don't you speak English?" In the environment in which I was working and living, I didn't have the opportunity to learn English.

In October of 1947, the farmer returned. His absence had lasted about a year, almost as long as I had been working on the farm. It was also nearly a year into my contract, so I asked him for my back wages, but the farmer said, "You know, I don't have the money to pay you. I cannot pay you."

Dissatisfied with the work conditions on the farm, I did not want to continue to work another year like that. I could not work there for free. So, I asked the farmer to pay me my overdue wages and set to leave the farm. Eventually, the farmer paid me $120 for eleven months of work on the farm, amounting to an average of $10.90 per month, claiming that he did not have the money to pay for my work. He agreed to take me to Calgary to search for new employment.

When the farmer's son, Les Hambling, who was a driver and had a car, brought me and my two large suitcases full of Polish books to Calgary, we stopped by the Cecil Hotel because we didn't know anyone in the city. We went for a beer to talk with the locals and to find out if there were other Poles in the city. Inside the beer parlour, where there were men only, we found a few Poles. They told us that there was a Polish community hall located at 313 4 Street NE, where the local Poles were congregating. Hambling took me and my suitcases there and left me in front of the building. Not knowing what to do, I sat on the stairs, observing the people and the passing trains going uphill. Across the street, I saw a man working on the rooftop doing some repairs. After a while, a woman came out of the home and with a loud voice called, "Walter! Supper!"

The man must have heard her calling and started descending the ladder. I noticed that he was not heading home, though. Instead, the man crossed the street toward the Polish community hall, where I sat on the stairs. "Veteran?" he asked, approaching me.

I was a little hesitant, but confirmed. Then the man took one of the suitcases by the handle and gestured me to take the other. I obediently followed the man. "Didn't you hear? She called supper," the man said in Polish.

The two of us walked across the street and the train tracks. When we got into the house, the man announced, "Anne, we have a veteran for supper," and turning to me, he commanded, "You, put down the luggage. Do you see this carpenter's shop? There is a bed. If you don't have a place to sleep, you can sleep there. Now, go wash your hands and come upstairs."

The man showed me around as if he had done it many times before. "Do you see this girl?" he pointed at a girl, around ten years of age, who slept in one of the rooms. "This is my daughter, Klara. And this is Anne, my wife. What is your name?" he asked me.

"Antek. Anatol Nieumierzycki."

"And I am Walter Chuchla. I am Chuchla! Call me Walter. Sit down, here is a plate, and here is the supper. Eat!"

While we ate, we talked about my plans. What was I going to do next? Where did I want to live? Why had I come to Calgary? And was I going to look for a job? Did I have a place to sleep? I answered all Chuchla's questions. Chuchla said that he had several beds he specially prepared for the Polish veterans returning from war, and if I needed a place to stay, I could sleep there. There were also beds in the carpenter shop if I preferred that instead. Later that day when work hours were over, I met a few Polish veterans who stayed at Chuchla's home.

I found this of significance that on the first day in Calgary, the first man I met was a Pole. Chuchla was a member of the Polish Alliance. That was also the first time I was introduced to the Polish community in Calgary. Also, that day I ate the first Polish supper, and I slept in a Polish home. This illustrated the strength of the Polish community in Calgary.

The next day we went out together to look for a job for me. We took a train to an Alberta Government Telephone (AGT) building, and because I'd trained as a telemechanic while in the army and graduated from a radio-technical school in Rome after the war was over, I was offered a job on the spot as soon as I filled out a job application. When the officer looked at my qualifications, he said, "God must have sent you to us! When can you start?"

I started the new job at 8:00 a.m. the next day. However, my employment at AGT lasted only three or four days. I was informed that because I was not a Canadian citizen, I was not allowed to work there.

The next day, I went again with Chuchla to search for another job. On 9th Avenue and 8th Street, there was a big sign above the electric shop— Electrical Contractors. I entered it with intention to ask for a job. A man inside looked at me carefully and getting up from behind the desk, he called out to me, "Tony! What are you doing here?" and seeing that I didn't recognize him, added, "Remember me from Ancona, Italy? We worked together."

I was surprised to see my former colleague Howard who'd served in the Canadian communications division at Ancona, Italy, while I was serving in the II Polish Army Corps in telecommunication. We worked together at the central military communication hub where we communicated using an encryption system to pass coded strategic military information, and we knew each other well. We used a secret code system to prevent the enemy from making spoofing calls, pretending that they were the Allies. The secret code helped conceal our highly confidential conversations in case of enemy eavesdropping, and that made our communication effective and safe. When we served in the army, occasionally, the Polish and the Canadian soldiers met together to get to know each other to prevent unauthorized radio contacts with people we didn't know. During one such meeting, I'd met Howard. So, he was happy to see me in Calgary.

"I am looking for a job," and trying to explain my situation, I added, "I quit farming, and I started working at the telephone company, but I am not a Canadian citizen. The closest profession to my education is electrical work." Because of my qualifications and experience, I was hired on the spot as an electrician in my colleague's company.

However, my employment as an electrician did not last more than a month because after the company reported to the government that they had filled their vacant position, as it was required of them, a representative of the government ordered me to finish my two-year farm contract first. I wasn't allowed to take any other job but farm help. Howard, my colleague, promised that my job would wait for me until I finished the farm contract.

When the next day I reported to the government to find another farm on which I could work for one more year, the officer shamed me about disappearing from the farm to which I was assigned and leaving my contract work ahead of time, even though I had promised to work there for two years. "Are you a Pole? You promised that you would work on the farm for two years. How about it?" and he repeated, "How about you finish the contract? Where is your ambition?"

After I had complained to him about the work conditions on the farm, the long distance from Calgary, as well as the lack of pay, the officer asked, "Where do you want to work?"

"Close to Calgary."

"There is a Burns Ranch, and two or three guys are working there already. Do you want to work for the Burns?"

I had no idea who the Burns were and where the Burns Ranch was, but I accepted the offer to work there until the end of my two-year contract. I informed Howard that I had to work on a farm for a year to finish my two-year farm labour contract and then I would return.

"OK. The job in my company is waiting for you."

The next day, I reported to the Burns building; the five- or six-storey-high building located in downtown Calgary. After the necessary paperwork, I was taken with my two substantial suitcases filled with Polish books to the Burns Ranch. The conditions in the Burns Ranch located in the Bow Valley were much better than at the previous farm. I slept in a bunkhouse, I was fed, and I became part of the crew. There was a building for the workers to live in and a special dining room where we ate. A woman employed there cooked for all the workers. The next day, the foreman showed me around the ranch and where the farm machines were, and told me about my duties. As the youngest there, I was assigned to get up earlier, milk the cows and bring the milk to the kitchen before breakfast for everyone to have fresh milk. After the morning meal, I worked on a tractor in the fields cutting grass for hay because I had experience operating tractors. Later, I was assigned to work at a feedlot where hundreds of cattle were fattened up and prepared for sale.

At the time of my farm-work contract with the Burns Ranch, there were other Polish vets and war veterans working there. Occasionally, they drove to Calgary where they met friends. I was also allowed to take

Nieumierzycki's first lesson: this is a tractor. [Courtesy of Anatol Nieumierzycki]

some time off of work on the weekends, and I started making more contacts with other Polish veterans. While visiting Calgary, I met other vets who were assigned to work on farms located close to Calgary. After a year of work, my contract with the Burns Ranch was finished, and I thanked my employer for the experience. Instead of being paid $45 per month, I was paid $150 for each month of work. I used this money to buy a car, a 1939 Dodge. It was in good condition, and I had it for a few years. I returned to Calgary to work as an electrician for the EC&M Company owned by my Canadian colleague from the Italian Campaign.

The Burns Ranch is now Fish Creek Provincial Park, where the Bow Valley Museum is located. The bunkhouse in which I lived, when I worked on the farm, is part of the heritage site. When I visited the site, I saw the bunk bed on which I slept.

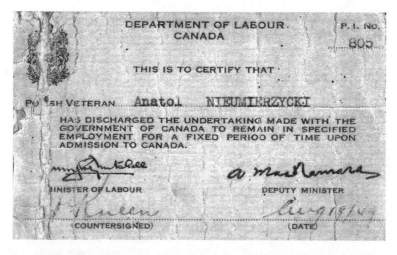

DEPARTMENT OF LABOUR.
CANADA

P. I. NO. 805

THIS IS TO CERTIFY THAT ·

POLISH VETERAN Anatol NIEUMIERZYCKI

HAS DISCHARGED THE UNDERTAKING MADE WITH THE GOVERNMENT OF CANADA TO REMAIN IN SPECIFIED EMPLOYMENT FOR A FIXED PERIOD OF TIME UPON ADMISSION TO CANADA.

MINISTER OF LABOUR

DEPUTY MINISTER

(COUNTERSIGNED)

(DATE)

Nieumierzycki's discharge document, proving that he finished the two-year contract working on farms in Canada. Issued August 19, 1949—on that day, he became a landed immigrant in Canada. [Courtesy of Anatol Nieumierzycki]

After I finished my two-year farm contract and returned to Calgary, I worked as an electrician for the EC&M Company from 1948 until my retirement in 1985. I took a four-year-long program at Southern Alberta Institute of Technology that allowed me to work as an electrician. After that, I continued upgrading my skills by taking continuing education courses. During my career at EC&M, I was responsible for such projects as the brewery and the Calgary Zoo. I am a member of the International Brotherhood of Electrical Workers.

Since 1948, when I started organizing the library at the Polish Alliance [later the Polish Canadian Association of Calgary], I have been involved in the Polish community centre in Calgary, serving in many executive positions and on committees. For several years, I was the secretary, financial secretary, president and vice-president, and treasurer of the organization. I was a member of the Cultural and Entertainment Group, Central Reconciliation Committee, Polish *Biuletyn* Committee, Building Committee, Polish Parish Requirements Committee, Audit Committee, Trustee Committee, Development and New Construction Committee, and Arbitration Committee, and for several years I was the editor of the Polish *Biuletyn*. Moreover, I was a founding member of the Polish Combatants' Association No. 18 in Calgary, formed on November 11, 1947.

I came to Canada for a two-year farm contract, and I was discharged from the undertaking made by the government of Canada in August 1948. Landed-immigrant status was granted to me in December of 1948. I was granted Canadian citizenship in November 1956. I fulfilled the terms of the contract, but I did not become a farmer.

The John Paul II Polish School in Calgary offers its students studies in Polish. On November 20, 2010, I was invited to give a talk about the Polish population deported from the eastern territory of Poland to Siberia and Kazakhstan on February 10, 1940. That was the day when my family and I were deported. I titled my speech "A Testament of the Deported to the East." I told the students that the history of Poland had many moments to which the words of Adam Mickiewicz, regarded as a national poet in Poland, Lithuania and Belarus, could be applied: "If I forget about them, O God in heaven forget about me." Some say that we, the Poles, have a predilection for contemplation of what was our misfortune, disaster. They say this is not right for the shared memory and for the collective imagination; that it is better to remember what was victorious. Perhaps there is a particle of truth in that, but on one side, we need optimism, a sense of power and self-confidence. On the other hand, we need the wisdom contained in the oft-quoted words attributed to Marshal Ferdinand Foch, "The homeland is the land and the tombs. Nations, losing memory, lose their lives."

So how to forget our fellow citizens, who on the morning of February 10, 1940, were dragged from their homes and packed into cattle cars? How to forget the men, the women and the children who visited the hell of Siberia and Kazakhstan? Hundreds of thousands of impoverished people, deprived of their country, died of hunger and cold. The homeland is the land and the tombs, but the most painful are those graves that are not there. About them, do not forget.

Remembering Anatol Nieumierzycki

During one of our meetings, Mr. Nieumierzycki showed me his Military Identification Tag, commonly known as a "dog tag," which he brought to Canada from the WWII Italian military campaign. Hanging from a chain, the two similar tags made from non-corrosive metal had a debossed inscription—Anatol Nieumierzycki 28/3 KAU 3—indicating his soldier number and the command restorations number to which he was assigned. "Every soldier on the war front had to wear a tag like that on the neck all the time," Nieumierzycki explained, while talking about his duties in the military communications unit. "If you talked on the radio you could not wait for a long time to move on because there might be a rocket sent your way," he said, describing work under constant threat of being shot at by enemy artillery or a sniper.

Nieumierzycki and other soldiers from his military unit were required to lay cables needed to maintain the radio communication between the command of all regiments and their own troops, with the artillery and their units, as well as with the central communication hub for the Allied forces. Laying those cables on the battlefield was very dangerous. Maintaining radio communication was imperative to fight the enemy and keep all Allied troops safe. Other veterans whom I interviewed said that sometimes during the Battle of Monte Cassino the Allied artillery shelled its own military positions by mistake, inflicting great and lethal casualties among the Anders Army soldiers who were in the trenches safeguarding their positions from the destruction inflicted by the German artillery and sharpshooters fortified in the bunkers around the hilltop sanctuary of St. Benedict of Nursia.

The Battle of Monte Cassino is considered the bloodiest battle of the WWII Italian Campaign. Holding Nieumierzycki's military dog tag was a profound experience, making me intensely aware that a soldier's life was under constant threat. The tag was one of the most personal items Nieumierzycki kept from the time he served in the Anders Army. Like every soldier, he wore it on his neck day and night and never took it off while on the war front. The military dog tag had a particular purpose, he told me. When a soldier was killed, a military official assisting in the collecting of the bodies pulled these tags until the chain broke. Then, one of the tags was removed from the chain and usually forced into the mouth of the dead soldier. The second copy of the dog tag was taken for the notification and administrative purposes conducted by the military. Nieumierzycki lived through the war, and his dog tag never had to be taken away from him in that way. Thousands of the II Polish Army Corps soldiers, however, were killed during the Italian Campaign, and they are buried in Polish military cemeteries in Italy, near the battlefields where they died fighting for freedom. Seventy years after the war, of the four II Polish Army Corps soldiers I found living in Calgary, only Nieumierzycki had kept his dog tag.

The other thing that Nieumierzycki shared that reverberated with me was his penchant for the 1937 book by Arkady Fiedler, a Polish writer and traveller. When I asked why he chose to come to Canada, he said, "When I was still in Italy, we had a Polish library where I found Fiedler's travel book. The way the author described Canada inspired me. I was always curious, even when we were forcefully taken to Siberia. Other people were crying and lamenting, but I was curious about where we would be going. I always liked new things, so I applied to work on farms in Canada as part of the Polish Resettlement Corps," and added, "I was never disappointed by how Fiedler described Canada in his book. Canada is a beautiful country."

I recalled how much I had also liked Fiedler's books, which I read growing up in post-WWII Poland. Just like Nieumierzycki, I read Fiedler's books from beginning to end in one sitting. Just like him, I was curious about the exotic and little-known places to which Fiedler travelled. Canada was one of those destinations. However, I had one more reason—I craved the freedom with which Fiedler was able to move around the world from one place to another, observe the life there, and write about the people he met and the places he had seen. His books offered a glimpse of what a free person like him could do. Through the travel stories, Fiedler described the freedom that I intuitively knew existed outside of a Poland ruled by a pro-Communist government. However, locked behind the Iron Curtain, Polish people like me were under the close surveillance of the inescapable Communist Party system, and travelling anywhere outside of the country was impossible. Fiedler wrote his book about Canada before WWII, almost twenty years after the time Poland regained its independence in 1918. This was the Poland in which Nieumierzycki was born. On the other hand, I read Fiedler's travel books as a teenager while living in a Poland harshly ruled by the pro-Soviet government, and I realized that freedom was a concept I could only imagine, not experience.

The other thing that I learned from Nieumierzycki was that he never stopped helping newcomers to Canada. "The Polish organizations in Calgary paid for the healthcare premiums for the Polish refugees who came to Calgary, Canada," he once told me, when I disclosed that I, too, was a refugee who arrived in Canada with family in 1990. "I was always actively involved in many Polish organizations supporting the Polish refugees coming to Canada," Nieumierzycki added, giving me a list of Polish organizations where he had served on the central executive committees.

This reminded me of my first week in Canada in 1990. The early February weather had rapidly changed from a warm day of chinook wind that swept away all the snow just a day or two before our arrival in Calgary to a cold day with the temperature falling to –40° C. On the TV screen, the red-lettered weather alert warned about the coming blizzard. I looked through the windows, watching the drifting snow. Someone on the street, bent in half from the force of the wind, was struggling to walk in the blowing snow. That changed my perception of Canadian winter forever. On one such cold and snowy day, our sponsor drove us to the Calgary Catholic Immigration Society office to pick up health-care cards for all five members of our family. "Your health cards are already paid for by one of the Polish organizations that took care of the premiums for six months," our family was told.

We were grateful for the help, but we had no idea who had paid. Still feeling hazy from moving ten thousand kilometres away from the familiar, we didn't even know whom we should thank. We needed these cards and medical help very much. My daughter was ill due to the harsh weather conditions and the exhaustion from the long travel from West Germany, where our family had first sought political asylum. With the healthcare card in my hand, I took my daughter to a walk-in clinic but unable to communicate in English then, I had scribbled a few words with the help of a Polish–English dictionary. After checking my daughter, and reading the words I wrote, the doctor brought us a bottle of antibiotic and sent us home to recuperate. At that time, little did I know that the 11 Polish Army soldiers like Nieumierzycki, were continuing their efforts to help Poles who had to leave Poland still under the Soviet influence and come to Canada seeking a better life for themselves and their families.

8

Władysław (Walter) Niewiński

(1918–2012)

Introducing Mr. Niewiński

I MET MR. WŁADYSŁAW NIEWIŃSKI in October of 2011 while working on a major assignment for my Canadian Studies undergraduate program at the University of Calgary. To graduate, I was required to undertake several projects related to a community. One assignment called for examining one's heritage and culture and talking about it with an elder member of the community, and I realized that I knew no one to whom I could turn. For over twenty years, my family and I had lived in Calgary. However, we had never managed to develop a sense of belonging, even though we were busy all the time. Starting a new life in a new country was challenging. My husband, our three children, and I were refugees who, in 1988, escaped from Poland, which at that time was still under the influence of the Communist Eastern Bloc. After almost two years in West Germany seeking political asylum, we made Canada our new home.

It was fall 2011, and the deadline for my assignment was
approaching. Determined to find out more about the Polish community in Calgary, I turned to the Internet where I came across a
website of the Polish Combatants' Association. The existence of
the Polish war veterans' organization intrigued me, and I wanted
to know who its members were. However, the website offered no
information about the veterans or combatants. Nevertheless, there
was one vital piece of information—the organization was formed
in 1947. Immediately I saw the opportunity to do something for
those people—help celebrate the upcoming sixty-fifth anniversary.
I decided to look for veterans willing to participate in a university
research project. The president of the association directed me to
one of the founding members, Władysław Niewiński, who had been
in the II Polish Army Corps where he fought in such battles as the
1944 Battle of Monte Cassino. When Niewiński came to Canada
after the war, he worked on farms in Alberta, and for many years
was involved in the building of the Polish community in Calgary.
In a short telephone conversation, Mr. Niewiński invited me to visit
him at home.

Mr. Niewiński and his wife Nancy waited for me at the door of
their small, comfortable bungalow surrounded by carefully trimmed
bushes. Niewiński led me to a room dedicated to the memories of
the time when he was a soldier. On the walls, there were war medals
and badges with his military ranks carefully organized in frames.
A large framed collage of pictures of Niewiński and his friends,
wearing Polish military uniforms from the time they served in the
Polish army, took a prominent place. There were books on the topic
of WWII, many of which I saw for the first time because they were
published outside of Poland. Mr. Niewiński sat on a modest chair
that showed many years of use. Behind him, on the wall, there was
a badge honouring the couple's fiftieth wedding anniversary and a
photograph of the couple with their two grandchildren.

I asked Niewiński in which language would he like me to conduct the interview during which we would talk about his life. With no hesitation in his voice, he answered, "In Polish," and proceeded to begin his story. "I am ninety-two years old. I have been living in Calgary, Alberta, since 1947. Before coming to Canada, I was a soldier in the II Polish Army Corps during WWII. The army was also called the Anders Army, since we were serving under General Władysław Anders. I fought in such battles as Monte Cassino," he said. Then he went on to say how they fought against the overwhelming power of the Nazi occupants during WWII.

He continued telling the story of his life in a well-organized manner. His voice was loud and his memory sharp, as if the events of war had taken place recently. While I followed his story I thought to myself, "I cannot believe I'm meeting a soldier who fought in the Battle of Monte Cassino!" The lyrics and music of a well-known Polish military song from WWII, "The Red Poppies at Monte Cassino"[1] came to mind. The song was composed on the eve of the last and victorious attack of the Anders Army on the monastery on Monte Cassino and was a tribute to those killed fighting for freedom. Performed with pride outside of Poland, it became a clandestine independence hymn inside postwar Poland. The poppies grew on the battlefields and, according to the song, instead of water the red flowers drank the blood of Polish soldiers who died on the battlefield. The song carried the message of the soldiers' courage and the sacrifices they endured. In postwar Poland, Anders' soldiers were considered renegades by the official pro-Soviet government and the dictatorial Communist Party leaders. At that time, the only real heroes of war recognized by this government were the Red Army soldiers and the 1 Polish Army soldiers led by General Berling, who fought alongside the Soviet Red Army, liberating Poland and taking Berlin in 1945. Almost daily on the single-channel, state-run TV, WWII documentary films praised the courage and the heroism of the Polish army fighting alongside the Red Army liberating Europe. The message was clear: to acknowledge and honour the ultimate sacrifice made by those who lost their lives liberating Europe from Nazism, which included Polish as well as the Soviet soldiers. However, nothing was ever said by the official media or the government about the soldiers of the II Polish Army Corps and General Anders. This version of WWII history had not been taught in elementary or high school when I attended schools in Poland.

Niewiński continued his story, describing his personal experiences as a young soldier who lived through the events of WWII and was drafted against his will into the Red Army. When he opposed the Russification of Poland, he was sent to a Soviet heavy-labour camp where he spent many months of the harshest winters on record. Eventually joining the II Polish Army Corps formed in 1942 in the territory of the USSR, he fought along side the Allied armies liberating Europe.

While listening to Mr. Niewiński talk about his experiences and his later involvement in the cultivation and preservation of Polish heritage and culture in Canada, I realized that his resolve was deeply rooted in patriotism. In his voice, which sometimes modulated when he was talking about a particularly challenging time, I could hear the sense of loss brought about by the displacement he experienced after the Soviet Union invaded Poland on September 17, 1939, and later when Polish citizenship was taken away from him in 1946. However, his enthusiasm grew when he talked about the many years he spent fighting for freedom. Later, we talked about why he came to Canada in 1946 as a stateless person and about his effort to create and cultivate a Polish community of inclusion.

After the interview, we chatted a little more as his wife set the table with tea and her speciality, banana bread, treating me more like a long-awaited guest than a scholar. Mr. Niewiński sat across the

Władysław Niewiński, wearing a Polish military uniform after he joined the II Polish Army Corps. [Courtesy of Władysław Niewiński]

table and looked into my eyes for a long time. Then he said, "I heard that the Communists gave people a good education."

Niewiński's comment took me by surprise. In an instant, it reminded me of the decades I spent in Poland ruled by a pro-Soviet government. I realized that he was talking about people like me. The sudden jolt of his words pushed me to think deeply. From the first moment I met Niewiński, I had never sensed a language or cultural barrier between us. The common factors that brought us together were being born in Poland, the thousand years of history and speaking the same language. However, his words brought back the realization that we were separated by the decades each of us had spent in a Poland that was similarly geographically situated in the centre of Europe, but was ideologically different for him and for me. Politically, Poland was a different country when Niewiński was born in 1918. That year, Poland regained its independence after 123 years of being partitioned between Russia, Austria and Prussia. In 1918 the first war that caused colossal human and material losses ended and this brought hope for freedom and peace. The Polish people were especially elated and looked forward to living in a new and independent country. Twenty years later, however, wwii started and lasted for six years. Even before the war ended, it brought fundamental political, social, economic and cultural changes not only to Poland and Europe but also to the entire world.

I was born in post-wwii Poland, in a country that was denied to Niewiński, where he could not return after he had fulfilled his duty as a soldier fighting for freedom, supporting the Allied efforts on the the Italian Front. Because he fought in the Italian Campaign and refused to return to a Poland ruled by the pro-Communist government, he was stripped of Polish citizenship. Postwar Poland was under the influence of the Communist Soviet Union where freedom of expression was repressed, or non-existent, and historical facts were erased or twisted to support the overpowering Communist

Niewiński in the Polish Fusiliers Company, training in Brześć nad Bugiem in 1939. [Courtesy of Władysław Niewiński]

ideology. I grew up, went to school and started my family in a very different country than the one Niewiński knew from his youth. Looking at him sitting from across from me, I pondered the reasons each of us had to leave Poland.

As a teenager, I read many books and visited the only municipal library regularly. I appointed myself the family's book-borrower in charge of bringing home the maximum allowed, eight books every two weeks. For me, each visit to the library was a celebration during which I walked slowly among the rows of tall bookshelves tightly packed with books. I touched the spines of every book on each shelf reading its title before making my choices. Many books described how Nazi Germany had invaded Poland, how they had killed millions of people in concentration camps, how the Red Army had defeated Hitler's army and liberated the world, and how Poland had been rebuilt after the war with the help of the Soviet Union. Some books described the heroism of the Polish soldiers fighting alongside the Red Army to defeat the Nazi regime.

With the new order in Europe, a new and different history had been written for those living in postwar Poland, tightly shut out from the rest of the world. There were no books about the invasion of Poland by the Soviet Union that I later found out took place on September 17, 1939, or about the annexation of the eastern part of Poland by the USSR, and about the forced deportation of the Polish population to Siberia or Kazakhstan. I never found books or information about the II Polish Army Corps, about the Battle of Monte Cassino, or about General Władysław Anders. We were not taught at school about those soldiers and the events in which they were involved. As a teenager, I only learned about the existence of the II Polish Army Corps when I overheard some whispering. None of this part of Poland's history was part of the school curriculum. Sharing any knowledge of Anders' soldiers was forbidden. If someone did talk about these soldiers, then that person risked being prosecuted for enticing anti-Communist propaganda, spreading false information, or for treason against the country's political interests.

All these memories started coming back to me while I was sitting across Mr. Niewiński and listening to him talking about the past. At this moment, I realized that I had now met one of the legendary soldiers from the II Polish Army Corps that I'd heard only whispers about, and that they truly did exist. What follows is what I learned about Niewiński's life as a Soviet detainee, a Polish soldier, a stateless WWII veteran and a newcomer to Canada.

Władysław Niewiński

Władysław Niewiński was born on March 9, 1918, in Bielsko Podlaskie, in the Podlaskie Voivodship, Poland, to a family of five children living on a small piece of land in the Malinówka village. The following story is based on interviews, a memoir, personal documents and photographs.

> Poland will exist, and we will return to our homeland.
>
> —Władysław Niewiński

When WWII started on September 1, 1939, with the German army invading Poland from the west, I was twenty-one years old. Before the war, I served in the Polish Fusiliers Company in Brześć nad Bugiem where I had been sent for military training.

Soon after the annexation of the eastern part of Poland by the USSR on September 17, 1939, Russia had announced in the newspapers that all Poles who lived in that region were now Russian citizens. All young Poles born in the years 1917 and 1918 were automatically Russian citizens, and were conscripted into mandatory service. I was of conscription age. On April 20, 1941, I received a letter that said I had to appear at the *Voyenkomat* NKVD, the Soviet military conscription commission, in Bielsko to be drafted into the USSR's military service. As ordered, I reported to the conscription commission on April 30, 1941. The Great Hall of the People's Commissariat building was filled with many young men waiting their turn to be seen by the military commission. I was registered and checked by the army's doctors and officers, and my head was shaved to ensure that I didn't run away. I was commanded to pack essential belongings, say goodbye to my family and report the same day to the military command in Bielsko for a swift departure. When I arrived at the army's command that evening, I joined a group of four hundred other Red Army recruits. I saw many familiar people my age from around the

Bielsko district. I remember looking at their faces and each of them had a look of sadness, depression and agitation. Above all, however, they were frightened because we didn't know what would happen to us and where we would be taken. Among those recruited to the Soviet army were Poles, Jews, Belarusians, Russians and Lithuanians.

Early morning on May 1, 1941, a reveille sounded. At the railroad station in Bielsko, we were loaded into eight freight wagons, and the train moved toward Białystok, where more railcars full of new recruits were attached. The train continued to Grodno where it stopped; again more wagons with more new army recruits were attached. We travelled towards the northeast, and that evening the train reached the Jdryca station. We figured out that we were close to the Latvian border, in the Kalinska Oblast. There we were unloaded from the train and marched a few kilometres on a forest road to a large military camp set in a dense forest. We received Red Army uniforms and were assigned to various military formations. I was assigned to the communication group. We lived in small temporary tents where we lay almost on the ground. Soon, military training started. It was hard to get used to the Russian system of training in addition to the new language. We lived in isolation, and the outside world was closed to us.

The only thing that allowed us to cope was that we were all from this same region of the eastern territory of Poland, and we could meet and talk about the situation in the camp and about hopes that our country would exist again, and we would return to our homeland. I was always trying to lift my colleagues' spirits. However, someone overheard our chats and apparently reported to the Red Army political officer, who was our commander, that I was spreading propaganda in the military camp. One day, a Red Army political officer stood in front of my tent and called my name, ordering me to come out. When I came out, he led me into a dark and dense forest, where he ordered me to sit on a tree stump. He sat on another tree stump, about six metres away from me. He took his pistol out of the holster and put it close by. Speaking in Russian, the officer yelled, "You Polish *svoloch* [scum]! If you are going to talk about how Poland existed before and it will exist again, I will kill you like a dog. No one will know. Do you see this pistol? By tomorrow morning, coyotes will gnaw your body. As you cannot see your ears with your own eyes, you will never see Poland."

I was young and quite frightened because the danger was real. I realized that the political officer could kill me anytime and would never be held responsible. By the time, I returned to the military camp I had calmed down a little. I told my close colleagues that we had to be vigilant because we might lose our lives. In this camp, besides the Jews, the Ukrainians and the Belarusians, there were about five hundred Poles from Lvov (Lwów) and the Mazowieckie Province. After this experience, I became quieter, and often my colleagues asked me, "Why are you so quiet?" I never told anyone about the encounter I had with the Red Army's political officer because I never trusted anyone anymore. I didn't know how our talks about free Poland were reported to the Russians since we spoke only in Polish.

For the next two weeks, we continued the military training. One early morning, the entire squad was ordered to report to an alarm muster. The political officer, speaking from a raised platform, informed us that the Fascist army had crossed the Russian state border, and were bombing Russian cities. Then he called out, "Our troops repelled massive attacks of the enemy. Don't worry! Our victory will prevail, and the enemy will be defeated!"

I noticed that the faces of the Poles brightened up a little after they heard this news. A full alert was declared, the soldiers were ordered to form marching columns, and we marched into the interior of Russia, as part of a strategic retreat of the Soviet troops. We walked for three and a half weeks and reached the city of Gorky (Nizhny Novgorod) on the Volga River. All the soldiers were exhausted. I remember that when we came to the river, I lay down on the grass on the riverbank and drank water directly from the river. Nothing happened to me. After that, I fell

Niewiński (R) wearing a Soviet military uniform after he was forcefully drafted into the Soviet army. [Courtesy of Władysław Niewiński]

into a long and very deep sleep. I don't know how long we all slept on the ground.

In Gorky, we were put into military barracks, and soon after, we started military training to prepare for a transfer to the front line. Before going to the front line, we were told that we had to take Russian citizenship. "How come? We have Polish citizenship," we protested. Most of those Red Army recruits of Polish origin like me refused to take Soviet citizenship.

After we had finished the two-week training, we were loaded into a train that took us to the front line. The train stopped in a forest near Harkov (Kharkiv) where the front line was so close that we could hear the roar of the artillery and see the flashes of explosions. We thought that if there was an opportunity, we would surrender to the Germans as POWs, or we would hide somewhere on the front line. We were careful to keep our plans to ourselves since we were assigned to military units with soldiers of various nationalities. That evening, after we unloaded the heavy military equipment, the unit commander called an emergency muster, during which he started reading aloud soldiers' names from a big long list. One by one, those who were called out had to step forward. After he had finished reading, there were about five hundred of us standing in front of the rest of the soldiers. We were ordered to march to the forest. I realized that all men called out by the officer were Poles who refused to give up Polish citizenship. We were being withdrawn from the front line. Our weapons, ammunition, maps and compasses were taken away from us. We were allowed to keep our military uniforms. Again, they loaded us onto a train that took us back east. The atmosphere on the train was quiet. We started to have different thoughts and worries about our situation, especially that they took away our weapons. We felt gloomier coming back from the front line than when we were going there because at least in the chaos of a battle we had some hope of breaking free from the Red Army.

I remember that our train arrived in Moscow at night. That was the first time the Germans bombarded Moscow. At the beginning of the attack, a squadron of German aircraft dropped spotlights to illuminate the city. It was so bright that one could find a needle on the ground. We jumped out of the boxcars, seeking cover in the nearby anti-aircraft trenches. We were so overtaken by panic that, instead of sitting in the trenches, we were jumping from one dugout to the other. We heard the buzzing of the planes flying above us, and the roar of the anti-aircraft artillery shooting at them. The railroad tracks were destroyed, and our train could not leave Moscow. Almost five hundred of us were left without any commanding officer or anyone else in charge. We stayed there for three days, and during that time, we ate only candies, which were in abundance everywhere in Moscow. After the railroad tracks had been repaired, we were loaded back on a train that headed east, taking us back to Gorky. We crossed the Volga River and the train took us to Chelyabinsk and Sverdlovsk. After a journey that lasted a few days, I was taken with others to Novosibirsk and from there to a nearby large detention camp where they told us the real reason why we were there.

"Our Russia has enough troops to fight the German enemy on the front, but it does not have enough auxiliary battalions to work to help combat the enemy," the political officer told us when we arrived in the camp. He told us that our assignment had been changed because Stalin ordered the Poles to be sent to labour camps and serve in work battalions. While in the camp, we were still part of the Red Army. It didn't matter to us if the explanation the political officer gave us was the truth or a lie; it was kind of a relief to hear it from the military since at least we knew why we were sent there. What he said uplifted our spirits a little. We were assigned to heavy-labour tasks, and I was assigned to work on laying the narrow-gauge railroad tracks, where I worked until February 1942. We started our workday at four o'clock in the morning. I laid the railroad tracks on the frozen river for the small, narrow-gauge wagons used to transport trees cut in the forest back to the river for the runoff when the river would be free of ice. When the trees in the area were cut down, they moved the detention camp to a new place.

The conditions in the labour camp, located in remote Siberia, were physically harsh in addition to the freezing temperatures during the winter. I had to work outside unless the temperature dropped below −65° C. There was no wind, and the air was dry. The tree trunks in the forest split now and then because of the severe cold and when splitting they made a *tra, tra, tra, tra* noise.

There was not much to eat. To stave off hunger, the young men dug out the roots of the trees and ate them. We lived on the tree bark, and we ate it because it was sweet. It was tough to survive such conditions, and many detained soldiers died of exhaustion and illnesses. The bodies of those who died were thrown out into the forest where wild animals tore them apart and devoured them. These scenes and the sounds were horrible.

In the camp, we lived in long wooden barracks made of tree trunks. The walls had wide cracks between the wooden boards. Each barrack contained military bunk beds for seventy soldiers. I slept on a top bunk bed, and each morning when I woke up, above me there was a pile of ice formed out of the moisture coming from my breath. In the middle of the barracks, there was a round iron stove where we burned coal. After we came back from work, we took off the quilted Soviet army jackets we called *fufajki*, wrapped them around the stove, first shaking the lice off, which dropped onto the hot stove making a constant *tatatatatatata* noise. The next morning, we put our fufajki back on and went back to work.

We had been entirely isolated from the political news, so we didn't know what was happening in the world. One day at four o'clock in the morning, they called a reveille for everyone, ordering us to report for an early muster. There were about three thousand detainees in the camp; all sent there were under suspicion of some wrongdoing against the Soviet Union. Among the detained were Russians sent there long before the war started, Poles who were resettled there during the forced resettlements in 1940, the Jews, the Kirgiz, and many from other Soviet republics. A high-ranking political officer, wearing a Soviet military uniform with a big red Soviet star affixed to the left sleeve, approached us. He stood in front of us and started reading names from a list loudly shouting each of them. Then he called, "Vladimir Karlowicz, *vystupi!*"— "Wladimir Karlowicz, step forward!"

He referred to my father's name, as was the custom in Russia. He called the names of about five hundred detainees. We thought that they would take us somewhere again. Then, I realized that all those who were called were Poles. I didn't know what they did with the rest of the detainees, but they separated us from them and left us in the forest. Two other Red Army political officers came, and I recognized the one who told me that as I couldn't see my ear with my eye, I would never see Poland exist again. The other officer that accompanied the one I recognized said, "Soldiers, boys, *rebiata*, today, you have..."

Niewiński stopped telling his story. Even though seventy years had passed, the emotions tied to those events made him unable to speak for a few minutes. Choking back the emotions and tears, he tried again, "Polish..." and he stopped again unable to utter a word. After a few moments, he returned to telling his story,

We didn't believe that something like this could happen. No news reached us. Then we heard the officer saying, "General Sikorski made a settlement with Stalin that you will go to the Polish army."

We asked, "Which army?"

The officer replied, "You'll go to the military! Now, you'll get a good breakfast right away. You'll get *lapsza* to eat today," he said, announcing a better food, and continued, "We're releasing you from the labour camp, and you'll go to the Polish army that's being organized on the territory of the USSR."

I have always been assertive. I walked to the political officer I knew and, staring at him, asked, "Comrade. Political officer, what's happening? You told me that Poland would never exist." The officer started to say something, however, I didn't want to talk with him anymore.

They lined us all up into marching columns, and we marched to the railroad station that was about five kilometres from the camp. There we got some salted fish, and an abundance of kipiatok ladled from big steaming barrels that were everywhere, to wash the fish down. They loaded us onto freight boxcars, and after a few hours of waiting, the train started moving towards the southwest. We had travelled for five days when the train stopped at one of the railroad stations. Then the train was moved from the main railroad tracks to a siding. We stayed there for three days. Again, we were given a little salted fish and water. Hunger began to tease us. Some of the soldiers started leaving the wagons in search of food. They found a boxcar on a nearby siding that was loaded with wheat. They managed to make a hole in its wall and took the grain in the small metal cans in which we had fish before. They mixed the seeds with water, warmed them up on the stoves in our wagons, and after the seeds swelled and softened a little we ate them. The train started moving again, and we travelled for two more weeks.

On February 5, 1942, after several weeks of a long journey of walking and riding a freight train, experiencing hunger, cold and exhaustion, we reached the station called Czepak where we were ordered to leave the wagons. Until the very end of our journey, we didn't believe that we would join the Polish army. When I saw the Polish soldiers and officers in British uniforms standing on the railroad platform, I was happy. Even though their uniforms were not familiar to me, I recognized them as Polish because they had little eagles, a symbol of Poland, pinned to their lapels and their military hats. The army camp was about eight kilometres from the Czepak station, and we marched there. There, we met many Polish soldiers who greeted us cordially and assured us that we were in the Polish army now. We were so happy to hear our mother tongue.

There we took off the fufajki and the old shoes, washed, and received new British-style military uniforms. After a short rest, we were sent for military training.

I spent two weeks in the Czepak transition camp, and there I met Sergeant Penski, my close friend, whom I knew from the 1939 military campaign in Poland when Hitler's and the Red Army invaded our country.

"My dear Władziu," he called me by my nickname. "What are you doing here?"

"Same as you are," I answered.

"Now, we will fight together against the Germans."

I was assigned to the heavy artillery. Penski was assigned to the supplies and provisions company. He had to go to the nearby kolkhozes to purchase supplies of meat for the troops. During those trips, he managed to get alcohol from the local Uzbeks. Sometimes, my friend came for a visit to my tent, and each time he brought alcohol with him. We drank a little and one day after such a visit I wasn't able to go for a military drill. As a punishment for drinking alcohol, I was assigned to bury corpses of those who arrived in the camp recently and died of exhaustion and illnesses. Six soldiers dug out long trenches. Four other soldiers, including me, carried the corpses with our bare hands and placed them beside each other in the freshly dug mass graves. Then, another group covered the bodies with earth to bury them. These graves are still there in Czepak. A lot of soldiers and civilians died of typhus, dysentery, typhoid, and exhaustion. Their bellies swelled from the illness and turned blue, and after that, they died. They were dying like flies. I attribute my immunity to those diseases and my survival to the alcohol I drank with my friend.

In the transition camp, the military command had been organizing the Eighth Military Division, and I was assigned to the heavy artillery. We were still on Russian territory, and even though we received military uniforms, we weren't given weapons. When we received an order to move

Niewiński (R) in a military camp in the desert close to Tehran, Iran. [Courtesy of Władysław
Niewiński]

to the Middle East, I left the camp in the first transport. We were loaded
onto a train and taken to Krasnovodzk by the Caspian Sea. On April 5,
1942, we said farewell to Russia and greeted the Middle East when we
boarded one of the two Russian ships that took us to the Persian seaport
of Pahlavi. The ships were not only used to transport the soldiers but
were filled with refugees, many of them children. The civilians carried
bundles packed with their possessions. The trip over the Caspian Sea
lasted about two hours. When the ship arrived in Pahlavi, it stopped
about half a kilometre from the harbour. To get to land, we had to board
small boats operated by the local Persians who took us to the shore.
After we had landed in the Pahlavi port, we were taken to a camp set up
on the beach where we went through an admission process that required
us to take off our uniforms, take cleansing steam showers and undergo

A group of Polish soldiers on a British destroyer en route from Alexandria to participate in a battle for Tobruk. The plans changed and they returned to Alexandria without reaching their destination. [Photo by Władysław Niewiński]

delousing, when they fumigated us with a cleansing smoke. After that, we received new military uniforms. Even though our military uniforms were still good, our clothes were thrown onto one-storey-high heaps, and the British soldiers set fire to them.

After that, the Polish army soldiers took an oath of loyalty to the homeland and the Polish government in London, and we finished our pledge with the words "God, Honour, Fatherland." Then, the commanding officer announced, "Soldiers, today is Easter in Poland."

That was the first time we were allowed to celebrate any religious holiday. Before, we had no idea when a Sunday, Christmas or any holiday was. To celebrate the first Easter in Pahlavi, we bought the only fruit available, dates, from Persian merchants. We went to the beach where we sat on the sand and ate the dates. Yearning for our home and homeland, we talked about past Easter celebrations in Poland before the war when we gathered together with our families to share a holiday meal. We talked about our families, wondering what had been happening with

Niewiński (centre) and the soldiers from the II Polish Army Corps in a field of flowers.
[Courtesy of Władysław Niewiński]

them since we still didn't have any news from those left behind. Far away from Poland, and sitting on the hot sand during our first Easter celebration, our hope of Poland regaining freedom grew.

After we had rested for a few days in Pahlavi, we were loaded onto large Persian trucks. The local truck drivers took us through the mountains to a camp close to Tehran, the capital city of Persia. My division was ordered to depart to England where we were to join the I Polish Army Corps under Allied command and General Stanisław Maczek, after we trained in the Persian camp for this mission.

While in the camp, I met Tworkowski who was a doctor in Bielsko Podlaskie before the war. I knew the doctor since I'd gone to school with his daughter. He was organizing the third Polish hospital in the camp. We were happy to see each other. The doctor was afraid for my safety

Recovering from injuries, Niewiński is seated second from the left. [Courtesy of Władysław Niewiński]

There were no cemeteries in Iraq. Soldiers who died in Iraq were buried in the desert.
[Photo by Władysław Niewiński]

and offered me work as a medical orderly to stay with him in Tehran.
He said, "Władziu, listen! Son. It's dangerous to go to England since the
German Luftwaffe regularly bombs ships, sinking many of them. I'd like
you to stay here and work with me." I took the job, but I worked there for
only about two months because I was unable to deal with the sight of
blood and wounds.

At that time there was a Polish–British expedition organized in Persia
to help repatriate the Polish families detained in Russia and transfer them to the British colonies. Taking the advice of Dr. Tworkowski
who said that because I knew how to read and write, I should consider this option. I applied and joined the expedition made up of three
Polish and three British soldiers. For this mission, we were assigned a

twelve-passenger aircraft with a pilot, and flew to Russia. After the plane landed on Russian territory and we had our documents checked, we travelled to places where there were large concentrations of displaced families to organize their evacuation. First, these people were taken to the railroad stations and from there they went by train to Krasnovodzk, then through the Caspian Sea by ships to Tehran, and later they were sent to the British colonies. This mission lasted until Stalin broke off diplomatic relations with the Polish government-in-exile after Germans discovered the mass graves of the Polish soldiers and officers murdered by the NKVD in the detention camps in Kozielsk, Starobielsk, and Katyń.

I kept a record of those displaced people the Polish–British expedition helped evacuate from Russia while the mission was still operating. Between 1940 and 1941 among those deported to Russia from the annexed eastern territory of Poland were 300,000 children and youth up to seventeen years of age. The number of Polish orphans had reached 30,000. Between 1941 and 1942, in the Soviet Union, there remained 160,000 to 180,000 Polish children and youth up to seventeen years of age. By 1945 the number of children had been reduced by 50 per cent because some evacuated, but many died there.

The following information comes from the documents Niewiński left behind with his notes from his involvement in the repatriation mission of soldiers, civilians and children from the USSR to the Middle East, as well as activities he witnessed in the Czepak Camp in South Kazakhstan.

The first evacuation of the soldiers from Russia to the Middle East took place on March 19, 1942, when initially 30,000 soldiers and 10,000 civilians were to be evacuated. After representatives of the Polish government-in-exile had talked with the Soviet government, the number of evacuees was increased to 33,069 soldiers, 10,789 civilians, and

During the military campaign in North Africa. Niewiński appears on the right. [Courtesy of Władysław Niewiński]

3,100 children. The civilians and the children were to be sent to Tehran, Kenya and Uganda.

The second evacuation from Russia took place in September 1942 when the Polish government demanded that all Polish military personnel be allowed to leave. At that time, 60,000 women and paramilitary youth involved in the auxiliary service were allowed to leave. Moreover, the Polish government asked that the families of soldiers be authorized to leave in addition to 50,000 children, and 5,000 mothers and caregivers. The Polish Embassy in Russia demanded that Russia provide care for the rest of Poles.

The last transport of displaced people from Russia came to Pahlavi on September 1, 1942, when 69,247 people were evacuated to Iran. Among others, this transport included 25,501 civilians and 9,633 children.

In the last evacuation from Russia, 115,742 were sent to the Middle East, including 78,470 soldiers, among them officers, petty officers, paramilitary youth and nurses. Ten per cent of those who were evacuated from Russia were not of Polish nationality and included Ukrainians and Belarusians, but most were Jewish: 4,300 Jewish soldiers were evacuated from Russia to Palestine. However, upon arriving in Palestine, 3,000 of them deserted. General Anders decided not to look for and prosecute them.

At the end of the humanitarian mission, after the intervention of the US and Britain, Russia allowed civilians, and especially 13,948 children and 5,737 youth, to be evacuated. The total number of children and young people was 19,685. The Polish government had difficulties helping with the evacuation of individuals who were not of Polish nationality because the Russian government did not allow those people to leave.

Most of the civilian population evacuated from Russia was moved to East and South Africa and settled in Kenya, Uganda, Tanganyika and Rhodesia where 22,000 were sent. Part of the Polish civilian population was sent to India, where 10,000 people, including 5,000 orphans and 5,000 children with families were evacuated. In 1943 New Zealand accepted 700 children and all of them stayed there after the war; none returned to Poland. Ten thousand Polish refugees were settled in Mexico, sponsored by the US government. The first transport of the Polish refugees arrived in Mexico in October 1943 in Santa Rosa near the city of Leon. A few thousand refugees were settled in Palestine, Libya and Syria. The biggest concentrations of Polish refugees evacuated from Russia were in Jerusalem, Tel Aviv and Nazareth.

When the repatriation mission of the Polish population from the Soviet Union ended, I returned to the transitional camp of the Polish Corps in Gedera close to Rehovot in Palestine to undertake the next military duty. I was accepted to the aircraft division to learn to operate military aircraft. However, playing soccer one day, I was injured and had to stay in a hospital for two months. After being discharged from the hospital, I was assigned to an Independent Armoured Brigade in the II Polish Army Corps as a *plutonowy* (platoon leader) and participated in two attacks conducted by the Polish troops on Monte Cassino, where I drove a tank providing support for the Polish Carpathian Infantry Division. The preparations for this attack took two weeks while the sappers dug out tunnels where they stored water and ammunition.

Our preparations didn't go unnoticed. The Germans, who tried to break the spirits of the Polish soldiers, installed loudspeakers on top of the mountain and called to us in Polish, "Poles, we know that you are preparing the assault positions. There are not enough of you to take on the monastery. Why would you want to fight for your country, when it is sold already? Drop your weapons. Cross to our side. You will return to your families. Be respectful of your life."

We weren't discouraged by this *wanda* (propaganda) and continued our training to deal with the enemy. After a few weeks of preparation, we were ready for the attack. One night, at eleven, a massive attack on the monastery started. I was in the tank watching the area through binoculars ready for an assault. Then, in one second, four thousand artillery cannons fired at once. It was as bright as in the day. For each square

Standing on the platform, General Władysław Anders (L) and Field Marshal Harold Alexander (R) review a parade of the II Polish Army Corps in preparation for the coming battle, 1944. [Photo by Władysław Niewiński]

metre, four artillery missiles fell. After the artillery attack, there was a mortar attack. At four o'clock in the morning, we could hear the roar of the approaching airplanes. Consecutive formations of eight planes in each line flew above the abbey, dropping bombs. About four hundred bombers dropped bombs that night on the Germans, but they held on to their positions. Despite our efforts, the first attack wasn't successful. We had to withdraw. Four thousand Polish soldiers died that day. Among them were the members of the tank crew I commanded. They perished when the artillery hit the tank. I was standing in the command

Field Marshal Harold Alexander, inspecting the II Polish Army Corps. [Photo by Władysław Niewiński]

Recovering from injuries again. Niewiński is seated second from the left. [Courtesy of Władysław Niewiński]

stirrup observing the battlefield and directing the driver where to go, and because of that, I was able to escape. I was lightly wounded in this attack on Monte Cassino, and I was still able to participate in the coming battle.

After this unsuccessful attack, General Anders decided that we would try to take the monastery on Monte Cassino where the German soldiers fortified themselves once again, and he ordered that we start the preparations. All higher-ranking soldiers had a few days of training. Polish soldiers killed during the first attack were replaced with new recruits.

The second attack in which the Polish troops were involved took place about a week later. General Anders changed tactics and included the tanks

Sightseeing in Italy. Niewiński is seated. [Courtesy of Władysław Niewiński]

in the assault on the monastery, located on top of the hill from where the Germans were shooting at anyone who took the road below. There was a warning sign in Polish on the road *Nie bądz głupi, nie daj się zabić* (Don't be stupid, don't let yourself be killed). Soldiers walked there with their heads down, and the military Jeeps had their roofs taken down while driving through that part of the road to avoid being shot. I was in the Independent Armoured Brigade, and during the second attack, once again I was a commander of the tank and its crew. The Germans shot the tank in front of ours, disabling it. Unable to move farther, the tank was blocking the narrow rocky path, and we couldn't drive uphill. We had to push the disabled tank from the mountain, and it fell into the abyss below. That tank, the artillery, and the Jeeps are down there today. I drove up that steep road. The soldiers from the Carpathian Brigade moved closer to the top of

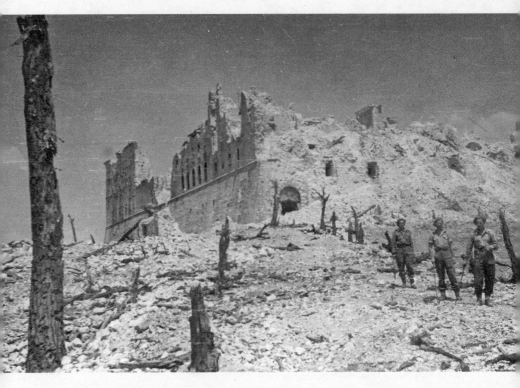

The Abbey Monte Cassino, founded by St. Benedict of Nursia, after the battle. [Photo by Władysław Niewiński]

the hill, taking cover under our fire. To avoid being shot, the soldiers ran toward the monastery bent in half or on all fours.

At five o'clock in the morning, we took the monastery, and put the Polish flag on top of its ruins. One of the Polish soldiers standing on top of the hill beside the Polish flag said, "I can see the tower of the Mariacki Church in Kraków from here." It was a huge battle, and many died there. The Germans were no longer in the monastery. They were hiding in the bunkers.

Before the last attack on Monte Cassino, I'd been put in charge of another tank and appointed commander of its crew. The Germans had stretched thin metal ropes across and above the path where we

A piece of a stole from the monastery on Monte Cassino, courtesy of Władysław Niewiński.
[Photo by Aldona Jaworska]

drove our tanks. The metal cables were dangerous and beheaded anyone standing in the command stirrup who didn't notice them. I had to
keep my head down. During the last attack that led us to victory, the
tank I commanded was hit by a phosphorus bomb that made a big cav-
ity in the outer wall. When the missile was inside, it burst into flames,
engulfing the tank's hull and trapping everyone inside. I was in the
commander hatch and managed to leave the tank. I rolled over on the
ground to extinguish the fire raging on my back. The four other soldiers
from my tank were killed. I was the only one from this crew who survived. I was severely burned, and I had to spend some time in a hospital.
Since I was unable to return to the active military, I was assigned to work
in the corps headquarters where I worked at distributing supplies for the
entire II Polish Army Corps. During the Battle of Monte Cassino, I lost
two tanks and two entire tank crews of which I was a commander, and
I was wounded twice.

Before the battle, the monastery was beautiful. When the artillery
and aircraft attacks took place, the monastery started sinking because of

The medals awarded to Niewiński for his service in WWII. [Photo by Dale Flemming]

the impact of the bombs and the artillery shelling. I went to see the monastery after the battle was over, and I found a liturgical vestment and other ceremonial artifacts that had been torn apart during the bombardment. I found a stole, from an ecclesiastical vestment, amid the rubble. I took a piece of it with me, and later I carried it to Canada. For my military service, I was awarded the General Service Cross—Monte Cassino Bar with two wound stripes for my involvement during the Battle of Monte Cassino. I received the Polish Army Medal—Medal of Merit, issued to all Polish veterans for fighting in battles abroad. For detention in Siberia, I received the Siberian Cross. The British government awarded me the 1939–1945 Star Medal, the 1942–1943 Africa Star with Bar, the Defence of Britain Medal, and the 1939–1945 War Medal. Moreover, I was the recipient of the bronze, silver and gold medals issued by the Polish Combatants' Association in Canada. I visited Jerusalem during WWII, and received the Knighthood of the Holy Sepulchre Medal.

I kept my Polish military uniform that I received after joining the Anders Army, and I brought it with me to Canada. It has always given me a sense of national pride and belonging. This uniform is an integral part of my heritage. I was a soldier bound by an oath to fulfill my duty and

On May 25, 1944, near the Monte Cassino monastery, in the presence of the 5th and 3rd Divisions, General Harold Alexander held an investiture on behalf of His Majesty George VI of Great Britain, conferring on Władysław Anders the Order of the Bath. [Courtesy of Władysław Niewiński]

moral obligations to my country. I made personal sacrifices. That was the cost of war.

After the war was over, the II Polish Army Corps stayed in Italy for a year. In 1946 the British government declared demobilization of the Polish armed forces under their command. General Anders shared the news that we could not return to a free Poland, as our country was under the influence of the Soviet Union. The outcome of the Yalta Conference was not in our favour. We didn't have a place where we could go. The soldiers and the officers of the Polish corps were disappointed and sad. A great confusion followed. When I worked at the corps headquarters, General Zygmunt Bohusz-Szyszko, who was the general officer commanding II Polish Corps in Italy in 1945–1946, proposed to General Anders that the II Army Corps take the weapons in its possession and go to Monte Cassino, stay there, and defend ourselves there. General Anders did not approve of this.

Once again, while Niewiński was telling this part of his story, tears filled his eyes. All soldiers and officers of the II Polish Army Corps were disappointed at the treatment they received from the British government that pressured them to return to a Poland that was under the influence of the Soviet Union. After a few moments of silence, he started telling his story again.

Later we learned that there was a possibility for the soldiers from the II Polish Army Corps to move to the British colonies. Also, the British command allowed us to form the Polish Combatants' Association in Italy. Right away, the recruitment camps were organized for those wanting to move to Canada. I joined the Polish Resettlement Corps, formed to help us find a place to go to, and I had to undergo a practical test to determine if my agricultural knowledge and experiences were sufficient for me to be accepted into the program. I was asked to demonstrate if I knew how to milk a cow and if I knew how to plough a field using a walking plough drawn by an ox. Based on the aptitude test, I was accepted into the program. Each soldier who was accepted to this program had to sign a two-year contract to work on farms in Canada. Because of that, the Warsaw regime took away Polish citizenship from us. We were given a letter in which the Polish authority pressed us to report to the Polish consulates and return to Poland to undergo rehabilitation. They gave us only one week to make the decision if we wanted to go back to Poland. Otherwise, we would automatically lose Polish citizenship.

11 Polish Army Corps soldiers. Niewiński appears second from the right.
[Courtesy of Władysław Niewiński]

The Polish Camp Canada, Italy, 1946. The 11 Polish Army Corps soldiers on their way to ploughing a field using oxen, a mandatory test to qualify for work on farms in Canada.
[Photo by Władysław Niewiński]

Niewiński (R) and his friend Józef Magadzia (L) in Italy. The two men were separated after they arrived in Halifax and never met again. Niewiński kept this photograph on the wall in his house. [Courtesy of Władysław Niewiński]

Soon after the agricultural tests were finished, we were demobilized from the II Polish Army Corps, and we boarded a warship in Porto Recanati, Italy, on November 3, 1946. After ten days on the ocean, we arrived in Halifax on November 12, 1946. The immigration officer asked me, "Do you have any close friends from the army who are also on this transport?" When I pointed out my close friend Józef Magadzia to the officer, he made a note of my friend's name. When we boarded the train, my friend was sent to Ontario, and I was sent to Lethbridge in Alberta. We had hoped to be placed together on the farm or nearby so we could keep in touch or visit. I always wondered about what had happened that day, and now I understand that we were separated on purpose. Later, I searched for my friend Józef Magadzia, but I never saw him again.

It took five days to travel from Halifax to Lethbridge, where I was sent. Our train arrived at the camp for the German POWs. We were housed in the quarters previously occupied by them. On the day we arrived, it was frigid and snowy outside. The barracks weren't heated and Lieutenant Karchel, who also was sent to Lethbridge, and I went to look for some coal to heat up the place. Even though we came to a free country, we came to a camp, but this time to a German camp. Farmers started arriving to pick up soldiers. They were picking us up like piglets, like slaves. I was there for a week, and nobody came for me. There were only a few of us left. We were sent for a medical exam. The doctor said that I had tuberculosis, and sent me to the Currie Barracks in Calgary. Ten ambulances were waiting in Calgary at the railroad station to pick us up. We felt healthy, and it was strange for us to be ordered to stay in bed all the time. Walter Chuchla and his wife, who were very active in the Polish community in Calgary, visited us in the hospital. We weren't allowed to get out of bed because we were told that we were very ill. This misunderstanding was cleared up after a colonel of Polish origin from the Canadian regiment in Edmonton helped me explain to the doctor that I'd suffered from pneumonia when I was in the labour camp in Siberia during the winter of 1942 and that had left some marks on my lungs. The next day, I was sent to peel potatoes in the hospital kitchen.

After I left the hospital, I was assigned to work on a farm near Cremona. My experience of working on a farm that first year wasn't positive. My duties included milking the cows and performing general farm labour. I was housed in a barn, and the farmer didn't provide enough food. He had a big family and several young children. By the time I finished milking the cows in the morning, and I came to the kitchen, there wasn't much food left on the table after everyone else had already eaten. Because of that, I often went hungry. In secret, I started drinking the freshly milked milk, and to cover that up, I added water before bringing the milk from the barn to the house. However, my secret was found out when the tests from the lab indicated that there was too much water in the milk.

After the first year, I asked the Canadian authorities in Calgary to assign me to a different farm, hoping that the second year would bring a better experience. I was assigned to work on a farm near Mossleigh. After the contract finished, the farmer for whom I worked wanted me to stay longer and even offered to cede the farm to me. However, I didn't want to live in isolation on a remote farm. After finishing the contracts, young veterans started fleeing from the farms to Canadian cities. They began a new life and formed the local branch of the Polish Combatants' Association. New members joined the organization. In almost every city where Polish veterans could be found, new veteran associations were established. Energy and life blossomed, parties, weddings, baptisms... everybody was in a happy mood.

I had been enthusiastic about the prospect of a new life and new opportunities in Canada. However, I didn't want to stay on a farm, and I wanted to find a job, start a family, buy a house and have children. When I came to Calgary after my mandatory farm-work contract ended, I dis-covered a Polish community hall. Six other Polish veterans lived there in a few rooms set up for people like us. The other young veterans wanted to enjoy themselves and have a good time. However, I wanted to settle down as quickly as possible, and I was careful with my money. The other veterans trusted me, so I did the shopping for everyone, and kept track of money for all of us. I was their banker. I got married, and had children. I found a job in a small company working with brass, and I stayed there for six years. However, working with metals caused problems with lungs, and it wasn't healthy for me. I got another job in a small factory where I stayed for almost twenty years. Over that time, I took a half-day off from work when I was ill. I bought a house for the family.

In 1947 the Polish Combatants' Association in Calgary had 160 members. We met at the community centre located in Bridgeland. I wanted to keep the Polish traditions and values alive. We wanted to have our Polish place, so we could dance, sing, or speak Polish without fear of being chastised for it. The Polish soldiers started the Polish church too. They bought a piece of land and built the church. Now, in this place, there is a different church. Outside of the Polish community hall, we didn't feel that this was our place, our homeland. We wanted a place where we could share our common traditions and talk about our history. That was important to us. I became involved with the Polish community in Calgary and actively participated in the building of the new Polish Canadian Cultural Centre. The help I received from the Polish community in Calgary upon my arrival allowed me to start a new life in Canada. For fifteen years, I served as the secretary and treasurer of the Polish Credit Union, established to help Poles coming to Canada start a new life. For many years, I was the secretary and treasurer of the Polish community hall, and I participated in the building of the new Polish community hall.

For the children who were born in here, it is their country. However, even today, I feel that we still are living in a foreign land. Wherever someone is born, that is where his or her homeland is.

We, the soldiers who served in the II Polish Army Corps in WWII, felt like we were the ambassadors of a free and independent Poland. We lived our lives with a hope that the day would come. I lived long enough to see that day, but not everyone did. We have to bow our heads before those soldiers. We should be proud of our achievements. When Lech Wałęsa, the first president of Poland was elected in a free election, our watch was done. In December 1990 at the Royal Castle in Warsaw, Ryszard Kaczorowski, the president of the Polish government-in-exile in London, symbolically handed Wałęsa the constitutional power, and our duties as ambassadors of free Poland were done. Our dreams of free Poland were fulfilled that day. It would be a shame if our rich history were forgotten in Canada and Poland. Today, we are veterans only. I would like the history of General Władysław Anders and General Władysław Sikorski, and the involvement of the II Polish Army Corps soldiers in bringing freedom to the world to be put on display in a museum. There, the names of those who fought for freedom would be posted, along with a sign in two languages: *Walczyli i polegli za Waszą i Naszą Wolność* (They fought and died for your and our freedom). There we could put our medals, our military uniforms, and the photographs, as a lasting memorial. Such a place would serve and inform the younger generations about the past. There, they will learn more about Poland's involvement in achieving freedom. We are getting old, and we will be going to eternity, but we always stood by the military oath we gave to our homeland.

Remembering Władysław Niewiński

On Wednesday, July 11, 2012, I had an appointment with Mr. Niewiński to continue the interviews. However, I never managed to say a last goodbye to him. On July 8, 2012, following a very brief illness, Mr. Niewiński suddenly passed away. For the past few months, I had been working with Mr. Niewiński, collecting material for my master's thesis. His wife Nancy said that he had looked forward to this meeting during which we were going to look through the photographs he took while serving in the II Polish Army Corps. With the small allowance he had received for his army service, he had bought a camera and took pictures of the many events in which he participated. These photographs offer a unique insight into the life of the soldiers at that time.

Over the time I worked with Niewiński, I experienced moments that provided an intimate and unique look at the life of a soldier. During one of our visits, Niewiński showed me his military uniform and the shirt that he had been given when he joined the II Polish Army Corps. The dark green felt fabric had not changed at all. On the left sleeve of his uniform, a badge with the Mermaid of Warsaw holding a sword in one hand and a shield in the other—the insignia of the II Polish Corps. On the right sleeve, another crest with a golden cross symbolizing the British Eighth Army. On each sleeve, above both insignias, "POLAND" was written in capital letters. On each of the epaulettes, there was one star indicating military rank. It touched me that these stars were hand cut from a piece of white plastic and affixed to the material with a bent pin. The uniform had all its buttons, each impressed with an eagle, a symbol of Poland. It was a great privilege to examine Niewiński's military uniform, which he wore on special occasions. Perhaps he had worn it when he travelled to Canada. Niewiński told me that he wore the military pants that were part of the suit during the winter when he worked on the farms in Alberta. He had had to throw them away when they became tattered, but he kept the jacket.

On another occasion, Niewiński opened a drawer of his desk and took out a small box. When he opened it, I saw the stole he found in the monastery ruins after the Polish troops took the abbey on Monte Cassino. He handed the box to me. When I touched the stole, something unexpected happened—I felt as if I was almost in that monastery. This small piece of liturgical vestment was a bridge between the decades past. Once again, I thought about the different Polands in which we grew up and about what brought us to Canada.

During my research, I was able to find information about Niewiński's friend Józef Magadzia with whom he had come to Canada. However, Niewiński's sudden passing prevented me from sharing with him that I had found the obituary that said Magadzia died in 2006 in Ottawa.

I learned a lot from Niewiński during the time we spent talking about his life and experiences: as a Polish soldier in the 1939 military campaign, with the Red Army, as a detainee in the labour camp in Siberia, as a soldier in the Anders Army and as a newcomer to Canada. Learning about the life of Niewiński prompted me to write a book about soldiers like him and share his story.

Władysław Niewiński was buried in Calgary. Police officers accompanied the funeral procession and stopped traffic at all intersections leading to the cemetery. All police officers involved stood at the entrance to the cemetery saluting the hearse carrying Niewiński's body, honouring him as a war veteran. Special tributes were also given to Niewiński by Polish veterans, members of the Polish Combatants' Association in Calgary. The flag of the association was on display during the ceremony. Niewiński's son-in-law is a police officer in Calgary, and his daughter works as a citizenship officer in Calgary.

A small museum commemorating the WWII Polish combatants and veterans was opened at the Polish Canadian Cultural Centre in Calgary on November 11, 2015.

9

Zbigniew (Leo) Rogowski

(1927–)

Introducing Mr. Rogowski

I MET MR. ROGOWSKI AT the seniors' club meeting where
I shared my findings on the topic of the II Polish Army Corps veterans in Calgary. Mr. Rogowski was wearing a black military beret
that had an eagle with a crown, a symbol of the Polish military
during WWII. "When I was young I was a soldier, and I fought in
the Battle of Monte Cassino," Rogowski said, eager to talk with me
even though he had to use oxygen to help him breathe. "I joined
the seniors' club a few years ago; before that, I used to go to the
Canadian Legion No. 1, where I became a member after I was discharged from the Canadian military following a two-month atomic
bomb survival training in 1963. Because I was a soldier during the
war, I also wanted to become a soldier in the Canadian military and
be like my father. I liked the military life. But my wife was ill, and
I had to take care of her, so they reclassified me a military reservist.
The Canadian soldiers I met in the Legion didn't know that Polish

soldiers liberated Monte Cassino," he said and proceeded to tell me how he met his wife.

"It was sometime in the 1960s. I was returning home from work. In front of the building where I lived, I saw a woman sitting on the stairs. She was wearing a dress only. It was freezing outside. She was crying. When I asked, she said that her husband beat her and she was afraid to go back home. They had two almost grown-up children, a daughter and a son. She was born in Greenock, Scotland. During the war, she had been a soldier in the British army. I told her that she could stay with me, cook for me, and I would pay her. She stayed with me for a few years, helping me at home. Then her husband found her and wanted her to come back. He threatened to beat us both. I helped her apply for a divorce. We got married on February 19, 1970. We were happy together. Sometimes, we cooked a pot of soup and we took it to the homeless people sitting on 17th Avenue. We wanted to help them. My wife lived for a few more years, then died. She was buried in the Field of Honours. After she died, I was sad. I have no family in Canada."

Listening to Rogowski's story made me think of his selflessness when dealing with human suffering and his willingness and readiness to help others.

Zbigniew Rogowski

Zbigniew Rogowski was born on November 15, 1927, in Gródek Jagielloński, Mszana township, Lwów province, Poland. His father Henry Rogowski served in the Polish cavalry from 1914 until 1925, and from 1926 until 1939, he was a police officer. His mother Anna was nineteen years old, and his father was thirty-two years old when they got married in 1927. The following story is a reconstruction based on the interviews, a rudimentary memoir, personal documents and photographs Rogowski shared with me.

> People ask me why I wear my black military beret every day. I wear it, so I never forget who I was, and who I am. I wear it for all the soldiers who did not make it through the war and died for us so we can have a better life. They gave their lives for us and for peace. Lest I forget, I was a soldier.
> —Zbigniew Rogowski

On September 1, 1939, I was to start grade five at the Augustyn Kordecki School located on Kordecki Street, in Lvov (Lwów) Poland. The other boys called me "philosopher" because I always gave good answers in class. My father was a police officer and worked at the nearby police station. When I was growing up, I thought that I would be in the military for twenty years and after that, I would be a police officer, like my father. Once, my dad told me, "You have to study hard if you want to be a police officer in the future."

However, on the first day of school, w wii started, and we couldn't go to school. Soon, the air raids started. The manager of the building in which we lived asked that I join the *Liga Obrony Powietrznej i Przeciwgazowej* (air defence league of the country). I was eleven years old and the only young boy still residing in the building. The manager gave me an armband with the league's logo, and I was to check if anyone needed help or direction to an air-raid shelter, or was wounded, or killed during an air attack. During one of the Russian airstrikes, the building that was close to where I stood was bombarded, and I could smell the gunpowder. I saw parts of human bodies flying in the air...the legs, the arms, and the heads.

After the Russian army took Lvov, at two o'clock in the morning, the Russian police officers in blue uniforms came to our home to arrest my father. I was still in bed. As they were taking my dad away, he looked at

me and nodded toward my mother and my three younger sisters.
I understood that he wanted me to take care of them. I looked through
the window, and I saw a big truck loaded with many Polish police
officers.

Two weeks later, the Russian soldiers came to our apartment and
ordered my mother, my three sisters and me to leave. My younger sisters
were eight, seven and four years old. My mum packed some of our belongings, carried my little sister in her arms, and we left the house. There was
a truck waiting for us outside, and there was a family of another Polish
police officer in it. A woman who stood nearby told me, "Run."

I looked at my mother and my sisters, and I thought that they needed
me, so I stayed with them. I was the oldest child in my family—almost
twelve years old. The Russian soldiers loaded us into an empty freight
wagon with eight or nine other families. It was a long journey, and we
were locked up inside all the time. The soldiers who escorted us sat on
the roofs of the wagons and watched us continuously. If someone tried
to run away, they would shoot and kill that person. Sometimes the train
stopped, and the soldiers would come to our wagon and order me to
take a bucket and bring hot water. They took me to a place where there
was *kipiatok*, as they called boiled water in Russian. After I carried the
bucket full of hot water back to the wagon, a soldier would lift me up
to help me get inside. Then, the soldiers would give us a loaf of bread
to share with everyone in the wagon. It took us one month to travel to
Kazakhstan, and throughout this time, everyone was sad, and people
cried that they had lost everything. But we could do nothing. I had my
twelfth birthday while we were travelling by boxcar train to Russia. We
arrived somewhere in Kazakhstan. The railroad tracks ended there. It
was mid-December, it was cold and we had to walk to the place where
we were supposed to live. The Russian soldiers pushed us with bayo-
nets to make us walk faster. We arrived at a small kolkhoz, Karakol in
the province of Kazakhstan. The kolkhoz was located along a river, also
named Karakol. There were about fifteen small buildings and huts made

of mud and set far away from each other. There was also a school. The population of this kolkhoz was about fifty people. They had lived there from the time of the tsar. They believed in God, but after Stalin became the leader of the Soviet Union, they had to hide their religious beliefs. Later on, when I talked with them, I was told, "There is no church here, there is no religion here, and there are no doctors here. Children go to school and learn differently."

Stalin was like a god to them. "He does everything here. If you need help, go and pray to Stalin and thank him for everything you have," we were told, and if we didn't do what we were told to do, then they would kill us or put us in jail.

Upon our arrival, the Russian chairman of the kolkhoz, who was in charge of distribution of food or any other goods, said that there was no place for us there, except a dugout about three metres deep. We were told that we would stay there until spring. When we were inside the dugout, we couldn't reach the ceiling even with an outstretched arm. This dugout was about eight to ten metres wide, and twenty-five to twenty-seven metres long. The stairs leading inside were made out of mud, too. This ditch was covered with wooden planks and tree trunks, and spruce branches were put on top of them. Later in December, when the snow fell onto the roof, there was no air inside, and it was hard to breathe. Taller boys stood on each other's shoulders to reach the ceiling, and made small openings in the snow that covered the roof, to let in a little bit of fresh air. By the time they managed to do this, two older people had died. Their bodies were left inside for a few days before someone from the kolkhoz came to take them away. The stench of rotting corpses was hard to bear. This place served as a home for ten families. People as old as seventy lay directly on the ground. There was nothing there. Many people were ill and dying. We were destitute.

We were hungry. Once a day someone threw a loaf of bread inside for everyone to share. People fought for food, and the older boys ripped the bread into pieces. We got just a morsel of food. That was everything we had to eat for the entire day. When we arrived, we didn't even have water. We waited for the snow to fall. Only later, we got some hot water. We lived in these conditions until the summer when they told us that we had to move out and find a new place for ourselves because they wanted to bury the dugout. My mum found a small empty hut on the other side of the nearby, knee-deep river. The local Kirgiz shepherds used it during the winter, but they allowed us to live in it for two months during the summer when they moved to their yurts closer to the pastures where they took their sheep. We lived in this hut with two other resettled families.

Soon after we arrived, the kolkhoz chairman told us that my sister Luba, who was nine years old, and I would have to go to the Russian school. Luba sat at the front of the class, and I sat at the back, with the other boys. There were eight or ten children there. The teacher asked the class, "Who believes in God, arise?" I raised my hand and stood up. My sister kept sitting down. She looked at me and whispered, "Sit down."

Everyone in the class looked at me. The teacher said, "Our god travelled by train abroad, and will never come back." Then she asked me, "Can your god give you candies?" and when I said nothing, she added, "Comrade Stalin can." After she said that, I thought to myself that they don't have any god here. Later that day, the teacher told me not to come to school anymore. That was my only day of school in Russian. During the spring and summer, when I passed the school as I took cattle and sheep to pastures, the children watched me through the windows. Once a boy called out to me to not let the cows eat grass because they would get sick and die of it.

My sister Luba died that winter, at the age of nine. She was very ill with a fever, and I got sick too. Even though I wanted to help her, she didn't want to use the bucket, set in the middle of the dugout, which served as a toilet for everyone to use. I told her, "Sis, I will cover you with a blanket, no one will see you."

"No, I want to go to the river," Luba kept saying. As I lay ill on a wooden bunk covered with a little bit of straw and a jacket, Luba stubbornly went outside. My mother followed her. After about three hours, my mum came back alone, and told us this: "The mud by the river was slippery. Luba was disoriented by the fever and fell into the river. I pulled her from the frigid water, and took her to the closest hut. She was vomiting and bleeding from her mouth, and soon after, she died."

My mum paid some locals to make a small box and bury my sister in Karakol. Once, my mum showed me the slight protuberance in the steppe marked by a small wooden cross. It was made from two pieces of wooden arms tied together with a twine. It wasn't even a cemetery, but an empty place where they buried people who didn't have money for burial. After a while, Luba's grave was overgrown with grass. It was terrible there. I survived the illness without medicine, without food and without doctors. It was my fate to survive.

I wanted to help my family, so during the summer, I worked for the peasants taking their cows and goats to the pastures. For a day of work, they would give me an egg or a piece of bread. One day, one of the peasants called me inside his hut, wanting to show me something. He took me to a place where there was a calendar hanging on a wall. "Do you see this?" He moved the wall calendar aside uncovering a hole behind it. Inside, I saw a statue of Jesus. "I come here to cross myself. But, if my son saw me, then I would be arrested. It is forbidden to make a sign of the cross in here." The man told me he could show me what he kept behind the calendar because he knew that I believed in God. I felt it was strange that the people there weren't allowed to believe in God.

That summer, I found a job in the nearby kolkhoz where I helped with the collecting of the hay that was needed to feed about three hundred sheep during the winter. Tractors equipped with a wooden rake picked up the hay from the fields, and I was put in charge of synchronizing their work. I was given this job because I could whistle loudly and communicate the change of the rake with the other tractor drivers over a great distance. We built big haystacks from that hay. My mum received the money for this work, but at that time, I didn't know that. I was given food. I just wanted to work to help my family and bring the food home. During that summer, I collected many pieces of bread that were given to me as payment for my work. I didn't want the food to rot, so dried it. I often worked until late at night and came back home when it was dark. My mum kept a light in the window to help me find the way back. Once, I saw some lights in the barn. At first, I didn't know what they were but my mum told me that they were the glowing eyes of a wolf that had followed me home. I got frightened. From then on, I was cautious and always watched my surroundings.

In November we had to move out of the hut. The Kirgiz shepherds wanted to come back to their home. We put the money I earned during the summer together and, with other families, hired a driver with a truck that took four families to search for a new place. We decided to move to Ayagoz, located a few hundred kilometres from Karakol. There wasn't even a road there. We drove through the steppe following the tracks made by the trucks that sometimes came to the kolkhoz. That evening, the driver stopped the truck and came to the back, where we were sitting. He lit four torches and placed them on the truck's sides. I asked the driver why.

"We will be going through an area where there are a lot of wolves. You will see their glowing eyes later, watching us. Once a soldier rode a horse here, and the wolves attacked him. They ate the horse and the soldier. The only thing left of the soldier was a shoe with a little bit of flesh and small bones inside the shoe. This is a very dangerous place," he said. When I heard that, I started to fear wolves again.

We arrived in Ayagoz. It was a big city. There were small empty homes there. Together with the other families, we found an abandoned house and moved in. The house was made out of mud. It was painted white. Inside there were two rooms. We had one big room and the other family, which moved with us from Karakol, took the other room. The other two families found another place for themselves. No one bothered us there. The floor in the room was made out of wood. In the kitchen, the stove was made out of mud. There was no firewood, and I collected dried cow pies to burn them in the stove. We boiled some water, added the dried bread to soak. Then we added a little sheep's milk. That was everything we had to eat. We ate in the morning only, and sometimes we had a piece of bread at night. It was a harsh life.

I started looking for a job, and I went from restaurant to restaurant in the city. I asked if I could wash the floors and clean the place for a piece of bread. I understood the Russian language a little, but I only knew how to say a few words. When the man asked me why I wanted to work, I told him, "*pozhaluysta* (please)...they took us from Poland to Kazakhstan. We don't have any food. My mother is ill, and I have two little sisters."

The man gave me a big broom and a bucket full of wood shavings to scatter on the floor where they would mix with the slush. He told me to sweep the dirt and clean up the floor. I got some bread for two hours of work. I went to another restaurant where I washed the dishes. There, I got more bread and an egg. At the third restaurant, I got borscht for my work. After I brought home the soup and bread, my mother couldn't believe that I received so much food for my work. She asked me if I ate.

"Don't worry about me. Eat. I will go again," I told my mother. I wanted my mum and sisters to eat. I went back and found a bakery where people waited in line to buy their ration of bread. I observed that women coming out carried a small piece of bread on top of a loaf. The loaves weighed less than their food ration, so a small piece was cut and added to make up their allowance.

"*Pozhaluysta, dayte mne kusok chlieba,*" I asked in Russian for a piece of bread from one woman leaving the bakery. She looked at me, then at the piece of bread sitting on top of the loaf and handed the small piece to me. That day, I collected about twelve slices of bread. Back at home, I shared the food with everyone, even with the other families. We dried the rest of the bread over the stove to prevent mould. I always had to work to help my family. I worked like that for a few months. Once my mother asked me to take my sister's dress to the people who lived in the nearby house and exchange the dress for milk.

"*Pozhaluysta, moloko*," I asked the woman who opened the door. The women looked at me and poured milk into a small tin can. My mother gave the milk I brought to my younger sisters. I didn't want to eat. I drank water instead. We suffered like that until 1942.

In the spring of 1942, I was fourteen and a half years old. I heard that Stalin had declared an amnesty. We weren't allowed to return to Poland, but those Poles incarcerated in Siberia and in Kazakhstan were free to join the army, and young men could sign up for cadets. I asked my mother for permission to join the army cadets. She agreed but asked that first I collect a stash of cow pies to use for heating the house and cooking.

In Ayagoz there was a corporal who wore a Polish military uniform. He met with two boys, who also wanted to join the Polish army, and me. The corporal explained that cadets went to school for a half a day and the rest of the day was spent on military training. After I finished the training, I could sign up for the military. I signed up. My mother took me to the railroad station, bought me a ticket to Tashkent, where the Polish army was being formed, and she gave me thirty Russian roubles. I didn't want to take the money, but she insisted and said that I'd worked for this money in the kolkhoz. She followed me to the wagon, walking behind me and turning her face away from me, so I didn't see her crying. When I saw my mother crying it made me sorrowful. I felt terrible. I hoped that God would help and I could join the cadets and bring my family to me. On the railroad station platform, there were many other families like ours, who had brought their sons to the train.

When I boarded the train, I saw no place for me to sit with the corporal and the other two young boys, so I had to find a place to sit on a bench in the next wagon. We travelled the entire night, and the next morning, when I went to visit the Polish corporal, their wagon was no longer there. When I asked about them, the conductor told me that during the night someone in their wagon fell ill with typhus and that they had to unhook that carriage and quarantine all the people. When we departed from

Ayagoz, my mother had given my train ticket to the corporal, so now I was left without my train ticket. We travelled for a long time, and when the train stopped somewhere, I asked the conductor if it was Tashkent.

"Tashkent?"

"Tashkent."

He said that it was Tashkent so I jumped out of the train. However, there was nothing there, no buildings, only one light pole with a single lamp sticking out from the tall grass. It was getting dark. I could hear the wolves howling, *houuuu, houuuu, houuuu*. I was alone, and I didn't know what to do. I got closer to the light pole and thought that if the wolves came closer, I would climb up it. I saw something big, like a horse, walking toward me. Then I heard a voice ask, "What are you doing here?" and I saw a Russian peasant wearing a huge sheepskin and carrying a big walking stick. He must have been watching a herd of sheep close by.

"I am going to Tashkent," I told him.

"Tashkent is far away, two hundred kilometres from here. It is dangerous here," he said and added, "You wait here. In half an hour, there will be a train. You will see its lights. When it stops here, you jump inside and hide behind the door. Stay there until you come to a big city. There will be many lights. That will be Tashkent. Don't be afraid of the conductor. He will be drunk. He always drinks." Then, the shepherd left.

When the train came, I jumped onto the wagon and hid behind the door. From my hiding place, I could see the conductor sitting in the company of two women and drinking with them. One of the women noticed me. She came and pulled me up by my ear.

"What are you doing here?"

"I want to go to Tashkent."

"Do you have a ticket?"

I tried to explain my situation: "Two days ago, the corporal had my ticket, and the wagon he was in was unhooked from the train."

"Why Tashkent?" she asked.

"I am going to the Polish army," I told her.

"No," she said. "You have to get off the train at the next train stop."

The conductor was very drunk, and she didn't say anything to him. The train was already moving so they couldn't kick me out. When we stopped in the morning, they pushed me out of the train. It was not Tashkent yet. While I stood on the railroad platform, not knowing what would happen next, I noticed a soldier in a Polish uniform. He had three stripes. He was a sergeant. I went to talk to him.

"Soldier! Sir! Are you a Pole?" I asked. "I was supposed to go to Tashkent from Ayagoz, to sign up for the cadets, but I lost my train ticket and they threw me from the train," I said.

"You want to join the cadets?" he asked.

"Yes!"

"Come with me," he said. The soldier took me to the military barracks, where they fed me buckwheat topped with lard, and I was allowed to sleep there overnight to rest a little. "Tomorrow, I will take you to the railroad station, and I will find a place for you on the train," the sergeant told me.

The train we took was filled to capacity with Russian soldiers wounded on the front who were being transported to the hospital in Tashkent for treatment. The Russian soldiers wanted to kick me out. "Leave him alone," the sergeant said sharply to them and added, "He is going to the military." After that, they left me alone. However, the Russian soldiers didn't believe that I was going to join the cadets because I was little.

"I have to get off the train at the next stop to return to my company," the sergeant told me. "You'll have to continue the trip to Tashkent by yourself. You'll see big lights. When you get off the train, ask the orderly at the station to help you find the Polish officers who come to pick up their mail," he instructed me.

The train reached Tashkent, and there were many lights there. When the train stopped, I jumped out onto the platform, and I asked one of the workers about Polish officers. He said to me, "Every morning at ten o'clock, a Polish officer, a lieutenant, comes to the station to pick up the mail. But, you can't wait here."

I had to wait until the next day for this officer to come. I left the railroad station and started walking on the adjacent street, as I wasn't allowed to stand by the station's building. I sat on the ground nearby. A Russian soldier looked at me closely, lowered his eyes, looked at my feet, and then he looked back at my face. Then he came closer, sat beside me on the sidewalk, and pointing toward my shoes, asked, "Where are your shoes? Is that all you have?"

I was wearing old *valenky*, boots made of wool felt. They were wet and had holey soles though which the rags in which I wrapped my feet were showing. I was almost shoeless. I was practically walking barefoot. The Russian soldier took off his big military boots handed them to me and said, "Put them on." The boots he gave me were so huge that my feet almost drowned in them. The soldier took out another pair of leather shoes from his backpack and put them on. "Are you hungry?" he asked me.

"I haven't eaten for the past two or three days," I said to him. The Russian soldier gave me one rouble to buy pancakes and left. I bought two pancakes. I still didn't know where to spend the night. A local Russian boy my age told me about a place he knew where I could stay. He led me to an abandoned warehouse about two kilometres from the station. When we got there, it was about eight o'clock at night. The concrete floor was packed with homeless people. They lay so close to each other that they looked like sardines. When I tried to find a spot for myself, they chased me away. It was still dark when I went back to the railroad station and waited outside, sitting in the same spot as before. I had my new big Russian boots on my feet, and my old valenky were still in the same place where I left them. No one had taken them.

I sat near the railroad station waiting. Then I saw a military truck stop in front of the building. A Polish officer, a captain with three stars on his shoulder pads, came out. I approached him, "Sir, I would like to join the cadets. Where do I go?"

"Wait for me by this military truck. When I come back, I will take you to the cadets." The captain took me to a place called Tartak Plaza. It was surrounded by a tall wall. Inside was a big plaza with a pool of water in its centre. There was a high building. There were Polish sappers and cadets, and there was General Sulik. The officer took me inside where I signed up for the cadets. I had to take off all my clothes, which were burned later. I took a hot shower. Then, they put some powder on me to delouse me and kill any insects. I got a uniform and put it on. I was sent to my first training. There were four of us learning how to use a gas mask. An officer put something into a barrel that created a sweet but stinky smoke. The air was bad. We had to put our gas masks on, and we kept them on for a long time. The officer told us to remember the smell and put on gas masks as soon as we smelled it again. Then, he took us to an empty field and asked us if we saw anything there. We didn't see any-thing but tall grass, shrubs and bushes. Then the officer gave a signal, and we saw that many soldiers were hiding there after they rose follow-ing his order. They were camouflaged, and we hadn't seen them at all. After this training, we rested for a few days, sleeping in military tents, and then we were taken to a bigger army camp in Tartak by Tashkent, where our company was staying in a long brick building. There were many cadets. The cooks prepared food for us. The camp was surrounded by big trees, and there was a pond close by. We went to classes and got basic military training.

When we were in the army camp in Tartak, I remember some Polish soldiers cheating. They drank the condensed milk we got in our rations, put water into the empty cans and resealed them. Later they sold them to the locals for one rouble. The Russians got angry and reported this to the commander who came to look for the person. They found him, took him away, and he got some punishment. I didn't see him after.

I started to think about my mother. I wanted to go back to Ayagoz to bring my mum and my sisters to the camp. I saved a can of beans and a can of soup that we got there and asked other soldiers to give me cans of food if they didn't want them. I kept all I collected in my backpack. I wanted to give this to my family. I asked if I could leave, and our corporal said that this was the military. "Go, ask General Sulik for a permit to leave," he told me.

I went to see our general who was in charge. I entered the office saluting him, "Sir General! May I ask for permission to travel to Ayagoz to bring my mother and my two sisters here and take the cans of food I have for them?" I didn't get the permission to leave for Ayagoz. Instead, General Sulik said to me, "Sorry, son, tomorrow we are leaving for Iran."

I broke this news to the other cadets from my company, and everyone was excited that we were going to Iran. They called it Persia at that time. I packed two cans of food, two blankets and a pair of pants into my backpack. We marched for a long time from Tartak to the Krasnovodzk seaport. We rested at night and walked again during the day. I carried my bag, and I noticed that the lad beside me couldn't walk anymore. The boots he brought with him were too heavy for him. I told him to put his boots in my bag, and I carried them for him.

In Krasnovodzk we boarded a tiny Russian ship that was to take us to Iran. The higher-ranking soldiers lay down on the deck, and the cadets sat. On the sea, many people got sick with stomach aches and diarrhea. I, too, got sick. There were no toilets. I didn't want to soil myself. I lowered my pants and sat on the railings holding onto the iron bars so I wouldn't fall into the sea. I stuck my buttocks out to the sea. I was sick, got dizzy, and almost fainted. One older soldier called out to me, "Do you want to drown?" then helped me get down from the railings and found a place for me to lie down. "What happened?" he asked.

"I was thirsty, and I drank the sea water. I thought I could." He left, and when he came back, he brought a cup of water for me. At first, I was afraid to drink it. He assured me that it was safe water. They used a special machine to make it from the seawater. I got better. When the ship was in the middle of the sea, we had to leave it because it was too small for the number of people on board, and it started sinking. The water flowed over the deck. A big ship was brought to us, and we had to climb a rope stretched from one ship to the other. There was an opening below, between the two ships, and I could see the waves. We could use our arms, but some also managed to hook their legs onto the ropes. When we made it to the other side, they caught us by our legs to help us. Even though we had to rush because the ship was in danger of sinking, no one fell into the water.

After we arrived in Iran, we were unloaded from the ship and taken to a camp set up on the beach. There were three rows of wooden poles buried in the sand on which the canvas was stretched to protect us from the sun. The entire company lay on the hot sand, and it made sleeping at night difficult. We used our blankets to cover up at night. An outdoor toilet was about fifty metres from the beach. It was a deep dugout with no walls. Many of us were sick, and we walked there throughout the entire night. There were jackals by the toilet. They loudly howled all night.

They told us to be careful when we took off our boots and socks before going to sleep. We had to check them in the morning, before putting them on, to see if there were scorpions inside. Once, I picked up my boot and a scorpion came out of it. I was frightened because when a scorpion stings you, you die.

The water was brought to the camp in big tanks. A military cook prepared food for us. Each of us had a dinner pail that we used for soup and hamburgers. Once, our company went for a short sightseeing trip to Tehran, the capital of Iran. I visited a mosque there and had to take off my shoes before entering it. I sat there watching people pray. Even though I didn't understand what they were saying, I tried to do what they did.

Then they moved the troops by big trucks through Iraq to Egypt where we stayed for about a month. Then, we moved to Palestine, close to Tel Aviv, and then to Haifa. We stayed there for about six months from 1943 until January 1944. In this camp, I met soldiers returning from the battlefields in Italy; some of them were wounded.

We lived in a military camp in tall, square-shaped military tents. There were six of us living in each tent. It was hot there, even at night. They told us that in the desert, when the wind blows, the dunes could change, and we might not recognize them afterward. I didn't know that, so I learned something new. In the cadet training camp, we were at school half the day, and after that, we had military training. All that I learned helped me later when I became a soldier. I wanted to be a soldier.

One day in January, General Władysław Anders came to visit the cadet camp located close to Haifa. Our company stood in rows ready for his inspection. He looked at us and said, "Some of you can sign up for the military because you are too old to be in the cadets."

I just had my sixteenth birthday on November 15, so I volunteered. I was assigned to the Third Company, and I moved to Palestine. They took us for training to a place where there was a small hut, in which we were told enemy soldiers were hiding. Our officer told us to capture this place. We were divided into platoons. Those inside the hut shot at us while we attacked them. We were given blank bullets for our rifles, and we thought that the soldiers in the hut had blanks too. "This is a real bullet. It whistles," I said to my colleague. "They shouldn't be shooting at us," he said.

The corporal went to the soldiers in the hut, took the real bullets from them, and gave them blanks. Later, they showed us how to stand on guard. They taught us how to behave in real combat, how to camouflage during the day and at night. They told us not to eat things like garlic and not to smoke because a sniper, who is a professional soldier, would be able to smell it. A sniper sits in the bushes and listens, we were told. If anyone walks on leaves or gravel, making a noise, the sharpshooter will hear it. At night when the moon is out, we shouldn't stand in its light, but look for cover behind a tree trunk or a rock. We should give signals using our hands, instead of talking to each other. On the front line, we would have to follow the orders given to us by the corporal or the lieutenant.

After the training, they selected those who were doing well. "You will go to Naples and then to a mountain called Monte Cassino. You will go by train. We don't know how long it will take you to get there," they told us.

We said goodbye to the rest of the cadets and boarded a passenger train. There were about eighty cadets on that train with me, and more wagons were added. After about four hours, the train stopped at the end of the railroad tracks in Naples. We moved to the big, three-ton trucks covered with canvas that were waiting for us. The trucks took us about ten kilometres from Monte Cassino. There was a plaza where the trucks bringing the soldiers parked. This place looked like a desert. We could see the monastery from a distance. Trees surrounded us where we stood. That night, a heavy rain came down. We had to stay in the trucks overnight because we couldn't leave them. In the morning, they told us to collect our belongings and stand in three rows. We stood in six-inch-deep mud. An officer called out, "Who wants to go to Monte Cassino tonight? Step forward, three steps!"

I looked to the left and right. I thought that I had nothing to lose. I looked around and made three steps forward: one, two, and three. To my left, my colleague Adam stepped forward, too, and moved closer to me. At the end of the column, one more soldier also stepped forward. "Only the three of you?" the officer called. From about three hundred soldiers, only three of us volunteered. They took our names. "Where would the other soldiers be going?" I asked. "They are going to the cavalry, where they will learn how to operate tanks."

I hadn't known that. No one had told us. "Tomorrow morning, three of you will go to Monte Cassino. When the mules come to take the food for those on the mountain, you will go with them. The rest will go to the cavalry to learn how to operate the heavy tanks," the officer announced to us. The soldiers were loaded onto several trucks and taken away.

In the morning, local peasants came, bringing with them five or six mules. Each peasant pulled one of the animals by their bridle. The corporal said to us, "You will go with us. We are taking the food for those on the mountain. There are three companies there: First, Second and Third."

Then, pointing at me, he said, "You and your friend will go to the Third Company, and the third soldier will go to the First Company." The three of us walked uphill, following the mules. On the way up, about one kilometre from Monte Cassino, I saw the dead body of a soldier lying on the path. "Why is he here?" I asked the corporal.

"We walked by this place yesterday, and he was dead already. There was no one to take the body down from the mountain," the corporal answered, and continued walking uphill. We reached the middle of the mountain. To the right, there was a house made of red bricks. Once, it had to have been someone's home, I thought. There was a small, round and empty plaza beside it. I thought that once it had to have been someone's garden. Now, the ground was flattened, and the clay there was hardened. Not even a blade of grass grew on it.

Our guide told us to wait by the house while he walked the mule farther to deliver the food. He called the third soldier to accompany him, and they left. They went to First Company, taking a downhill path to the left of the hut. The Second Company had its positions in the middle of the mountain. No one from our group was taken there. After a while, the guide returned by himself. He called my friend Adam to go with him and told me to wait. The two of them went to the left. The guide returned by himself and asked me to give him my rifle. He walked to the right. I waited for several minutes. The guide returned and gave me back my gun.

"Now, go by yourself uphill. There will be a sergeant waiting for you," he instructed me. I went to the very top of the hill where the Third Company held its position. On the way, there were no trees, and the ground was barren. On the hilltop, a soldier was waiting for me.

"Follow me!" We walked uphill. "Wait here!" he ordered, "I will call the captain," he said and left. I looked around. There was nothing there, only rocks and barren hills. The sergeant returned with the captain. "This is the new recruit, from the cadets. Sir!"

I saluted the captain, "Zbigniew Rogowski, reporting to the Third Company."

"How old are you?" the captain asked.

"Sixteen years and three months, Sir."

The captain looked at me and said, "Ah, youth, youth!" I looked at the captain. He was young too, twenty-four or twenty-six, I thought. He is only nine years older than I am? He looked at me, then turned to the sergeant, and said, "Sergeant Król, show him where his place will be."

The sergeant took a few steps from where we stood and said me, "Do you see this hole to the left? It is yours. Go and repair it! You will be standing in the middle of it. I want to know where you are. If I need you, I will come and get you. We have people everywhere in this place. You don't see them now; they're hiding in their holes. At night, when we go on a patrol, or change the guards, you'll get to know them."

I looked inside the hole. Three walls surrounded it, and in the middle of the hole, I could hide behind a higher and slightly longer wall. I sat there all day. At six o'clock that evening, it began to darken. Sergeant Król came to my hole and ordered others nearby and me to follow him. One of the soldiers asked, "Sir! Sergeant! May I stay a little longer and dig out more to make my position a little deeper? I worry my hole is too small and that they will shoot at it."

"OK! Stay and work! In the meanwhile, we will set up the guards for the night in the woods to prevent the Germans from taking our hill," said Sergeant Król. The soldier returned to his hole to continue digging. We had taken no more than ten steps away when the artillery shot came, *zuuuuu*. Sergeant Król yelled something. We stood there watching as the shell hit the soldier working on improving his position.

"Dammit! If he was with us, he would still be alive," Sergeant Król said, and looking at us added, "Don't you ever do something that stupid in the future." The sergeant put me on guard close by his position, situated behind a small hill made out of broken rocks.

"May I smoke?" I asked him.

"What? Do you have a coat? Hide under it. Then you can smoke. Don't show light from the cigarette, because they will see and shoot at us," Sergeant Król said.

I lit the cigarette under the coat but started choking on it, and couldn't continue. The sergeant took me to a big spruce tree nearby. He showed me where the light of the moon would fall, and said, "Stand in the tree's shadow, and when it moves, you move with it, so the Germans on top of the mountain cannot see you. On the Cairo Hill, there are Germans, they have an observation point there, and they could see us from their position."

I realized that we were surrounded by the German troops. The only place the Polish troops had was where our battalion was located. At night, Sergeant Król came by to check if we were alert. When I heard him, I called out, "password?" and the sergeant gave me the password. Later, he ordered us to start returning to our positions in our holes— before daybreak so the Germans wouldn't see us moving around.

In our company, there were three Gurkha soldiers. They were fearless and vicious. At night, they would go on a patrol around the mountain looking for German soldiers. They moved quietly and touched the sol- diers' shoes. If there were shoelaces in their boots, they let them live because they were Allies. If the soldiers did not have laces in their boots, they killed them because they were Germans. The Gurkhas kept to them- selves and always sat together. They never talked with us.

Third Company was located on top of a small hill between the Germans on the Monte Cassino and the Allies on Cairo Hill. The Allies were behind the position where three Polish companies were placed on guard. The Germans occupied the top of the Monte Cassino and shel- tered themselves in the monastery. They were also in the little town nearby. Their troops were all around us.

In our Third Company, there were about 110 soldiers. The shelters that could accommodate only one soldier were located close to each other. First Company and Second Company were located below the positions taken by Third Company. Only the hill guarded by these three Polish companies was ours. Hidden behind the trees, there was a first aid station for those who were wounded or ill. I went there when my leg became swollen and red after I'd had my boots on for a long time. It hurt. The paramedic cleaned my leg, gave me a shot and some pills, put on an ointment and bandaged my leg. I returned to my position after the treatment. It was hard.

Sometimes, when there was a lot of artillery fire exchanged between the Germans and the Allies, the mules couldn't bring supplies, and we didn't eat for two days or longer. We didn't know how long it'd take until the next mule came. That was my first week on the hill. I was hungry. We all were given a chocolate bar in a yellow metal tin, but that was to be our reserve, and we could only use it when we were starving. If we needed another chocolate bar, then they would charge us. I noticed in the nearby woods, a few metres from my shelter, three dead soldiers lying on the ground close to each other. I crawled to them. They had to have been there for a long time because their bodies stank. I don't know how they died. I touched their right pants pockets, checking for their rations. Only one soldier still had his chocolate. I lived on that chocolate for a few days. When you don't eat for two or three days, and you eat a small piece of chocolate that piece of chocolate can last you for the entire day. I kept my ration of chocolate for an emergency. We also had English military biscuits. They were as hard as rock; I couldn't bite into them. I smashed them with a rock to break them into little pieces, and I put a little water on that piece and licked it all day long. We kept the water in our water bottles. But, we had to be careful and conserve it, and we couldn't drink a lot of it. At the most, I had a few sips of water a day. When the mule left, there was no water. We took water from soldiers who were killed. Sometimes our throats were so dry, and there was no water, then I had to drink my urine. I had to do it. I had no other choice. If I had a handkerchief, I'd use it to strain it. Or I would swallow a few drops to wet my throat.

It stank on this hill. The stench came from decomposing corpses of soldiers whose bodies were scattered around. When their bodies lay in the sun during the day, they swelled, and at night, they collapsed, spilling out terrible fumes. The air was awful. I sat in my hole the entire day, and I couldn't see the sun. The Italians walked on the hill collecting the dead bodies and carried them down the hill on stretchers. They had their faces covered with handkerchiefs.

The only thing I thought about were the bullets flying by, and I listened to them all the time. I lived like that for two and a half months. I just thought one more day, maybe two. I didn't know how long I'd be there. I thought that any day I might be gone. Using the bayonet from my Tommy gun, I marked on the wall of my shelter the days I lived there. One, two, three, four, I wrote in Roman letters. When I was there for five days. I wrote a V for Victory. When I was there for ten days, I made a cross on the wall. I think that these markings are probably still there. If I could go there now and look how I lived then, I'd be frightened. It was terrible. I never knew if I would live until the next morning.

I could only go to the bushes that served as a toilet at night when I wasn't on guard. During the day, I peed into a can and spilt the urine outside of my shelter through a small opening I made. The urine flowed into the ditch. I did this so the Germans, who were observing us from the top of the hill, wouldn't see me. At night, I was on guard. At four o'clock in the morning, I would return to the hole where I sat. I didn't know anyone in the company. I was always by myself. The military life is hard. It is hard. I taught myself how to behave, how to do things and how to live. Being a hero is hard. You have to think and listen. I was always aware of the possibility of losing my life. Death was close by. I lived the life of a rat. The Germans shot at us from above every day.

A few times, when life pushed me to the ground, I thought about killing myself. I had my rifle in my hand. Once, someone came to my hole, looked at me and said, "I know what you are thinking. Don't do that stupidity." I looked at him, but the thought of killing myself stayed in my head. He talked with me. We went for a walk and drank some wine. I thought that my life was over. But after we talked, the thoughts went away.

During the time I was on Monte Cassino, the American troops tried twice to take it. Our duty was to defend our position for the American troops that were going to attack the mountain. However, the American troops couldn't succeed. Then an order came for General Anders to take the monastery. He tried two times. During the first attack, our soldiers didn't take the mountain. During the second attack that started early in the morning, we took our positions in our shelters. The artillery was heavy; the Germans were shooting at us. At times, the Polish artillery was aiming too close, and their shells fell on our positions too. The Germans had special grenades; we called them *garłacz*. When they hit the ground, they burrowed deep inside it, making an *urrr urrr urrr urrr* noise. This sound was terrible on the nerves. Then the grenade exploded. The Germans did that to aggravate us. I didn't think much about them, but when the Polish battalion started attacking the German positions, Adam came to my shelter. He was shaking from the bombs and the artillery shells flying above or falling around us. "Can I stay with you?" he asked.

I moved to the side to make some space for him. I kept my rifle close by. The artillery fire was massive. Adam looked at me and asked, "How is that you can sit so calmly, and smoke your cigarette when my hands are trembling?"

"Adam, I listen to the shells passing by. If they whistle, then it is okay. Those that don't whistle are the ones that I worry about because I am afraid that the silent one could hit me," I told him. After I said that, Adam got more frightened and ran from my shelter. I stayed there, and a moment later, a shell hit the ground a few feet away from my legs. The Germans above us had observed my position and targeted my shelter. Maybe they thought that it was a place where something important was happening, like a command point. In an instant, I saw the colours of the explosion like a rainbow...the red, the yellow, the green and the grey flew in front of me like several antennas spewing fire into the air. The energy of the explosion forced me out from my hole and threw me into the nearby bushes, about five metres away. My rifle was gone. I fell to the ground and rolled. The raging artillery fire around caused confusion. I had narrowly escaped death. I could hear our sergeant yelling.

"Rogowski! Crawl toward me!" He called my name repeatedly, "RRRROOOO-GGGGOOOO-WWWSSSSSKKKKIII!" knowing that the artillery shell had hit my hole.

"Where are you?" I shouted back.

"Fifteen, or twenty metres from you. Straight ahead!"

"I will try!" I yelled back and started crawling toward his voice. But something stopped me. I had a few grenades tied to my epaulettes. While I was crawling out of the bushes, a small branch caught a little safety pin ring attached to one of the grenades. The safety pin started coming out, dislodging the safety lever. It was halfway out when I noticed it. If the lever fell off, the grenade would explode and kill me. I stopped crawling. I broke off the branch, freeing the grenade. Slowly, I took the grenade into my hand and put the safety lever back into its place. I took my bayonet, pressed it into the slot in the pin to widen it, and I pushed the pin back. Then, I put the grenade into my pocket. I crawled into the hole where the sergeant was hiding. There were four of them already in one small hole squeezed tight like sardines. I crawled out from that place, moved to the other side, and hid behind a boulder.

That was the offensive. The artillery fire was heavy and never stopped. The soldiers attacking the mountain were jumping over our positions. They were paratroopers, commandos, infantry and cavalry. The fire was so intense that I didn't know what was happening around me. There was confusion all around. I didn't know which way to go. The entire mountain was completely smashed. I felt lost. The dead soldiers were everywhere around me. I couldn't comprehend what was happening. Then I thought that God gave me the strength to live through it. I felt renewed, as if I were born again. It was beastly around me. There was a lot of suffering. Some soldiers could not hear. Some soldiers lost their eyes. Some soldiers were wounded. Some soldiers didn't have their arms or legs. I came out unharmed. Only inside, I was sad. I thought about my family, and that I didn't have anyone. I didn't have colleagues. Everyone I knew was killed. During the attack, one of the soldiers was shot close to his heart. I stayed with him in his last moment.

"Zbyszek, remember me. Don't forget me," he pleaded, using my nickname. After he said that, he died.

The soldiers from the Fourteenth, Fifteenth and Sixteenth Polish Battalions were overtaking our positions. Soon after, I saw the Polish flag on top of the monastery. There was a Polish flag and the British flag there. Later the British flag was taken down, and only the Polish flag stayed on top of the monastery. I said to the sergeant, "It looks like we took the monastery."

It was about seven o'clock in the morning. When everything quieted down, I asked how many of our company had survived. They said only ten of us were still alive out of about one hundred and twenty. The rest of the soldiers were killed, and the captain was killed, too, when he ran with his gun to attack the German positions. From all three companies, there were about fifty or sixty of us there. We stood around the red brick building, and one soldier from my military unit took his Tommy gun and started shooting at a German helmet that lay on the ground. The Tommy gun's bullets were big and short and made a big hole in it. I laughed because I didn't understand why he was doing this. He was infuriated.

During the entire battle for Monte Cassino, more than three thousand Polish soldiers were killed. There is a vast cemetery close to Monte Cassino, where the Polish soldiers from the paratroopers, commandos, infantry and cavalry are buried. The soldiers from my company are buried there too. After the battle, they took us away by trucks to a place where we rested for about two weeks. We were hungry because they hadn't been able to bring food uphill for a long time, and we wanted to wash too.

After a break, they told us that Third Company would be returning to military duties. We had a new commander because our captain had been killed at Monte Cassino. The new one had the rank of a lieutenant. Many new soldiers were assigned to my company because most of those with whom I served had been killed at Monte Cassino. We were in the area of Predappio, in a small village. I was sent with some other Polish soldiers to check out the bakery there. Inside, I sensed something out of place. I saw something that moved a little. Then we saw a pair of German military boots. We walked up quietly and pulled off the covering...behind it was a German soldier. We took him as a POW.

Then, the lieutenant ordered me to stay on guard by the cornfield in the nearby village. He set up a machine gun aimed at the field for me to operate. "If you hear something moving in the cornfield, yell stop and if they don't obey, then shoot," he ordered. The officer was still with me when I saw something moving in the field. I called, "Stop! Who's there?" There was no answer, and something was still moving in the cornfield. I was ready to shoot. I had my finger on the trigger, and I started pressing it down. Then the officer saw a Polish uniform and started yelling at the soldier that he should answer when called. "I got lost, and I didn't know where I was," the soldier told us.

I had almost killed this soldier. I started feeling unwell. I blacked out and collapsed. They took me to a hospital. I had too much stress accumulated over time when I didn't eat much and couldn't sleep. I stayed in a hospital for ten days, and the doctors told me that my heart couldn't handle all that pressure. I was exhausted, and my heart started giving up.

When I was released from the hospital, my company was a few kilometres from Predappio, fighting to liberate the town where Mussolini was born. I joined one of the units heading this direction. However, the soldiers couldn't leave their current position because they were still defending their place from the Germans trying to take it back from them. The lieutenant put me on guard by the road. He told me to stay there until midnight.

"Watch! If you see that something is moving, give us a sign. If it is infantry then lift up your rifle; if tanks are coming, raise the gun's butt up." We went to where the company was staying overnight, and the lieutenant pointed at one of the soldiers and said, "You will change with Rogowski at midnight."

I stood on guard for a long time. It was dark, and the moon was high. I didn't have a watch, but I thought when it must be midnight, I went to the soldier who was assigned to replace me. "It's time to take your turn," I pulled his arm to wake him up. "OK," he said and got up and started walking away. I lay down close to where he had been sleeping and fell asleep. Suddenly, someone shook me by my clothes, pulled me up and started yelling at me.

"Dammit! You were sleeping, and the entire company could have been taken by the Germans!" I opened my eyes and saw the lieutenant holding his gun to my head and yelling at me, "You should be standing on guard, and instead you are sleeping."

"Sir, the other soldier should be there. I woke him up, and he went to take his turn standing on guard," I tried to explain to the lieutenant. "There was no one there!" he kept yelling back. The lieutenant wanted to kill me. "Come!" he barked at me and took me to a nearby place surrounded by trees and bushes. Pointing to an empty space along the trees, he ordered, "Run from this tree to that tree far away, and run back to me." I ran with my backpack on. In it, I had a metal bottle, a metal dinner pail and metal utensils, things that made a clunking noise. The other soldiers watched me run and shouted, "Come on, Rogowski! Come on, Rogowski!"

I was running back and forth from one tree to the other for a long time...I didn't know why. The lieutenant watched me from afar. Then, I realized that he was using me as bait to check if the Germans were close by. If they were near, they would shoot at me. After a while, he ordered me to go to a building half a kilometre away, where earlier that day, we had left our big backpacks.

"Go to that home and stay in the barn. Don't show yourself to the man who lives upstairs. We will send the mules to bring our backpacks," he ordered. I found the barn, went inside it, sat on the bags and waited. The large wooden barn doors were wide open, showing the dark night outside. There were no lights. The packs lay scattered around me. The moon started coming out a little. I could hear someone walking toward the barn. Branches and leaves were cracking under the heavy footsteps. I saw a big German soldier. He stopped by the door, undid his pants and started urinating. Oh, Jesus! I thought. Inside, a few metres away from him, I sat on a backpack pointing my machine gun at him ready to shoot. All the time, I observed the man. I thought that if he comes into the barn, I'd have to kill him. Then, I realized that if I killed him, then those who were with him would come after me and kill me. They would throw a grenade into the barn, and they would shoot the farmer and his family. It was a terrible situation. Then I heard someone calling, "Hans! Komm her!"

I thought that the German soldier had to be a part of some group because someone called him back. He turned around and called back. "Jawohl, Hoffman!" The German soldier went back to the house. He didn't look inside of the barn. I breathed out heavily.

It was still dark outside when the farmer came to the barn in the morning. When he saw me, he put his hands on his head and started jumping up and down, lamenting and wailing. "Mama MIA! Tedesco! Polacco soldato! Tedesco! Ayayay!" I thought that the Italian man had lost his mind. However, after I saw his reaction, I got scared too. He said to me that the German soldiers had asked if there were Polish troops close by, and he had told them that the Poles weren't here. The farmer was so distraught that I thought he would have a heart attack. The experience in the barn was the worst moment of my life. That was the time when I really thought my life was over.

The lieutenant came later and told me that they couldn't come earlier because the German troops were here and he had moved the company two kilometres away to stay safe.

"Lieutenant, they were here. They could've killed me. I was in the barn all the time."

"How did you survive? You were lucky."

After this experience, I felt exhausted, and I couldn't walk. The lieutenant told me to hold on to the mule's tail to help me walk uphill. When we reached Predappio, I learned that Third Company had taken the town.

On May 25, 1944, I was reunited with my company. After a long search, I found them in one of the farmhouses there. I found my officer. The lieutenant called me and said, "Sit down. You are the youngest in the company. What do you want to do when the war is over, and you return to the civilian life?" he asked me.

"I have nothing. Nothing, Sir."

"We'll teach you. Do you want to learn how to drive a big truck?" He sent Adam, my friend, and me to Forli to Material Park 45 (Park Mat) to learn how to drive. The emblem of Park Mat 45 was a brown bison. I received a military type of driver's licence, allowing me to drive big trucks and motorcycles. Then, the lieutenant assigned me to be a driver, to bring munitions for the artillery and to take wounded soldiers to the hospital. I drove a Jeep, driving General Sulik and other high-ranking officers for a while.

Once I was sent to take a Bedford truck back to Naples from Forli. There was a column of fifteen vehicles that had to be taken there. From Naples, I was to bring a Ford truck back to Rimini and then return to Forli. We drove for two or three days. On my way back, I got a Ford filled with six 500-kilogram bombs. I had to take them to the airport in Rimini. Then my truck ran out of fuel. The British military helped me with the fuel, and I continued driving until I lost my way and drove over a bridge where one of my front tires was punctured and exploded. I stopped on the bridge.

The British military police came to me. "You know that you have bombs on your truck?" they asked and one of them added "Booof!"

Luckily, the police helped me. They took my truck for repairs, gave me food and let me rest a little. After that, I was on my way to take the bombs to the airport in Rimini. But, I had to drive around to avoid the area close to Forli where Allied airplanes were bombarding enemy positions. I didn't get to the Rimini airport that day. Instead, I came back to Forli, still carrying the bombs in my truck. It took a while to find the Park Mat 45 company because in the meantime they had moved. They were surprised to see me bringing back the bombs. The next day, I went with one of the sergeants to Rimini, taking the missiles to the airport. I must have been away for a while since my ration of food and cigarettes was quite big. That was my last big assignment. I stayed with the Park Mat 45 until October 1946.

I joined the Polish armed forces under the British command in Italy on February 15, 1944, as a private after serving as a cadet in the Polish army. I served in the 1944–1946 Italian Campaign until I was honourably discharged on November 20, 1946, when I immigrated to Canada. I took an active part in the military operation in Italy from March 11, 1944, until May 2, 1945. The military wrote that I was honourably discharged, meaning I was a good soldier, and they were satisfied with what I did. I always followed orders given by the officers, the platoon leaders and the lieutenant. I was happy that they wrote that I was honourably discharged. They were happy, and I was happy. I didn't fight to get medals. I fought for my country because I loved my country. I thought that my life's purpose is to serve my country. I thought that my life is for my homeland, and this is why I put my life on the line. I was awarded a Polish Army Medal, the Monte Cassino Cross and the British 1935–45 Star, and the Italy Star. However, when I moved to Canada, someone stole my Monte Cassino Cross.

In 1946 they told us that we couldn't return to Poland, that we could only go to England or Canada, and that some people would come to

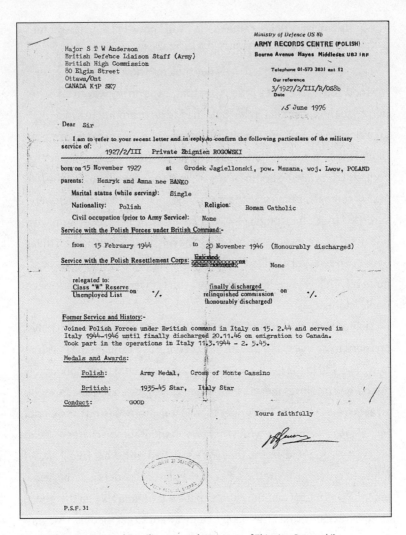

Major S T W Anderson
British Defence Liaison Staff (Army)
British High Commission
80 Elgin Street
Ottawa/Ont
CANADA K1P SK7

Ministry of Defence OS 8b
ARMY RECORDS CENTRE (POLISH)
Bourne Avenue Hayes Middlesex UB3 1RF

Telephone 01-573 3831 ext 12

Our reference
3/1927/2/III/R/OS8b
Date

15 June 1976

Dear Sir

I am to refer to your recent letter and in reply to confirm the following particulars of the military service of:

1927/2/III   Private Zbignien ROGOWSKI

born on 15 November 1927   at   Grodek Jagiellonski, pow. Mszana, woj. Lwow, POLAND

parents: Henryk and Anna nee BANKO

Marital status (while serving):   Single

Nationality: Polish   Religion: Roman Catholic

Civil occupation (prior to Army Service):   None

Service with the Polish Forces under British Command:-

from   15 February 1944   to   20 November 1946   (Honourably discharged)

Service with the Polish Resettlement Corps: ~~Enlisted~~   None

relegated to:
Class "W" Reserve   on   ·/.   finally discharged   on   ·/.
Unemployed List   relinquished commission
                                    (honourably discharged)

Former Service and History:-

Joined Polish Forces under British command in Italy on 15. 2.44 and served in Italy 1944-1946 until finally discharged 20.11.46 on emigration to Canada. Took part in the operations in Italy 11.3.1944 - 2. 5.45.

Medals and Awards:

Polish: Army Medal,   Cross of Monte Cassino

British: 1935-45 Star,   Italy Star

Conduct: GOOD

Yours faithfully

P.S.F. 31

Private Zbigniew Rogowski's military record. [Courtesy of Zbigniew Rogowski]

examine us. If I wanted to go to Canada, I had to know what grains like wheat, barley or oats looked like, because we were to go to Canada to work on farms. They put seeds on the table and asked me to recognize them. "Do you know how to plough with horses and a wooden plough? Do you know how to rake and sow?" they asked me. My father had a little farm when I was growing up, and I knew all the grains. "Good! You will

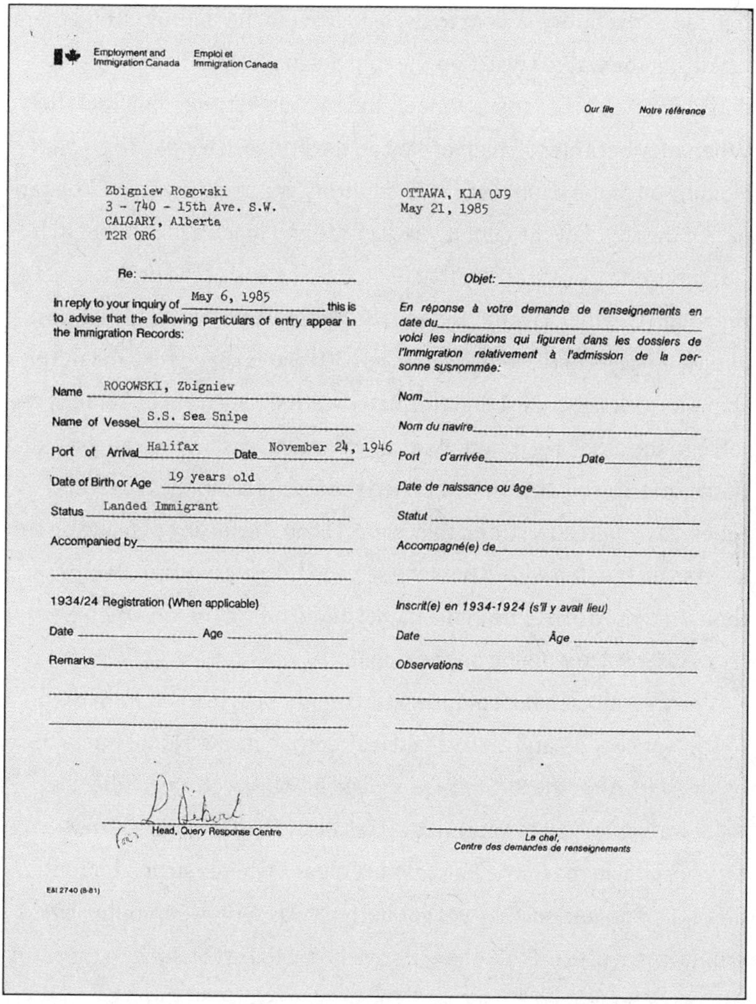

Employment and Immigration Canada   Emploi et Immigration Canada

Our file   Notre référence

Zbigniew Rogowski
3 - 740 - 15th Ave. S.W.
CALGARY, Alberta
T2R 0R6

OTTAWA, K1A 0J9
May 21, 1985

Re: ______   Objet: ______

In reply to your inquiry of May 6, 1985 this is to advise that the following particulars of entry appear in the Immigration Records:

En réponse à votre demande de renseignements en date du ______ voici les indications qui figurent dans les dossiers de l'Immigration relativement à l'admission de la personne susnommée:

Name ROGOWSKI, Zbigniew   Nom ______

Name of Vessel S.S. Sea Snipe   Nom du navire ______

Port of Arrival Halifax Date November 24, 1946   Port d'arrivée ______ Date ______

Date of Birth or Age 19 years old   Date de naissance ou âge ______

Status Landed Immigrant   Statut ______

Accompanied by ______   Accompagné(e) de ______

1934/24 Registration (When applicable)   Inscrit(e) en 1934-1924 (s'il y avait lieu)

Date ______ Age ______   Date ______ Âge ______

Remarks ______   Observations ______

Head, Query Response Centre   Le chef, Centre des demandes de renseignements

E&I 2740 (8-81)

Rogowski's Canadian immigration document. [Courtesy of Zbigniew Rogowski]

go to Canada," the examining committee told me. Some other soldiers didn't know the grains, and they were sent to England.

In October 1946, they took us to the railroad station in Forli and the train took us to a seaport. There, we boarded the SS *Sea Snipe* that took us to Halifax. The ocean trip lasted a few days. We slept on bunk beds below the ship's deck. I was curious, so I went outside and took the stairs that led to the bridge. I went to the very front of the ship and stood there, looking at the water. I watched the ship break waves and rock up and down. The waves became stronger, and seawater started falling on me. When they became too high to stay on the bridge, I decided to go back. Holding on to the bannister, I walked slowly, watching my steps. The captain of the ship saw me coming back inside and made a joke about it. He was amused by my curiosity that led me to the end of the deck despite the rough weather. I went inside to the mess, where we ate, and it was almost empty. There were long tables with plates set up for a meal. The ship was rocking so hard that the plates were sliding from one side of the table to the other. I was hungry, and I wanted to eat. The rough sea didn't bother me. During the trip, I watched the sailors climb the masts and the ropes. I admired how strong they were. I liked the feeling of being on the sea and on the ship. I liked how the sea and the ship worked together. I thought that I'd like to be in the navy. I asked one of the crewmembers, "How do you like working on the ship?"

"Very good!" he said. I didn't know English, but I learned from them to say "very good!" and always said it after that. It was a lot of fun to be on the ship. After the SS *Sea Snipe* arrived in Halifax on November 24, 1946, we were taken to Lethbridge. I fell ill and had to go to the military hospital in the Currie Barracks in Calgary, where I stayed for ten days. I had pneumonia. After I got better, I was sent to Edmonton to the employment office. From there they sent me to Fort St. John to the farm of George Bonefox, a French guy. The farm was located three kilometres from the town. On the farm, I milked the cows, fed the horses and chopped wood. I slept in a small hut where straw was scattered on the floor. That was my bed. At night, I covered myself with my military blanket. That was all I had. The roof of the hut was leaky, and pigeons came through the holes. The birds sat under the ceiling and soiled my bed.

I worked on this farm for two and a half or three months. There was nothing on the farm. One day, I had an appetite to go to town, to have a beer or something. I had the ten dollars given to us before we arrived in

Canada. I walked to Fort St. John and I saw a beer parlour. I sat there and drank a beer. Someone saw my military uniform and asked me if I was a soldier.

"Yes, I'm a Polish soldier from the British army. I was with the Eighth British Command," I told him.

"Were you in the war?"

"Yes. I was all over Italy," I said.

"Where are you working now?" he asked me.

"George Bonefox."

"He is no good," the chap said to me.

"I work there, but he doesn't pay me. He doesn't feed me well. I broke a handle of an axe when I was breaking ice to fetch water for the pigs, and he said that I had to pay him two dollars. You say he is no good?"

The Canadian man I met in the beer parlour must have reported this because the next day when I was chopping wood, a police car came to the farm. The police officers asked me to show them where I slept. When I showed them, the police officer said, "Dreadful. Go and request that the farmer pays you for all the months and days you worked for him. We will take you to the city and find another job for you."

I went to the house and knocked at the door. The farmer came out, asking what I wanted. "George, can you give me my money you owe me? And the police, they want to take me to town." I went back to the police officers and told him that he said, "No money."

"Ah. Wait," the police officer said to me and went to the house. I waited for half an hour, and when the officer came back, he was holding a cheque in his hand. I think the cheque was for ninety or a hundred dollars. The police took me to the city where they told me, "Go to a hotel and take a room there for ten days. You will pay two dollars a night. When we find you another job, we will come and take you there."

They found a job for me in Hythe, Alberta, close to Beaverlodge. I arrived at the farm of Bruce Robinson in April 1947. I had a place to sleep. He provided food for me while I worked there. The farmer said he would pay me at the end of the year. I didn't know how to deal with this, to insist that the farmer put the money I earned in the bank. He didn't give me anything. I worked there for six or seven months, and I didn't get any money. Then he changed, started to be angry with me and complained about my work speed. I got angry because of what he said and packed my belongings and left the farm. Someone gave me a ride. The driver asked where I wanted to go.

"Where is a large city?" I asked.

We went to Wembley. I sat in a beer parlour, angry. I was wearing my military uniform. Two young boys came and started talking with me. They were Ukrainians. I told them that I worked for Bruce Robinson and he didn't pay me for the entire time I worked there. The two lads had a car. "We will go with you to the farm," they told me.

They went home to change into suits and ties, and we drove to Bruce Robinson's farm in Hythe. They asked me to stay in the car while they talked to the farmer. In about half an hour, they came back, brought a cheque for $300, and said that the farmer told them that he would send me the remaining $50 later. But he never sent me that cheque. I gave the young lads twenty dollars for their help and bought them a beer. When I heard that one of them worked at the railroad tracks, I wanted to find a job there too. "There is a Ukrainian who works at the train station. Go and talk with him; he is a foreman," he told me and added, "They always hire people there."

The foreman hired me to work on the railroad tracks as a helping hand. "You'll sleep in a small room in the building where other workers are staying. Early mornings, you'll clean the railroad switches to ensure that they operate correctly. After that, you'll drive the spiller wagon to examine the tracks and adjust them if they're misaligned," he told me. I liked working there, and they liked me too. But on Sunday, the immigration officer came to me and said, "You aren't allowed to work here. You have to finish your contract of working on a farm for a year."

The foreman paid me $150 and told me to put the money in the bank. I gave it to a woman who worked at a bank who said that if I came in on Monday, she would give me a deposit receipt. But the immigration officers took me away on Sunday. I never went to the bank. Because I didn't have any document proving I gave her the money, I lost it. The immigration officers took me to their office in Spirit River. They found a place for me in Rycroft. The farmer was a Pole. He had a small hut with one room and a kitchen. He showed me a place where I was to sleep on a couch near his bed, which he shared with his wife. I worked there the entire winter. I didn't like it there. I couldn't sleep at night. Often, I felt uncomfortable there, and I had to go outside where I smoked a cigarette. It was difficult because I had to get up early in the morning to work. I told him that I didn't want to work for him. "You live with your wife in this same room as me. I can't sleep at night." He took a two-by-four and wanted to hit me with it. I told him, "Put it down. This is foolishness." I left his farm with a few dollars in my pocket, which I'd earned at the previous place. I went to the city and looked for a hotel. I started looking for a job. A few days later, the farmer's wife came asking me to come back and work for them.

"I can't do that. It's not good for me. You don't have a place for me." After a few days, the immigration officers came to me and asked why I left the job. I told them that I couldn't live in one room with a farmer and his wife and sleep on a sofa that is near their bed. The officers laughed at me and asked, "What do you want to do?"

"I want to work in a forest." I found a job cutting down trees and clearing them of branches. I cut tree logs, nine, ten or twelve metres long. They paid me forty-five cents for each tree that I had to cut down, clear of branches and cut into three smaller logs. I loaded these logs onto a cart driven by a horse, and I took the wagon to the sawmill. In the mill, I cut the logs into boards. Then I had to take the boards to the railroad station and load them onto a train. They paid a few cents for thousands of those boards. The winter came, and this job ended. I found a job on a farm again. I worked there for three months. The farmer said that I didn't need to work hard on his farm. He didn't have the money to pay me. I worked there for food and the place to sleep. I helped him plough the fields and clear them of rocks and roots. Then, in spring, we sowed wheat. After I'd finished, he gave me $50 and told me to go to town and look for a job.

I found a job in a sawmill. But I worked there for two hours only. The manager didn't want to pay the workers for their work, so the police came and told them that he had to pay us for a full two weeks of work. Back in town, some people said that there were jobs in the far north and they needed people there. For that, I had to go to Edmonton and then travel far north.

"What is up there?"

"The Canadian military. Maybe you will get a job there." I'd met two Canadian soldiers in a beer parlour. They said they were from Whitehorse and that they were going back. I wanted to go with them and look for a job there. They asked me if I knew how to drive a truck. "You will drive, and we will sleep," they said to me.

They slept on mattresses stored at the back of the truck. I drove on the Alaska Highway. The road was straight. It was about three hundred kilometres. When we came to Whitehorse, they told their military officer that I drove the truck from the Watson Lake to Whitehorse and that I wanted to be a driver. I was given a job in the kitchen washing dishes. I lived in the barracks where I had a bed. I worked from early morning until nightfall. Later on I drove a truck taking mattresses to Watson Lake or Wembley. Then the military moved to Edmonton, and my job with them ended.

I found a new job in the forest cutting down trees. They were nine or ten feet long. They wanted me to make a thousand cubic feet piles. I didn't know how much that was. They showed me piles three metres by three metres and explained that that was a thousand feet. They estimated the size of the piles of trees I made and paid me. I earned $200 there.

Then, one day a Pole came looking for a job. He was born in Canada and spoke a little Polish. I told him that I'd just got this job, but if he wanted to help me, I would pay him using the money I made. I helped him. We ate together. We worked together. When the job ended, we went to Whitehorse and lived there together. He got a job with the air force washing dishes. I couldn't find a job there. I even thought of going back to Fort St. John and looking for work on farms. Then I decided to go to Edmonton. I travelled to Fort St. John and from there to Edmonton, the capital city of Alberta.

I found a job setting up electric power poles. I dug big holes in the ground into which I put the poles. Other workers installed the transformers and the cables on them. I thought that I could do that too. "If you want to try, put on the metal climbing spikes and climb up," the foreman told me.

He liked what I did and asked me to go up and set up the wooden arms that go on top of the pole. Then I installed the pins for insulation and the wires. They paid me a few cents for each pole I set up. After we had finished this work, we moved to Drumheller, Creek Mile and to Hannah. All the farmers in the area got electricity.

I came to Calgary where I worked in a warehouse, preparing mail orders of dinner plates for shipment. I packed them into big boxes. After that ended, I got a job making crackers for the Independent Biscuit Company on 12th Avenue. I worked with a machine that made cookies that had different designs. On one end of the machine, they put the dough in, and I was in charge of operating the machine. However, this work finished soon too. I found a job as a courier, driving a truck for the Rapid Reproduction Company where I worked delivering documents all over the city for ten years until I retired. When I worked, I never took vacations, not even one day.

When I came to Canada, my life was tough. I didn't know the language. I didn't have anyone to talk to because there was no one else where I was. I learned the language from Natives and other people I met in the beer parlour. I didn't have a radio when I worked on a farm. I was by myself at night. I lay down and didn't know what was happening to me. I suffered. I suffered. I suffered. Sometimes, I thought about committing suicide because life had pushed me so nastily.

Despite all the challenges, my life was better in Canada than in Russia. In Canada I didn't have to panhandle. I worked here. In 1950, when I came to Calgary, I joined the Polish Combatants' Association, but I didn't get involved. Later, I joined the Royal Canadian Legion where I met Canadian veterans. In 1957 I started attending the celebrations held in Memorial Park on November 11 where I went wearing my black military hat and my military medals. I listened to the speeches and watched the officers salute those who died in the war to commemorate their sacrifices. After that, everyone went his or her own way. Before 1957 I could not mark Remembrance Day because I worked on the farms and later on I worked far up north setting up power lines. I didn't talk about the war with other people, I never told my stories to anyone until now. No one in Canada knew that I was in the military during the war. Anyone I met didn't seem interested in my stories, so I kept those stories to myself.

After the war, I looked for my family in Europe through the Red Cross. I found only one sister, Jadwiga, alive. She was living in Poland and visited me once in Canada. She is a widow. Her husband was a high-ranking Polish military officer. She told me that my youngest sister Janina died when she was six years old. She passed away in my father's arms, soon after he reunited with them in Ayagoz. I never visited Poland, and I never saw my parents again. My mother died on March 3, 1968. My father died on February 24, 1978.

I thank God for my life. I lived through many difficult situations. Even though my health isn't good now, I'm still alive, perhaps, because I helped many people when I was young. Now, I'm eighty-seven years old.

I just have a few photographs of my family. My sister Jadwiga gave them to me. I started writing a book about my life. But, I became

Rogowski with the author at the convocation ceremony at which she received her Master's in Arts in Communications and Culture at the University of Calgary, November 10, 2014. This occasion was his first visit to the university campus. [Courtesy of Aldona Jaworska]

nervous and tore up the pages I wrote. I started drinking too much. When I began recalling all these times I lived through, I started feeling very poorly. That was my life. When I talk about it, inside my body, I feel the experiences that I lived through, even if all that happened a long time ago.

People don't know that I was a soldier. They ask me why I wear my black military beret every day. I wear it, so I never forget who I was, and who I am. I wear it for all the soldiers who didn't make it through the war and died for us so we could have a better life. They gave their lives for us and for peace.

Lest I forget, I was a soldier. War is terrible. You don't go to war to shoot and kill but to defend the people you love. You go to war for the love of peace. You give your life for all that.

Remembering Zbigniew Rogowski

When I met Mr. Rogowski for the first time, I saw a modest-looking man sitting at a table in the company of other seniors attending their monthly meeting. Beside his chair, there was an adult walker where he kept a large bottle of oxygen with the extension tubes stretching to his face. With slightly laboured breath, he told me the story of his late wife. The way Rogowski described this part of his life not only showed his love and dedication to a woman in need, for whom he opened his home and heart, but also the profound sense of loss he felt after she died. In his life, he witnessed and experienced first hand the death of many people due to starvation, illnesses, hardship and battle. The relationships he had with his family when he was a child and with his wife when he was an adult were vital to him. His willingness to help others allowed him to experience the happiness that human contact, no matter how minimal, brought to him. Rogowski's sensitivity to other people's suffering allowed him to see a human face even when confronting enemies on the battle-field. Once, he told me, "I don't know if I killed someone. I was shooting, but I never wanted to see if I killed someone. I was shoot-ing to defend myself."

The story of the abandoned house and the trampled garden of Monte Cassino, which Rogowski walked by on his way to the mili-tary post in the trenches after he had volunteered to fight the enemy, moved me. The way Rogowski described it was as if he could see the garden in its fullest glory of a summer day in Italy. Every time, I listened to this story, the pain Rogowski experienced seeing the utter devastation of this place was palpable. I, too, could imagine the garden full of flowers, vegetables and trees that used to grow there before the military offensive took place. Even though the young soldiers didn't see the fruits of the labour of people who toiled in this garden, but instead saw its complete annihilation, through their pain and longing for a better world, I could see butterflies circling above the blooming flowers and bees working hard to help produce the harvest. That was the feeling of gratitude and hope people like Rogowski offered to the countless millions who now live in peace. Mr. Rogowski never travelled to Poland or anywhere else in the world after coming to Canada. He never took vacations. Polish citizenship was taken away from him in 1946, and he was a stateless person until he received Canadian citizenship in 2005.

10

Stefan Koselak

(1921–1960)

Introducing Mr. Koselak and His Family

ONE OF THE MEMBERS OF THE Polish Combatants' Association in Calgary called me to set up a meeting with a woman whose husband fought in the Battle of Monte Cassino. "You have to meet Mrs. Ewa Koselak. She is ninety-one, and her daughter Krystyna has photographs and documents," he said excitedly.

We were to meet after Sunday mass at the Polish community hall adjacent to Our Lady Queen of Peace Catholic Church, known as the Polish church in Calgary. I wondered how I was going to recognize the caller and the women I was to meet. However, even in the busy teeming place, I needn't have worried about finding the right person because I was the only person they had not seen before. The man who set up our meeting introduced himself as soon as I stepped through the door and led me to a table where a few coffee cups were already prepared for the meeting. However, Mrs. Koselak was not at the table. Only her daughter sat waiting.

"My mother is mingling with her friends, as she usually does after the Sunday mass. She hasn't seen them for a week. There is a lot of catching up," Chris Fisher said, explaining her mother's absence. "I brought with me a photo album my father put together when he was still alive. Some pictures are missing, but these are most of the photographs of my dad and his colleagues from the time when he was a soldier in the II Polish Army Corps serving as a gunner in the 4th Armoured Regiment while fighting on the Italian Front."

After several minutes, an elderly woman with a broad smile on her rosy-cheeked face approached the table ready to finish the coffee that awaited her. Mrs. Ewa Koselak was wearing a colourful dress that not only matched the sunny fall weather outside but also her outgoing personality. She had a bottle of oxygen to help her breathe, but despite this, her body was beaming with optimism and joy. It was evident that she belonged to this big congregation and to the place where they gathered, as much as this place and these people were part of her.

When I asked her to share the story of her late husband from the time when he was a soldier in the Anders Army during WWII, she told me, "My husband didn't talk about the past with me. For many years, I had to work two jobs. In the morning, I left for a job when my husband and our daughter were still asleep. I came home for a short break before going to another workplace. When I came back at night, they were already asleep. I didn't have many opportunities to talk with my husband. Any free time I had after work, I spent taking care of the family, cooking, cleaning and doing the laundry."

"Mama did not talk much about this with my father," Chris confirmed.

Despite the limited information about Stefan Koselak's life when he was a soldier during WWII, I felt that his story as told by his surviving family would provide a unique perspective on

Stefan Koselak. [Courtesy of Chris Fisher]

the time he spent working on a farm and later organizing his new life in Canada.

Ewa Koselak

Ewa Koselak (née Kulawska) was born to Konstantin Kulawski, a railwayman and Anna Ostkierko, a seamstress, on May 20, 1922, in Nowogródek, Poland. Her father and brother were detained by the Soviet army that invaded Poland soon after WWII began. During the summer Ewa usually stayed with her maternal grandmother who lived near Horodeczno, Polesie voivodship, Prużana county (Powiat Prużański), Poland. In the summer of 1941, on the way to a store in Horodeczno, Ewa was detained by Gestapo soldiers during a massive systemic roundup of the civilian population. After a two-week detention, a large group of youth, women and men was transported to forced labour in Germany; Ewa was sent to a farm where she worked until the end of WWII. During the invasion of the Allied forces on Germany, she was wounded. Throughout those years, she didn't have contact with her family. After the liberation, not wanting to return to Poland, Ewa stayed in Germany and worked for the British Red Cross. When immigration officers from different embassies came to examine people for possible admission to their countries, Ewa decided to come to Canada. She arrived in Halifax, Nova Scotia, on October 30, 1948. On arrival, she was granted landed-immigrant status and assigned to work as domestic help on a farm near Pincher Creek, Alberta. Ewa met Stefan Koselak during the 1948 New Year celebration in Lethbridge, Alberta. They got married on November 26, 1949, in Twin Butte, Alberta. The couple had one child, a daughter, Christine. From July 1957 until retirement, Ewa Koselak worked as a ward maid at the Calgary General Hospital.

I listened to Ewa Koselak telling her own story of immigration to Canada, working as a domestic help on a farm in Alberta, meeting Stefan Koselak just a couple of months after she arrived in Canada. "I had red hair, and I came from Germany. So, when I went to church, people said that another ryża Niemka (pejorative Polish slang meaning "ruddy German") had arrived and come to church," Ewa said, adding, "This was my natural hair colour, and I spoke German because I'd had to learn to speak the language when I was sent to forced labour in Germany. Later, I was told by one of the local women that the young men who came to church, too, were interested in me."

Ewa continued talking about her life in Canada and said, "Also I had to speak German when I was working on the farm in Pincher Creek. The Canadian family of German descent had eight children I took care of, and there was a lot of other work on the farm. When I spoke Polish with their children, the farmer's wife told me that I had to speak German because they didn't understand Polish. I was paid twenty dollars for each month of work, I had to buy my own clothes and I was given a bed and food at the farm."

Browsing through the family photo album. I looked carefully at the photograph of Ewa affixed to a bright yellow temporary travel document (in lieu of passport for a stateless person and person of undetermined nationality) issued by the Office of the Military Government of Germany. Numbered 75944, it was dated August 31, 1948, in Bad Salzuflen, Germany, valid until February 28, 1949, and it had entitled Ewa to come to Canada. In this photograph, I could see Ewa's sunken cheeks, sadness in her eyes, and lips turned downward. All this gave an impression of the concern she must have had about her uncertain future. The signature under her photo was written irregularly, showing perhaps that she had spent little time in school. Ewa had paid twenty German marks for the issue of this military exit permit. The next pages of official stamps proved several doctors' examinations conducted by the Department of National Health and Welfare of Canada, showing her health was sufficient to immigrate. She had also saved her Canadian Immigrant Visa, issued on July 21, 1948, and extended until November 28, 1948.

When I asked her to tell me about her journey to Canada, Ewa explained, "After the war, a lot of people in Germany went to Canada. It was sad because we didn't know where we were going. But what can you do? After we had arrived in Canada, they separated us. Some people went to British Columbia or to other places. I was sent to Pincher Creek, Alberta, to work on a farm."

The next pictures of Ewa in the family photo album are with Stefan Koselak. In every photograph, Stefan seems to be lovingly courting her. Ewa looks happy in all of these pictures, her face radiating a big smile. Stefan is gently holding her hand or arm while the two of them walk along a river or picnic with some friends. In one of the photographs, Ewa is bravely posing over the barrier of an iron bridge stretched high above a fast-flowing river. There, too, Stefan holds her hands to make sure she is safe. In the next photograph, the two of them are in a tight embrace with the iron barrier between them. Ewa's bravery seems to say, "With Stefan by my side, I am not afraid of anything, and I can take on any challenge that comes my way." In many of those photographs, they look deeply into each other eyes, embracing a fateful young love.

Through Ewa's story, a picture of the life of Stefan Koselak began slowly emerging like light through a dense fog. The time this small family of three spent together had ended abruptly when Stefan Koselak died at the young age of thirty-nine of an incurable heart condition. "If they had the machines and medication we have now to cure his failing heart, he would still be alive," Ewa said with sadness. She died on May 20, 2016, in Calgary.

Chris shared the experience of growing up as a child whose parents were displaced persons in Canada. She talked about how the loss of her father, when she was only ten years old, affected her and how she turned away from the community in which she grew up. Chris had to deal with the challenges of adulthood without her father. The memories the wife and the daughter of Stefan Koselak shared with me carried palpable personal pain and a profound sense of loss still felt even though the loss occurred over half a century ago.

Stefan Koselak

Stefan Koselak was born to Wincenty Koselak and Rozalia Koselak (née Wierzbicka) on March 20, 1921, in Brzustów, Opoczna township, Kielce province, Poland. He was eighteen years old when Soviet forces took him captive on September 25, 1939, soon after the Soviet Union invaded Poland and annexed its eastern territory. After the defeat of the Polish army, Koselak was detained by the Soviets in the Szepietówka camp and later moved to the Równe–Lwów captive camp for Polish army soldiers and officers. He was held as a detainee from October 16, 1939, until the amnesty declared by the Soviet Union in August 1941. Soon after Koselak was released, he joined the II Polish Army Corps on September 2, 1941. Stefan Koselak fought in the WWII Italian Campaign, first in the rank of shooter and by the end of the war in the rank of a senior trooper in the 4th Armoured Regiment. On December 9, 1946, he signed the agreement to work on farms in Canada as offered by 1947 Polish Resettlement Act, and by undertaking this contract, he joined the Polish Resettlement Corps of the military, serving His Majesty the King. The declaration stated that he was single, a qualified farmer, that he would serve for two years as required, and that he could be held responsible under criminal law for providing misleading information. The Polish veterans were expected to treat their membership in the Polish Resettlement Corps as part of their military service. After he had finished the contract, he was granted landed-immigrant status. Koselak became a member of the Polish Combatants' Association on May 26, 1948. Stefan Koselak passed away at the age of thirty-nine on July 28, 1960, in Calgary.

I conducted interviews about Stefan Koselak's military service in the II Polish Army Corps and the time he spent working on farms in Canada as part of the Polish Resettlement Corps with Ewa and Chris. To fill in the missing information in Koselak's stories I used his memoir, photographs, written testimony of his tank commander and his medals which helped me to piece together the story of his involvement as a soldier of the II Polish Army Corps in the WWII Italian Campaign.

> What my father taught me in ten years, many people would not
> have learned in a lifetime.
>> —Chris Fisher

Ewa Relates Her Husband's Story

My husband's family described him as a religious young man who went to church and helped the priest. My daughter visited my husband's family in Poland twice and talked with his siblings. His entire family was very religious. From an early age, their mother and father taught the children to pray. At the time of my daughter's visit in Poland, his family asked the priest to celebrate a holy mass for my late husband. A lot of people who remembered him came to the church that day. Even his godmother, already an old woman, came. She hugged my daughter and cried a lot. Then they all went to the cemetery to visit the graves of his mother and father who had also passed away a long time ago. There were a lot of flowers and crosses and monuments at the cemetery.

Truck drivers' training of the 4th Armoured Regiment, part of the Polish Armed Forces in the East, Quizil Rabat, 1943. Koselak's driving licence indicated his military identification number, 280/III. [Courtesy of Chris Fisher]

Before the war, when he was still in Poland, he had a girlfriend and promised her that after he came back, he would marry her. But the war started, he was drafted into the military, and I don't know what happened after that. I was told by his family that from early childhood he had wanted to join the military. I remember that my husband liked being a soldier very much. But I don't know much about his life before he joined the II Polish Army Corps because he said nothing about the past.

My husband spoke of the Battle of Monte Cassino and shared his war stories with other veterans, colleagues who visited us and, who like him, came to Alberta. However, my husband never wanted to tell me

Members of the Skorpion tank regiment: Koselak is first from the left.

[Courtesy of Chris Fisher]

A photograph of Tank Commander Jurek Matykiewicz, dedicated on the back to Koselak:
"To Stefan—To the heroic shooter from Monte Cassino—'Tank Commander'."
[Courtesy of Chris Fisher]

the stories about the time when he was a soldier in the Anders Army
because he didn't want me to worry about things from the past and also
because his health was deteriorating.

He was proud of his military medals and said that he fought hard
for them, and he wore these medals during military celebrations like
November 11, or when there was a special mass for veterans held at the

Koselak served in the *Pirat* tank as a gunner. [Courtesy of Chris Fisher]

Polish church in Calgary. On those days, veterans, men and women, pinned on their medals and marched to the church. I was also very proud of my husband's military involvement during the war.

My husband was someone who was willing to work hard until his health deteriorated. He never complained. He fell ill with pneumonia

Members of the Skorpion tank regiment with the *Pirat III* tank (L). Koselak is standing first from the right. [Courtesy of Chris Fisher]

while he was in the detention camp in Russia due to the hardship and severe conditions there. This caused his health to deteriorate. When he fought in Africa, he fell ill with malaria. In Iraq he underwent medical treatment to nurse him back to health, and he somehow recovered for his transfer to Italy. However, all this caused heart problems later.

I met my husband during the New Year's party organized by the mayor of Lethbridge for the Polish veterans who came to work on farms. It was free of charge. A lot of people from the farms came. It was a nice party; we got small gifts like scarves and perfumes.

The remnants of Koselak's tank, destroyed during the Battle of Monte Cassino. [Courtesy of Chris Fisher]

My husband and I, we got married on November 26, 1949, in Twin Butte, Alberta. The two farmers for whom we worked organized our wedding. His farmer bought the alcohol, and the farmer for whom I worked rented a school hall and made food for everyone. They liked my husband there. He loved to play sports, and the farmer's sons and other young boys from the neighbourhood came over to play soccer together. My husband liked working on the farm because the air in Canada was much better for him than in the United Kingdom where he had stayed for a while. He couldn't remain in England and had decided to immigrate to Canada because he couldn't handle the humid air. Malaria, contracted during the war, affected his health.

A picture of the ruins of the St. Benedict of Nursia monastery after the Battle of Monte Cassino with a Polish flag on the crumbling wall (L). [Courtesy of Chris Fisher]

My husband kept his Polish military uniform; it was green, and it was beautiful. During the winter he put it on to keep him warm while riding a horse to visit me. However, my husband's health started slowly deteriorating, and he couldn't work. When he was outside, he felt better. So, the farmer told him to check with a doctor to see if he could continue to work on the farm. My husband went to town, and the doctor who examined him said that my husband had a heart condition and couldn't keep working like that.

After my husband finished the farm contract, we moved to Coleman where I worked in the hospital's laundry. In 1954 we moved to Calgary. I cleaned offices. In 1957 I got a second job at the Calgary General Hospital

Monte Cassino Cemetery where Polish soldiers from the II Polish Army Corps were buried following the battle. [Courtesy of Chris Fisher]

The ceremony of laying of the wreaths at Monte Cassino Cemetery. General Władysław Anders is standing at the front, saluting. [Courtesy of Chris Fisher]

as a ward maid. I was paid eighty-three cents per hour. I was the only one working, and we had to buy medication for my husband. My husband asked if the welfare office could help him because he couldn't work as a labourer anymore. He was given an eight-month-long course to learn how to be a barber. After that, he worked as a barber at the Model Barber Shop at the York Hotel in Calgary, and he liked doing this. This helped us pay the rent. Many of his colleagues came to get a haircut or shave, and once in a while, the Polish priest came too. When his colleagues wanted to pay my husband for his service, he told them, "You have children, and you just started building a house," and he didn't charge them. He took money only from those people who he knew had the money.

My husband's health continued getting worse, due to his heart condition caused by malaria contracted during the war. Eventually, he couldn't lift his arms and was unable to work as a barber anymore. However, the welfare office didn't want to be involved in long-term assistance and wanted the military to help him. It was unclear which institution was responsible for my husband. The president of the veteran organization sent a letter to the army office in Britain asking for help for my husband, and they received a reply saying they had sent a healthy man to Canada and that was it. The welfare office wanted the military to take care of my husband because he had served in the military. My husband found himself caught between these two institutions. That was a very stressful situation for him. Eventually, unable to work, he received a small military pension.

Daughter Chris added, "When my dad was ill, he was sent to the Mayo Clinic, only because the Polish veterans took up a collection to pay for it and to see if there might be any hope for him. That was a lot of generosity when people didn't have much."

On December 7, 1953, my husband was granted Canadian citizenship. He was happy about this. However, he missed Poland very much and

DESCRIPTION – SIGNALEMENT

NAME
Nom ___STEFAN (STEVE) KOSELAK___

ADDRESS
Adresse ___CALGARY, ALBERTA, CANADA___

TRADE OR OCCUPATION
Profession ___BARBER___

PLACE OF BIRTH
Lieu de naissance ___POLAND___

DATE OF BIRTH
Date de naissance ___20th MARCH, 1921___

MARITAL STATUS
Etat matrimonial ___MARRIED___

SEX M   **HEIGHT** 5' 7"   **COMPLEXION** DARK
Sexe   *Taille*   *Teint*

EYES BLUE   **HAIR** BLOND
Yeux   *Cheveux*

DISTINGUISHING MARKS
Marques particulières ___NONE___

THIS CERTIFICATE HAS BEEN GRANTED **UNDER THE PROVISIONS**
Le présent certificat fut   *aux termes de*

OF SECTION
l'article ___10(1)___

DATED *7 December 1953*
Daté

[signature]

REGISTRAR OF CANADIAN CITIZENSHIP
Registraire de la Citoyenneté canadienne

Koselak was granted Canadian citizenship on December 7, 1953.

[Courtesy of Chris Fisher]

wanted to visit someday. He was planning to go there in 1960 and often said, "It is nice to be in your own country. Why can't we go there and change things there? Maybe it would be easier." Perhaps he was referring to the possibility of a different outcome of war or a different government in postwar Poland.

Whenever there was a holiday approaching, I would hand him some money, and after exchanging it into American dollars, he would send it to his family to buy presents for the children. His family always asked, "Stefan, when are you coming back or when are you coming for a visit?" But he told them, "I don't think I will ever come back," not because he didn't want to go for a visit, but because his health didn't allow him to travel. He died here. The veterans and the Legion organized a beautiful funeral for him. If he had gone for a visit and died in Poland, there would have been no money to do that for him.

My husband knew English because he had spent some time in Great Britain. Also, he spoke Italian that he learned while serving in the II Polish Army Corps fighting in the WWII Italian Campaign. When he talked in Italian with the people of Italian descent living in Calgary, they were happy. He helped at the Polish church in Bridgeland, working on the bulletin, and on Sundays, he served as an usher and collected money during mass. The children who came to the church liked him very much. He enjoyed playing soccer and skiing. When my daughter was six or seven years old, he bought skis and the two of them learned how to ski. They also went tobogganing. He didn't like to sit idle and always wanted to do something. He read the newspapers and took out books from the library. He never showed anyone that he was ill.

Before his death, my husband suffered three heart attacks. The welfare office sent my husband for tests to Edmonton where he had to lift heavy weights to check how his muscles worked. When he returned home, he was admitted to hospital. He died two weeks later.

When my husband died, someone from the funeral home came to take his military uniform. At my husband's funeral, there was a cushion

Monte Cassino Cemetery. After the burial ceremony, the soldiers marched in military formation carrying the flag, to pay tribute to comrades killed during the Battle of Monte Cassino. [Courtesy of Chris Fisher]

on which his medals were pinned. His colleagues put his military hat and some of the medals into his casket. He wanted his medals to be with him.

Chris Relates Her Father's Story

Soon after the war started, my father was imprisoned in a detention camp in Russia. Then the Russians came and said that they were free to go, but they didn't know where to go. So they organized themselves to go by trains. My father joined the Anders Army on September 2, 1941, in Trockoje, USSR, and from there was transferred to Iraq on board a British ship.

In 1943 my father was moved to Italy. After completing truck driver training to operate military vehicles in 1943, he served in the Fourth

Last honours given to the soldiers buried at Monte Cassino Cemetery. The II Polish Army Corps soldiers march enroute to Hill 593 and 575, under the ruins of the Monte Cassino monastery. [Courtesy of Chris Fisher]

Armoured Regiment, also known as the *Skorpions*, in the rank of shooter. He was a gunner in the military tank named *Pirat* and served under Lieutenant Białecki, who I heard was a hero of those battles. Later there were other military tanks called *Pirat* I, II, and III, after mines destroyed the first two. My father was awarded the Monte Cassino

Funeral for the Polish soldiers in Italy. [Photo by Władysław Niewiński]

Cross, the Medal of the II Polish Army Corps, and the Medal of the Fourth Armoured Regiment, the War 1939–1945 Star, and the Italy Star.

My father was wounded during the Battle of Monte Cassino. The tank in which he fought was blown up during the offensive. His tank *Pirat* was one of the British Sherman tanks and was not very well built, I was told. I remember my father saying that if they destroyed a German tank, the Polish soldiers would steal the German helmets because they would fit better in their tanks. They did that because the British helmets were too big and the soldiers wearing them couldn't move around in the military tank, which had little space inside.

LORETO _ POLSKI CMENTARZ WOJENNY

Loreto, Italy: The Polish military cemetery and memorial for the II Polish Army Corps soldiers who died during the Italian Campaign. [Photo by Władysław Niewiński]

My father said that on the Monte Cassino hill there was so much mud that sometimes the tanks couldn't move, especially during the winter when it rained a lot. It was hard fighting in the mountains. My father told me that the Germans laid the telephone lines and the Polish soldiers cut them at night so the Germans would not be able to communicate. He likened what they did to a chess game. The soldiers doing this were called sappers. That was one of the most dangerous and difficult jobs. The sappers crawled in front of the tanks, looking for land mines and bombs. When they found them, they would cut the wires to disable them. My father was in the army tank watching them doing this so he told me about these strategies used during the war. My father participated in the last offensive to liberate Bologna, Italy. As part of the tank regiment, he

After the Battle of Monte Cassino the soldiers spent time in Rome visiting museums, the Colosseum and the Vatican. Koselak is sitting in the third row, first from the left. [Courtesy of Chris Fisher]

Koselak on leave after the battles. [Courtesy of Chris Fisher]

also participated in the military actions to break the Goth Line, and he fought for Monte Fortino in 1944.

After the war, my father was afraid to return to Poland because of the repression and prospect of imprisonment faced by those who returned. No one heard from any Anders Army soldiers who went back to Poland.

11 Polish Army Corps soldiers pose for a picture after the Victory Parade in Bologna.
[Courtesy of Chris Fisher]

Those 11 Polish Army Corps soldiers who decided to go to England were not very welcome either. The Polish soldiers who had fought under the British High Command were not included in the June 8, 1946, victory parade in London.

After the war had ended, the British troops returning from the war front needed jobs, and the Polish soldiers who remained in England needed jobs too. The situation of the Polish soldiers who supported the Allied efforts during the war but refused to go back to Poland and stayed in England was a problem.

About ten years ago I started looking for more information about my father's experience from the time he served in the 11 Polish Army Corps

Koselak, on the left. [Courtesy of Chris Fisher]

Koselak being decorated with the *Krzyż Walecznych* (Cross of Valour) by General Rakowiecki. [Courtesy of Chris Fisher]

and later when he worked on farms in Alberta, and I started talking to Polish soldiers who came with him to Canada to work on farms. My dad came to Halifax, Canada, from England on board the SS *Sea Snipe*. When the Polish soldiers arrived there, armed Canadian guards escorted them from the ship to the railroad station to the trains that took them to the

Koselak, first from the left, at the unveiling of a memorial to the 4th Armoured Regiment. The memorial was built from a destroyed tank. [Courtesy of Chris Fisher]

Koselak in Europe before coming to Canada. [Courtesy of Chris Fisher]

On board of the SS *Sea Snipe* on the way to Canada. Koselak is second from the left.
[Courtesy of Chris Fisher]

different provinces to which they were assigned. I got information about the treatment they received upon their arrival from one of the Polish vets who came with my father. I understand that the government needed to be careful with all these refugees coming to Canada because one never knew who might be among them.

How humiliating the treatment must have been for the II Polish Army Corps soldiers coming to Canada because they had been with the Allies fighting against the common enemy alongside Canadian troops. It broke my heart that these people had to be escorted to the trains by armed Canadian guards. Yet, very few of them complained. My father was very

After the II Polish Army Corps soldiers landed in Halifax, some boarded a train that took them to Lethbridge, Alberta. Koselak (L) at the railroad station at a stop in Montreal.
[Courtesy of Chris Fisher]

diplomatic. Once he got here to Canada, he was just grateful, and he was the kind of person who would not hang on to grudges or anything and just wanted to move forward.

From Halifax, my father travelled to Montreal by train, and from there to Lethbridge, Alberta, where he was placed in an internment camp used to house the German POWs during the war. Then he was assigned to work on a sugar beet farm in Welling, near Lethbridge, along with many other Polish soldiers who came with him to Canada. I remember that some of the veterans I met later told me that they were housed in the chicken coop, that the farmer wasn't very kind to them and that in the winter there was ice on the walls inside.

Later my dad was sent to work on a farm in Twin Butte, Alberta, where he worked on contract doing general farm duties and tending the farm animals. My dad had a positive experience while working there. He loved working on the farm, and he liked working with the farm animals because he had been born, and grew up, in a village. He had knowledge of agricultural work. Despite his deteriorating health, he finished his two-year contract. He made friends with the people for whom he worked, and their friendship continued until he passed away. They even came to Calgary for his funeral. These people stayed in touch with my mother for many years afterward. Later they would bring me for summer vacations to their farm in Twin Butte, close to Waterton Lakes. These people were a family of Canadians of German heritage. They were religious people. Their place felt like home.

When my father arrived in Lethbridge, his only clothing had been his military uniform. Only later, when my dad started working at the farm in Twin Butte, did he get work clothes.

My father said that the farmer for whom he worked encouraged the Polish vets working there to get together every couple of weekends to socialize. They were given time off. The Polish vets kept in close contact with each other and met regularly. Also, the farmer took the Polish vets to church on Sundays, offering to drive. But my dad liked horses, so he

Koselak working on a farm. [Courtesy of Chris Fisher]

followed behind the farmer's car on a horse. The farmer and his family were very honest and good people. They didn't mistreat the Polish vets working for them like other farmers we had heard about. Even after my dad's contract was finished and my parents moved to Coleman to work in the coal mines where money could be made at that time, they still looked after my parents. In fact, we were in touch until a couple of years ago; now most of them have passed away.

My father bought a used car from the farmer. Because of his tank duty during the war, my dad knew how to repair heavy machinery, and after fixing the car, he was able to drive to nearby cities where he looked for contacts with other Polish vets, and to Lethbridge, where there was a big Polish community. He had joined the Polish Combatants' Association in May 1948 in London. Many other Polish vets in Lethbridge were also members of the association.

Koselak in Canada. [Courtesy of Chris Fisher]

On August 15, 1949, the Department of Labour Canada issued a document signed by the minister certifying that my father, Polish veteran Stefan Koselak, had "discharged the undertaking made by the government of Canada to remain in specified employment for a fixed period of time upon admission to Canada." Only after fulfilling their obligations were the Polish vets granted landed-immigrant status.

I remember my father as a brilliant, self-taught person, who knew several languages and who taught me a lot during the ten years I had with him before he died. Even though he was sick because of the heart condition, he never stopped being involved in the Polish community and helping new immigrants fill out forms, even going to government offices with them. He worked very closely with the Polish priest, Father Otłowski, in the church in Bridgeland.

I remember my father being on the phone looking for help for one of the soldiers with whom he worked on the sugar beet farm. After the agricultural contract, this man worked as a labourer in East Coulee near Drumheller, then moved to Calgary. The man had lost one arm and some fingers from the other hand in an industrial accident. Even though he and his family weren't established in the Polish community in Calgary, my father called many people from the Polish Combatants' Association, looking for help for him. I heard him saying, "This is one of our brothers. We need to do something to help him even though he hasn't yet joined our organization because this is really a tragic situation."

I never saw my father lamenting. He never succumbed to seeing his past as a negative experience, and he always stayed optimistic. I saw my dad counselling other veterans who, at times, were drunk and talking about their war experiences. I remember him as a vigorous and wise man, as someone able to give advice on how to deal with and overcome life's difficulties. He didn't have much education. He was only eighteen years old when he was taken by the military and then sent to Siberia. Growing up without him was sorrowful; I lost him so young. Now, I am at an age where I am beginning to believe that some people aren't meant to be here for a long time, especially people who have many gifts. I think that they are destined to pass through our lives and teach us something and then go. What my father taught me in ten years, many people would not have learned in a lifetime.

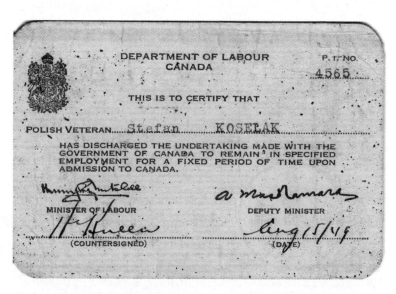

Koselak's discharge certificate, issued on August 15, 1949, proving that he finished his farm labour contract. [Courtesy of Chris Fisher]

We lived on 28th Street, renting a basement suite. I recall that the majority of the immigrants in Calgary settled in Bridgeland. This place became known as Little Europe, Little Germany, Little Italy, and after the war, Polish immigrants moved there too. It was a happy place because we were all poor and we didn't know it because we had such close connections with each other. There were three or four other Polish families on that block. My family lived the farthest from the Polish church. Walking to the church with all the other families joining us, maybe twenty or thirty of us by the time we got to the Polish church, was lovely. There was a great sense of community.

But when you crossed the bridge to go downtown and the other side of the city, then we saw we were not the same as the other people who lived there. We were considered DPs, displaced persons. Even though I was born in Canada, I felt the ethnic stigma attached to all immigrants and people like me. I recall that this was also evident when my father passed away, and the family had to deal with the funeral proceedings.

My father died on July 28, 1960, and was given a military burial in the Field of Honour in Calgary. His wish was to be buried in his military uniform with his war medals. We were Catholics and so we wanted to bury him in St. Mary's Cemetery where other Catholics were buried, believing it would be the way to honour him. The funeral director, Mr. McInnis from the Holloway Funeral Homes, was an Irish Catholic and a good friend of the bishop. When Mr. Holloway came to the house and saw that we had nothing, he said to my mum, "Why do you want to go into debt for the rest of your life? You have a daughter to raise, and you have nothing to pay for his funeral." Because my dad was also a member of the Canadian Legion here in Calgary, Mr. Holloway said that the Canadian Legion would help to arrange the funeral and pay for everything. "You will not have a choice of the casket or anything. But it is a very dignified funeral because of the Legion presence. The casket would be covered with the Polish flag and the British flag. There is a lot of honour in that," he said to convince us. At the time, it was the British flag, because we did not yet have our own Canadian flag.

I remember that the priest had a bit of a problem with burying my father in the Field of Honour because it wasn't a Catholic cemetery. Mr. Holloway spoke to the bishop, and the bishop said to the Polish priest, "Go. Bless the ground. This makes more sense." I felt angry at the time that there would be a question about it; I don't know why. I wanted him to have a fancy casket, a great big tombstone. My father was buried in his military uniform with most of his medals that he was awarded for his involvement in the Italian Campaign. I feel different about my father's burial today. Today I have a strong and unwavering sense of pride that my father is buried in the Field of Honour. All the tombstones are identical. There is no military rank there. It is an honourable place, and everybody is equal.

Also, I realized that for a long time I'd been disconnected from my heritage. I'd married into a Canadian family and that was my focus, but this realization prompted me to look for my roots. I started going through my father's documents and realized that I knew nothing about his history. I often wished for somebody with a gift for writing and interviewing because many of my friends agreed we hadn't asked our parents enough questions. They didn't want to talk about it. Therefore, now, when they are gone, the history is gone.

In 2006 I travelled to the place where my father was born, to learn more about him and about his and my roots. Finding information about the place he was born in central Poland was possible because of the Internet. *Dziennik Łódzki* published an article "From Canada to Pilce" about my travel there. "After 50 years Krystyna Koselak-Fisher, a Canadian citizen, found the family of her father Stefan Koselak from Brzustów, in Tomaszów county, community Inowłódz." The article tells the story of my dad's resettlement to Siberia, his involvement in the II Polish Army Corps, and the Battle of Monte Cassino. I met with the local television and other media, as well as with the vice-president of Tomaszów city, Grażyna Haraśna, and talked with her about Polish traditions and culture. Another article titled "In Search of Roots" was published in *Nowa Gazeta Tomaszowska*. Even though I was in Tomaszów for the first time, I felt as if I had lived there always. It was an incredible feeling to be in the place where my father had spent his childhood and youth. During the 1990s, I realized that the people who knew my dad from the time when he was in the military are getting older, so I started talking with them to learn more about my dad. Information that I have about my dad is mostly from those who served with him.

During some difficult times in my life when I was struggling to be strong, I often thought about the life of my parents, and I drew strength from their experience. I often reflect on the lives of the people who came to Canada. What my parents went through was a hundred times worse, and yet they persevered and found strength. I thought about how my parents' lives could be an example to me. I feel that the case of the II Polish Army Corps soldiers is a story of double betrayal and neglect, first, maybe not intentional, in England, and then in Canada. There was an absence of concern about what those people went through during the time of war, and these people asked for nothing. There were no English classes offered. They learned the language on their own. They were more than happy to take the assignments given to them, and they were grateful for whatever had been offered to them and said, "Thank you."

My dad and his friends became very proud and loyal Canadians because of the opportunities they were given. They worked very hard. They were not takers. They were givers and contributed immensely. They would take jobs no one would take, and they never complained. They were happy and grateful to have a job and found something good about their jobs. They were thrilled to work and they did so with passion. They maintained a positive attitude of moving forward and celebrating good times. I don't remember my father saying anything negative about his experiences in Canada. He was a helpful person by nature. His story was tragic. He survived the deportation to Siberia and the war, and then he came to this country for a new life with hope. Then he got sick and died at thirty-nine years of age. The whole time he was ill, there was no bitterness or complaining. He just kept the hope alive that something would happen that would help him live longer. He had a positive attitude every day. When he could not work physically, he volunteered to help new Polish immigrants during the 1950s who needed a lot of assistance in finding jobs. The priest would call my father and let him know that the new immigrants needed help. My dad helped a lot of people find work.

Now, I find I am going to more funerals, and fewer people are attending them because they are either sick or they are gone. I have made it a personal mission to go to as many funerals, to honour these people, as I could. My mum worried that when everybody was gone, there would be no one there to eat the lunch served after the funeral. I told her, "Mum, don't worry. I will eat the meal." That is how these people think: making sure that when somebody came by, they were hospitable.

Remembering the Koselak Family

During one of the meetings, Ewa Koselak talked about the trip her daughter made to Brzustów, Poland, in September 2006, looking for the family of her late father, Stefan Koselak. It was the first time Chris met her extended family. They took her to the cemetery to visit her grandparents' graves. "She saw many crosses and monuments at the cemetery, all adorned with flowers. It was beautiful there," Ewa said. The sadness and the nostalgia with which Ewa described this Polish cemetery located thousands of kilometres from Canada, which she only knew from her daughter's story, was palpable.

When I was growing up in post-WWII Poland, we were often reminded that six million Poles, including three million Polish Jews, and twenty-five million Soviet Union soldiers and citizens, died during WWII. There were many monuments erected to commemorate this immense loss of human life. Often these memorials were surrounded by the graves of Polish and Soviet soldiers who died fighting against the Nazi occupants.

Graves of ancestors have always played a significant role in the life of the Polish people. The first day of November is known as All Saints Day, a national holiday for people to visit the graves of their loved ones. Swept clean of falling leaves, the graves receive a lit candle and flowers. People also take care of graves that no one visits anymore. On the night of remembrance for the dead, the glow of the many candles light up the sky, and the scent of the candles envelopes the cities.

Even in Communist Poland, when the Church was severely repressed, many priests were present at the cemetery gate that day, taking requests for prayers. From the 1960s until the late 1980s in Szczecin, where the anti-Communist movement was strong, the cemeteries were also a platform of resistance against the pro-Soviet government. Family members and the public took special care of the unmarked graves of those brutally killed by the authoritarian government. Their graves were covered with many candles, making those graves glow especially bright. Many who came to the cemeteries also thought of people whose graves were nowhere to be found or were far away. From early morning until long past midnight, votive candles were set up by the cross in the middle of the cemeteries. These candles served as an expression of support for those who fought for democracy and lost their lives. The candles that burned out were quickly replaced by new ones. There were so many candles that soon the place beside the cross was filled up, and lit candles spilled onto walkways and continued for hundreds of metres, often stretching beyond the gates of the cemeteries.

Ewa Koselak told me, "My husband liked being a soldier and always told me that I should join the Polish Combatants' Association," as background for her own special overseas trip. "On May 18 to 20, 1979, I visited the Polish cemeteries at Monte Cassino, Italy to commemorate the thirty-fifth anniversary of the battle that took place there. I went there with many veterans from the Polish Combatants' Association in Calgary, and we visited four cemeteries. John Paul II celebrated mass; many priests, as well as the bishop, were there too. The Pope thanked the veterans for coming to the cemetery that day," Ewa said and stopped for a moment.

"So many of our colleagues were buried there. On every cross, marking a grave of someone who died there, there was a rosary. There were many flowers, and red poppies grew between the graves. Even if someone's body wasn't found, there was a monument. There were many graves of men, and I saw two graves of women. We drove by bus to four cemeteries where the soldiers from the II Polish Army Corps were buried. We cried a lot at every cemetery." Ewa stopped talking again and added, "I remember that it was scorching hot there and the sun severely burned my face."

The way Ewa Koselak described the commemoration of the thirty-fifth anniversary of the Battle of Monte Cassino made me once more ponder the stories that the Anders Army soldiers had shared with me. They spent many days in mud, but also scorched by the hot sun on the hills of the Monte Cassino stronghold. The monastery, as depicted in a nineteenth-century painting, shows green hills spreading below the abbey and many trees growing in the valley. During 1944, the monastery and all that surrounded it was turned into a stony desert from which only the odd burned tree trunk stuck out. On this bloody battlefield and site of massive annihilation, the soldiers defending their posts often had no water to quench their thirst. They experienced gruelling hardship under constant threat of being shot at by the enemy and even mistakenly shelled by Allied artillery. When WWII was near its end, and the geopolitical situation in Europe changed, Poland's pro-Soviet government rejected the II Polish Army Corps soldiers who fought for freedom and democracy. By doing so, the government that had sided with the Soviet Union also dismissed the ultimate sacrifice of those Polish soldiers who had lost their lives while fighting in the Battle of Monte Cassino.

During my research I was privy to Koselak's rudimentary memoir titled, "For Your Freedom and Ours," which contains brief information accompanying photographs of him, his tank regiment, members of the Polish army taken during the WWII campaign in Italy, and on board the ship to Canada. There are also photographs of Koselak taken during his first years in Canada. All pictures show Koselak wearing his impeccable military uniform. He always wore his military medals. Several photographs show the tank in which he fought during such battles as Monte Cassino. Also, his memoir has photos and names of those who were part of his tank regiment. Moreover, the pictures and captions illustrate his journey through the Middle East after he joined the II Polish Army Corps.

The comments under the pictures refer to places where he fought, destroyed enemy tanks and was awarded military decorations, and participated in a victory parade in Bologna. The memoir demonstrates how high a value Koselak put on being in the army and fighting in such battles as Monte Cassino and Monte Fortino, and on the Goth Line. Koselak included pictures of the monastery ruins and the cemetery in which the Polish soldiers are buried.

General Władysław Anders died on May 12, 1970, in London, Great Britain, on the twenty-sixth anniversary of the Battle of Monte Cassino. Anders' wish was to be buried alongside the 11 Polish Army Corps soldiers at Monte Cassino Cemetery. The internment of the casket carrying Anders' body took place on May 23, 1970. The tombstone of General Anders is positioned in front of the eternal fire burning in the centre of the sixteen-metre Virtuti Military Cross.

On the thirty-fifth anniversary of the Battle of Monte Cassino on May 18, 1979, Pope John Paul 11, the Polish pope, celebrated a Holy Mass at Monte Cassino Cemetery where the Polish soldiers from the 11 Polish Army Corps were buried. Six thousand people came to the cemetery that day from around the world, and thirty thousand came from Italy. Ewa Koselak attended this celebration along with twelve Polish veterans from Calgary. The annual ceremony at Monte Cassino Cemetery to commemorate those who died there was organized by the association of Polish veterans and, until 1990, in cooperation with the government-in-exile of the Republic of Poland.

During the Cold War decades, Poland was shut tightly behind the Iron Curtain, and travelling outside the country, especially to the West, was severely restricted for the general population by the pro-Soviet Polish government. Only those who closely followed pro-Communist principles and posed a low risk of defection were allowed to travel, and mostly on official business. Even in those cases, the travellers were briefed before departure by their immediate supervisors, members of the Communist Party, or government passport officers. They had their passports issued no sooner than three days prior to the trip and in exchange, had to leave behind their personal identification documents that were required to be carried at all times. Immediately upon coming back, they had to return their passports that were then carefully inspected. Information about unauthorized travel, especially to Western countries, called for possible surveillance, the cancellation of any future trip to a foreign country, or other severe punishment like incarceration under the suspicion of treason. I have heard from the Polish veterans in Calgary that visiting the graves of the Polish soldiers buried at Monte Cassino Cemetery was denied to those soldiers who fought in the Battle of Monte Cassino and returned to Poland after the war. Some of the II Polish Army Corps veterans in Calgary I spoke with expressed a desire to visit the Polish cemetery at Monte Cassino. However, none of them did.

I came to understand how people like Ewa Koselak who travelled to Monte Cassino Cemetery to pay homage to the II Polish Army Corps soldiers buried there, and the Poles locked behind the Iron Curtain who lit candles for those who lost their lives, were in a sense united. They all honoured those who died fighting for freedom and democracy at times when the official Polish government did not.

Honouring those who fought for liberty and democracy was important to all WWII Polish veterans I interviewed, as was finding family members they left behind. Some of them turned to the Red Cross shortly after the war. With the passing of time and help of new technology, almost fifty years after Chris lost contact with family in Poland, she found the daughter of her father's brother when conducting an Internet search.

When Chris travelled for the first time to Poland accompanied by her friend, whose father had also served in the II Polish Army Corps and come to Canada to work on farms, they were instantly embraced by the Brzustów community, the town where Stefan

Koselak was born. Their fathers had been friends, too, and had always wanted their daughters to visit Poland. Chris and her dad's story was featured in the local newspapers and on TV. The women met with the city's vice-president and shared their impressions of the people they had met, the places they had seen, and the culture they got to explore. However, many questions arose for those writing the story of Chris who followed the footsteps of her father in Poland. One of the newpapers Chris brought back with her asked, "What causes—after many years—people to start looking for their lost family members? Why do they come back to the places where their parents grew up? And, why do they want to renew their family relationships?"

In light of my research, I would add one more question. Why is it important to learn about the experiences of the 11 Polish Army Corps soldiers, who fought alongside the Allies and later came to Canada to work on farms for two years before being granted landed-immigrant status?

III

FROM VICTORY
TO SORROW

11

Understanding the Polish
War Veterans' Experiences

WHEN WWII POLISH WAR veterans came to Canada, the media
in Alberta covered few details of the challenges and struggles they
experienced as soldiers who fought on the side of the Allies against a
common enemy. The veterans had to come to terms with the trauma
of war experiences while struggling to start a new life in Canada.
The language barrier, in addition to the many other unfamiliar
aspects of life in Canada, added to those challenges. The media's
emphasis, however, was on them coming to work on farms. It would
seem that their farm labour was also all that mattered to Canadian
immigration authorities, who were focused on bringing help to the
farmers because Canadian soldiers coming back from war were moving to cities in search of a better life and the German POWs were
being sent back to Europe.

In 1946, upon their arrival in Halifax, the Polish veterans were
admitted as non-immigrants, escorted by the Canadian military
when disembarking and expected to provide fingerprints to be
granted temporary identification documents. The Polish veterans

were then assigned to work in different provinces, even if they hoped to be placed on farms together or near their friends so they could keep in touch. Niewiński reported that upon landing in Halifax, after the immigration officer asked him to point out his friend, the two of them were separated. Niewiński was sent to work in Alberta and his friend to central Canada. These two friends never saw each other again. Niewiński said that he wondered about it for a long time but researching newspaper articles later allowed him to understand. Martin Thornton in his article, "The Resettlement in Canada of 4,527 Polish Ex-servicemen, 1946–47," in the journal, *Immigrants & Minorities*, confirmed such "complaints from Polish ex-servicemen which included that they had been separated from other Polish-Canadians and, in some cases, their own relatives." Was this approach intentional on the part of the Canadian government or an example of poor practices? Alternatively, should it be viewed through the Canadian media's lens? The *Edmonton Journal* article "Plans Make Poles Good Canadians," claimed that such "block segregation" for the Polish veterans was promoted because of prior experience: "among Canadians of foreign birth much of the trouble developed when, not understanding English, and having no place to go, they crowd into Polish halls, and Polish societies."

After their arrival, the Polish veterans were placed in the Lethbridge detention camp still in use by the German POWs. (During the war Camp 133 housed over 13,000 German POWs, many of whom worked on farms.) Anatol Nieumierzycki recalled meeting some of them in November 1946, and said, "only then, I realized that by signing the farm-work contract, I was to replace the German POWs." This begs the question, was it specific to Alberta or were these practices country-wide as Thornton claimed: "Canada, in looking for replacements for German prisoners of war who had been working in the sugar beet fields of Ontario, selected 2,876 ex-servicemen of the II Polish Corps in 1946 from Italy."

Even though the Polish WWII veterans interviewed for this book didn't draw such a parallel, the conditions they experienced while working on farms in Canada are strikingly similar to those they had lived through in Siberia or Kazakhstan. Much of the time in Alberta, the veterans were housed in substandard accommodations such as chicken coops or badly built and uninsulated farm sheds, and they experienced malnutrition even while working on farms.

Many Polish veterans spent months in isolation, living in remote locations on the farms with limited contact with the outside world. They did not have access to any media. Some reported that the farmers left them alone for several months, tasking them with taking care of the farm. This arrangement made leaving the farm, even for a brief time, difficult or impossible. Because of the lack of opportunities to learn English, the veterans learned English from strangers they met in places such as beer parlours. When they spoke Polish in public they were chastised for doing so, and commanded to speak English.

The Calgary Herald printed an article on November 25, 1946, under a more positive headline, "Poles Settling Down to Canadian Farm Life," quoting Arthur MacNamara, deputy minister of Labour: "A definite understanding had been reached with each farm employer covering living and working conditions, including minimum wages." MacNamara also claimed, "Provision also was being made to keep in close touch with both Polish veterans and farmers so steps could be quickly taken should any difficulties arise between employer and employee." However, the reality was very different for many Polish veterans who arrived to work in Alberta. They had to deal with situations for which they were not prepared and for which it seemed there were no official governmental guidelines or policies in place. They were not informed of their rights or how they should deal with such issues as non-payment for their work, terms of their accommodation or inadequate food. No protocol available to them defined the responsibilities of the farmers, thus they sometimes felt

forced to take issues into their own hands. The only way they sometimes saw to resolve a conflict was to abandon the farm and seek
help or break the contract. In some cases, as a resolution, the veterans had to be moved to other farms to finish their two-year contract.
They were not aware that their contracts were expected to last one
year only and after that, a veteran was "free to accept employment
on a farm of his own choice for the second year of his undertaking,"
according to Thornton.

Many of the veterans reported that they did not receive payment for several months of their heavy farm labour, or that they
were severely underpaid. In some cases, such as when Rogowski
complained about the work conditions to people he met in a beer
parlour, his mistreatment was reported to the local police who inter-
vened with the farmer on his behalf. Nieumierzycki and Niewiński
decided to leave the farms where they worked and search for new
employment elsewhere. In their cases, however, the immigration
officers tracked their whereabouts and found other farms where they
were sent to work to finish their contracts.

All participants reported that they had to wear their Polish military uniforms for their farm work because they could not afford to
buy new clothing. When they had joined the II Polish Army Corps,
the military uniforms they received symbolized their hopes for the
rebirth of a democratic, free and independent Poland. Thus, the
need to use the military uniforms as farm-work clothing was perceived as a lack of respect for them as soldiers and veterans. Such
social, financial and labour conditions were experienced by most
of the Polish combatants, but never reported by the newspapers or
radio. There were only a few success stories. The *Edmonton Journal*
reported on a family reunion on November 22, 1946, under the
headline "Polish War Veterans Arrive in Edmonton." In this case, a
Polish veteran was allowed to work on a sister's farm because, it was

claimed, "where possible, all special requests in placement of the men were granted."

However, based on the information collected during interviews, except for Koselak, the Polish veterans did not have any contact with the other veterans or any other Polish community during their first year of the contract. In the case of Rogowski, the lack of contact with other Poles lasted throughout his entire two-year contract and several years afterward, when he was sent to work in a forest, and later when he took on the job of setting electrical power lines in rural Alberta. With the exception of Koselak's case, the contacts the veterans made with members of the Polish community in Calgary took place because of their initiative, not because they were encouraged. Most of the time these contacts were initiated when they were dealing with poor conditions on the farms. To seek help and plead their cases, they travelled to Calgary where they met other Poles. In the case of Nieumierzycki, he left the farm because he was not being paid yet was expected to take care of the entire farmstead.

When Nieumierzycki arrived in Calgary, he met members of the Polish ethnic group who had immigrated to Canada in the 1920s. The strong solidarity among Polish immigrants involved not only the group of WWII veterans but also other generations of immigrants. They were all welcomed and embraced by the local Polish community. Nieumierzycki and Niewiński reported that the Polish community already established in Calgary treated the Polish veterans very well; homes of the *Polonia Kanadyjska* (Polish diaspora) in Calgary were always open to the Polish veterans. The veterans were offered free accommodation until they were able to find a job and establish their lives in Calgary. And a few years later, when they started building their own houses, entire work teams comprised of WWII Polish veterans helped each other with such undertakings. The feeling of strong support and comradeship was always present during such times.

Through the contact with "the old Polish diaspora," Nieumierzycki met Walter Frank Chuchla, a 1920s Polish immigrant, who helped him find a job and provided free accommodation. Not only individuals but also Polish businesses helped with finding affordable housing and discounts. A barber named Rokita, who had a shop where the Calgary City Hall now stands, built a room behind his business and modest dwelling and equipped it with bunk beds for Polish veterans who could not afford or find suitable accommodation, due to a severe shortage of rental housing. The Polish veterans could stay there free of charge as long as they needed to. The help Polish veterans received from members of the Polish community was instrumental in allowing them to start a new life in Canada. This illustrates the strength of the Polish community and how it valued the sacrifices the veterans made during the war. Many members of the Polish diaspora never saw free Poland, because they had immigrated to Canada long before Poland regained its independence in 1918, yet they still cultivated Polish values and culture.

Each story in this book illustrates different experiences of the Polish veterans as Soviet detainees of labour camps or deportees to kolkhozes in Siberia and Kazakhstan, Polish soldiers, and farm workers in Canada. Rogowski's narrative could be seen as a representation of the incredibly difficult farm-work experience. There were other cases when veterans didn't finish their contracts because they went missing from the farm, were hospitalized or died. Rogowski was placed on four different farms, and each time he was not properly paid and lived in substandard conditions. Only after four negative experiences was he allowed to finish his farm-work contract working for a sawmill company instead. Rogowski's story not only reveals another dimension of his identity, namely his resolve to help others in need, despite his inability to negotiate terms of employment for himself, but it also illustrates the harassment, antagonism, mistreatment, and exploitation some veterans had to live through. Rogowski's narrative about his life in Canada indicates that he lived in isolation from a larger community for an extended time, and did not have any contact with the Polish ethnic community until the mid-1950s. He experienced a variety of problems caused by challenges of adjustment to Canadian society.

Lack of support for the Polish veterans who stayed in the West happened not only in Canada but in England as well, as indicated in a *Calgary Herald* article, "British Labor Averts Clash on Closed Shop," by Frank Swanson, reporting on October 23, 1946. Anti-Polish sentiments sounded loudly among the unions with regards to the "300,000 of General Anders's Polish army" for whom the British government had to find settlement. Shouts of "'Fascists', 'aliens,' and 'undesirable foreign elements' and worse" were heard directed at the Poles. Swanson also reported on clashes between Poles and Scottish villagers who declared, "If the government does not get rid of the Poles for us, we will do it ourselves." Only later, Swanson explained that the reference to the "Fascist" Poles had not involved all of the Polish veterans in the West but specifically a group of 20,000 Poles who were either "at one time in the enemy hands or actually served in German army, although against their will." Such a portrayal involving the Anders Army soldiers a month after the Polish veterans' arrived in Alberta could have influenced how Albertans received them.

The difference in how Alberta and the Canadian government viewed the situation of Polish veterans was apparent in the *Herald's* headline on November 25, 1946, "Poles Settling Down to Canadian Farm Life." Arthur MacNamara, deputy minister of Labour, was quoted as saying that the first group of 1,700 of Polish veterans who were placed in eight distribution centres were "very happy" to be in Canada and showed "every promise" of adjusting themselves quickly to Canadian life. Lieutenant Colonel J.P. Castle, who had commanded the Polish officers on the SS *Sea Snipe* said, "Canada is getting men who...will become excellent citizens." Was this contrasting information enough to change the balance of how the veterans were perceived in Alberta? The "Plan to Make Poles Good Canadians" as presented in The *Edmonton Journal* on how to deal with the Polish veterans' integration certainly had an adverse impact on their identity formation, just as the implementation of "block segregation" had devastating results on their adjustment to a new life in Canada, since they had felt so isolated.

Nieumierzycki talked a lot about his journey to Canada from Italy, bringing two suitcases of about two hundred Polish books that were his only companions while working on the farm. Soon after he finished his contract, he became involved with the Polish Canadian Association in Calgary, and from 1948 until 1953, he volunteered there as a librarian. He organized and maintained the Polish library to help preserve Polish heritage and culture, and promote the importance of remembering one's history and language, teaching it to the younger generation. The connections he made with the Polish diaspora in Calgary helped him start a new life in Canada.

Niewiński also looked for contacts with other Polish veterans when he left the farm. In Calgary, with other Polish veterans, he formed a branch of the Polish Combatants' Association in 1947 that attracted 160 members. They met at a community centre in Bridgeland. Niewiński also wanted to be involved in community life to keep Polish traditions and values alive. Having a place where Polish people could feel safe from prejudice, and comfortable with others who shared a common history and culture, was important to him. For Niewiński and Nieumierzycki, it was most important to speak Polish with their fellow veterans. Both of them maintained a strong resolve to communicate in their native language even sixty-five years after their arrival in Canada when they insisted on speaking Polish during the interviews conducted for this book. The help Niewiński received from the Polish community in Calgary upon his arrival allowed him to establish a new life in Canada and

later on, driven by his principles of maintaining the Polish culture, he became actively involved in the building of the new Polish
Canadian Cultural Centre at 3015-15 Street NE, Calgary.

Support for the Polish WWII veterans given by the Polish community in Calgary lasted for many years. Koselak's family reported
that he had also been involved in helping other veterans. First, he
provided his service as a barber free of charge to those veterans who
could not afford to pay. Later on in the late 1950s, when Koselak
could not work anymore due to his deteriorating health, he assisted
those Polish veterans who didn't speak or write English. On their
behalf, he wrote letters to the authorities regarding immigration
issues or labour-related matters. He also accompanied them during
their appointments, and helped plead their cases.

For years, the Polish community continued to help new immigrants. I learned from Nieumierzycki that the Canadian Polish
Congress, an umbrella organization formed in 1944, covered six
months of healthcare premiums for Polish refugees coming to
Calgary until the early 1990s and thus had paid my family's premiums when we came to Calgary in February 1990.

However, in cases where Polish veterans could not find contacts
with Polish communities, they were more challenged to establish
themselves in Canada. Rogowski had no connection with other
Polish veterans and rarely had contact with anyone at all because
of the conditions on the farms on which he worked as they were
located in the north and far away from any major city. He learned
English from people whom he met in beer parlours. After his farm
contract ended, he worked for several years in the northern part of
Alberta, setting electrical power lines. He reported that he did not
know any Poles when he moved back to Calgary. In 1950 Rogowski
joined the Polish Combatants' Association but did not get involved.
He joined the Royal Canadian Legion where he met Canadian veterans. It appears that the years apart from Polish community made

a mark on him and influenced his ability to get actively involved. In 2007 Rogowski became a member of the Polish seniors' club, meeting monthly in the Polish Canadian Cultural Centre. However, he said, "I only live from day to day, there is no happiness. Just sorrow!" Rogowski has no family in Canada. He was married from 1970 until 1976 when his wife, a war veteran from Scotland, died.

In his narrative, Rogowski portrayed himself as selfless, as someone who helped many individuals in need, including his own family while in Kazakhstan, his wife and many whom he met in Canada. Starting in 1957, after he moved to Calgary, Rogowski began attending Remembrance Day ceremonies in Memorial Park, wearing his military medals. He listened to speeches and watched officers salute those who had died during the war to commemorate them, but he noticed "afterward, everyone went their own way." Before 1957 Rogowski could not mark Remembrance Day because he worked on farms, and later on, in the far north. Rogowski said that he didn't talk about the war with other people, that he had never told anyone his life story until now, and so no one in Canada really knew that he had been in the military during the war. The people Rogowski met in his life were not interested in his stories, he claimed; therefore he kept these stories to himself.

Rogowski's story describing Remembrance Day illustrates how he felt forgotten as a war veteran. He said that he did not go to those events to memorialize his own involvement in the war, but on behalf of those Polish soldiers who died and whose deaths he witnessed. By commemorating November 11, he wanted to acknowledge their sacrifices. Even though seventy years have passed, Rogowski's memories of war events still feel raw to him, especially when he recalls providing consolation to comrades dying on the battlefield of Monte Cassino. In Rogowski's story, it appears as if the shrapnel wounds he witnessed are still open, and his wounded soul is still hurting. His body reacted physically while telling his emotional story. Time passing has not healed his wounds.

Rogowski says that now, when he visits Memorial Park on November 11 wearing his military medals and original military beret, young people come to him and say "thank you for your service in the military and for offering your life to defend the world." This simple acknowledgement from strangers seems to bring him satisfaction. This expression of appreciation is more than what he received for his military service when he came to Canada after the war.

Stories share information about events that were personally witnessed or experienced and shine a light on the larger social processes that affected the individuals involved. However, what if the story cannot be told, or it can only be shared with others who lived through similar experiences? Perhaps the story is difficult to share because the memory of it is too fresh, or the emotional load is too heavy. Reliving stories can evoke difficult memories and some veterans were not able to keep a safe emotional distance from those recollections.

People such as Nieumierzycki, Niewiński and Koselak had access to Polish communities and other veterans like them, and, if they needed to, they could talk about the past. Other people such as Rogowski, isolated from Polish communities, were not able to speak with others, especially if they did not share a language. Thus, it is possible that such stories were never shared with anyone; Rogowski confirmed this during our interview. This is perhaps why, only now and at the end of his life, Rogowski is reliving his stories from difficult times, and evoking powerful images. The way Rogowski told his story is fundamentally different from the way Niewiński and Nieumierzycki told their stories. Rogowski's stories are vivid, filled with pain, profound sorrow and suffering. They are just as raw as when he lay down alone and isolated in a sparse farm shed.

The way in which Niewiński and Nieumierzycki told their stories illustrates how they managed to distance themselves from what happened in the past. For Koselak the time gap was too short for him to tell his stories at all. Koselak's stories, as he would tell them himself, died with him. Koselak understood the pain associated with these stories but never "lamented," according to his daughter Chris Fisher. Instead, he counselled other veterans who, at times, "got drunk" and talked about their war experiences. Many Polish veterans, like many other war veterans, suffered substance abuse or depression, and what is now known as post-traumatic stress disorder, and Koselak was there to help and give advice on how to deal with life's difficulties. Wisdom came from those tough experiences, even for Koselak's daughter Chris Fisher, who learned a lot from her father.

Characteristics that contribute to the formation of relationships in communities include stories shared by a group. The identity of an individual is linked to that individual's relationship to others. People like Koselak, who did not share their stories, were most likely keeping silent to avoid the emotional stress of recalling those events. The stories of people like Niewiński and Nieumierzycki illustrate that they had built distance between themselves and the events because they had the support of the Polish community. The story of Rogowski shows that he was separated from the community and is still reliving his stories as they happened.

The reverberations of the article titled "Polish Vets Suffering T.B., Venereal Disease. Several in Currie Army Hospital for Treatment" on the front page of *The Calgary Herald* on December 14, 1946, continue to be felt by the Polish veterans and the Polish community in Calgary. The Polish Combatants' Association in Canada, Branch No. 18, celebrated the sixty-fifth anniversary of its inception in Calgary on November 11, 2012. The ceremony started with a speech delivered in Polish and in English by Barbara Gorzkowska, the vice-president at that time. Gorzkowska was born in Canada but her mother Marta Mańkowska is a veteran of the

1944 Warsaw Uprising. Gorzkowska talked about how the hurt-
ful article starts with a statement that some of the Polish veterans
who came to work on farms in Alberta had been diagnosed with
tuberculosis and venereal disease. The article was written in a sensationalized manner and was framed with a headline suggesting the
Polish veterans were endangering public health, safety and moral-
ity. To support the allegations, the author referred to the number of
infections and provided names of the officials involved in dealing
with this issue. This sensationalized approach was employed before
readers were subsequently advised "the danger to the Canadian population of this disease among the Polish soldiers is very very small."

Moreover, the article also undermined the qualifications of the
Polish veterans who came here to work on farms:

> The Herald also learned that although the government had declared that
> all the Polish soldiers had experience as farm workers, this was not true.
> The majority of the men arrived were not experienced farm workers and
> are learning the work from their new employers.

Bringing up this sixty-five-year-old article during the sixty-fifth
anniversary of the formation of the Polish Combatants' Association
indicates how the Polish veterans still feel about this unfounded
and uncalled-for representation. The speech was intended to illustrate how unfairly the Polish veterans and community had been
positioned in this article. The Herald had painted all the veterans
with one brush, and did not allow them a voice for rebuttal, thus, by
default, their image was altered by the media. During my interviews,
some of the Polish veterans had reported suffering from pneumonia during their imprisonment in Siberia and Kazakhstan that had
caused some concern about tuberculosis but cleared up immediately upon their arrival. They returned to farms to which they were
assigned soon afterward.

In this same issue, *The Calgary Herald* published a headline
"200 Prisoners of War to Stay Here" about a federal government
decision, based on petitions submitted by the German POWs and
their Canadian employers, to allow two hundred of them to stay.
Some Alberta farmers had petitioned for specific POWs who'd been
satisfactory workers to stay. Those German POWs would undergo a
careful screening and would be put on probation with the promise
of citizenship after a few years. Moreover, quoting *The Lethbridge
Herald*, remaining "German prisoners...would be given special training in some type of education camp," before they would be released
on parole. This favourable article about the German POWs was published on the same front page, separated by two columns, from the
article titled "Polish Vets Suffering T.B., Venereal Disease" that slan-
dered the morale and image of the Polish veterans.

It is not surprising that the Polish veterans who came to
Canada to work on farms as part of their labour contract felt that
they were treated more like POWs than veterans. Placing these
two articles—one about German POWs and the other about Polish
veterans—together on the same page of a newspaper suggested
a connection. Both groups had to do the same work, and both
were there by government decree. On December 20, 1946, *The
Calgary Herald* published another article, headlined "No German
POWs will stay in Canada," reporting the successful appeal by the
Canadian Legion, the Alberta government and Alberta's premier,
E.C. Manning, to extradite all Germans from Canada. However, was
this sufficient to undo the already inflicted hurt?

Not long afterward, on January 4, 1947, *The Calgary Herald*
reported a monumental change—the introduction of Canadian
citizenship—in a symbolic event. In a ceremony that day, Prime
Minister Mackenzie King was declared the first citizen of the
Dominion of Canada, saying, "The unity of Canada belongs not to
Canada alone, it belongs to mankind." He went on to say, "Only by

extending throughout the world the ideas of mutual tolerance, of racial co-operation of equality among men, which form the basis of Canada's nationhood, can nationality come to serve humanity." Moreover, he added, "In making nationality the servant and not the master in world affairs, Canada today is giving mankind its greatest hope for the future." Through his statement, King suggested a new attitude for Canada and Canadians. Furthermore, in the ceremony, the Canadian government paid tribute to those who built the country and to those who fought for freedom during the war by awarding citizenship to, among others, an eighty-seven-year-old Ukrainian settler from Alberta and a Winnipeg mother of a WWII pilot posthumously awarded the Victoria Cross.

However, the way the Polish veterans were treated and written about resulted in a negative transgenerational impact that still informs how the Polish diaspora sees itself in Canada. The Polish diaspora today is much larger and includes descendants of the veterans and those Polish immigrants who came here until the early 1990s when the immigration criteria for Poles changed after the collapse of Communism in the Soviet Union in 1989. It is a diverse community and naturally has to account for differing histories and experiences.

The description of the Polish veterans' community in Calgary— formed after the Polish veterans finished their farm contracts and settled in the city, creating and strengthening the Polish community—is in tune with the narrative of a supportive diaspora lending a helping hand to those in need. The veterans, unable to return to their homeland, moved to a foreign country. They did retain a collective memory of their home and cultivated their knowledge of its history and achievements. Also, they believed that they were not fully accepted by their host society and because of that felt alienated from it. Moreover, they regarded their homeland as their true and ideal home. Some reported that they believed that they should be committed to the restoration of the motherland and still hoped to return there. These beliefs led to their involvement in building and strengthening the Polish community in Calgary, which not only contributed to the growth of the Polish diaspora but also served as a form of support for them during their early years of immigration. The Polish diaspora in Calgary acted as a counterbalance to their sense of alienation and gave the Polish veterans a sense of belonging and positive identity.

The stories of Nieumierzycki, Niewiński, Rogowski and Koselak are about survival, loyalty, determination and moral values. They narrated their hopes from the time of their youth, their pain of losing their homes and family members when they were deported. They demonstrated their determination when, despite the high human cost of war they witnessed and experienced, they all put their lives on the line to fight for freedom, only to find themselves in another situation they did not deserve. After joining the Polish Resettlement Corps and coming to Canada, they were transformed from soldiers to supplicants with very little attention paid to their well-being, to the conditions in which they were housed and worked, before being given landed-immigrant status. After they fulfilled the terms of their two-year contracts, they went on to rebuild lives in a new and unfamiliar situation, with limited knowledge of the language and with little access to education, or counselling to deal with the effects of the trauma they experienced during the war. They were seen as undeserving of a similar status and assistance as the Canadian veterans received. For decades, in Poland, they were considered outcasts since they had never accepted the Soviet domination of their country. In Calgary, Alberta, Canada, their stories were not shared with the public. Thus, the stories told by the Polish WWII veterans here offer a way to share their personal and collective pain so Canada, as well as Poland, may remember their sacrifices.

Notes

Preface

1. *Stowarzyszenie Polskich Kombatantów (SPK) w Kanadzie, Koło Nr 18
   w Calgary.*

2. The Polish Combatants' Association refers to its members as "combatants."
   In Canada the word most often used to refer to a soldier who participated
   in a war is "veteran." In scholarly sources reviewed for this publication,
   the II Polish Army Corps soldiers who joined the Polish Resettlement
   Corps after the war were referred to as "ex-servicemen." Terms such
   as "combatants," "veterans," and "ex-servicemen" will be considered
   interchangeable in this book, referring to the II Polish Army Corps soldiers
   who fought in WWII.

3. For a detailed note regarding languages and translations in the book, see
   note 1 in Chapter 6. When referring to place names and names of people,
   for the most part, I used present-day Polish and Russian spellings.

4. The terms "pro-Soviet," "Soviet-influenced," and "Soviet-dominated" refer
   to Poland's Provisional Government of National Unity established on

June 28, 1945, in Lublin in the territory liberated by the Soviet army and the 1 Polish Army, and subsequent Polish governments in power until the summer of 1989, which marked the fall of Communism in Poland.

1 From Citizens to Prisoners

1. The phrase used in this book "on the territory of" refers to the fact that boundaries and borders shifted during wartime.

2. The expectations Poland had for Great Britain's and France's involvement were based on the Anglo-Polish Agreement of Mutual Assistance signed on August 25, 1939, and the Kasprzycki–Gamelin Military Protocol signed on May 19, 1939 in Paris.

3. The correct spelling for the name of the Polish President at that time is Ignacy Mościcki.

2 From Prisoners to Soldiers

1. As early as 1943, there were attempts to determine the number of those who died during the Nazi and Soviet attacks on Poland in 1939 and during their 1939–1945 occupation of Poland. *Polska 1939–1945 Straty Osobowe i Ofiary Represji pod Dwiema Okupacjami* (2009), edited by Wojciech Materski and Tomasz Szarota, provides the results of the latest research conducted by two generations of historians. It is believed the estimates of losses calculated before the collapse of Communism in Poland in 1989, were inflated "as Poland lost the war and was under foreign and imposed power."

2. Census data of 1921 and 1931. The mosaic also comprised Lithuanians, Czechs, Tatars, as well as the ethnic minorities Łemkowie, Bojkowie, Huculi.

3. This fact was discovered later, as documented in diplomatic papers. (See document 248, "Memorandum of Conversation, by the Under Secretary of

State," by Sumner Welles, dated February 19, 1943, Office of the Historian, https://history.state.gov.)

4. Wilno, Vilno, Vilnius—this is the same city known by Polish, Russian, and Lithuanian names. The Polish name appears in parentheses.

5. Per Materski and Szarota (2009).

6. Quoting this declaration by Molotov on November 2, 1939, Anders believed that about 300,000 Polish troops had been detained after the Soviet invasion of Poland.

7. Anders stated that of the 1.5 million Poles deported to the Soviet Union at the beginning of war, half were already dead from exhaustion, malnutrition or starvation, and illnesses at the time of evacuation. The others were working in labour camps and in kolkhozes.

8. PAI Force: Persia (modern Iran) and Iraq Force.

9. The Soviet decision detailed: "All inhabitants of the western districts of the Ukraine and the Bielo-Russian Soviet Republic who were therein at the time of their incorporation (November 1–2, 1939) in the Soviet Union had acquired Soviet citizenship."

10. Edmund Stevens was staff correspondent of the *Christian Science Monitor*, and had recently returned from a year's tour of duty in the Middle East.

3 *From Soldiers to Stateless Immigrants*

1. Tomasz Arciszewski was prime minister of the Polish government-in-exile in London at the time.

2. The government-in-exile existed from 1939 until December 22, 1990.

3. Norman Fairclough, Jane Mulderrig and Ruth Wodak, scholars of discourse analysis, argue, "Discourse is always connected to other discourses which were produced earlier, as well as those which are produced synchronically and subsequently." The role of discourse analysis is to uncover the

relationships between discursive, social and cultural changes, which are present in various forms of textual communication. The production of the text is linked to social and cultural practices that influence the text... Therefore, the press and newspapers are seen as platforms for creating of discourses.

4   *The Immigrant as Ethnic*

1.   Per American sociologist Talcott Parsons (1975).

2.   According to German sociologist Max Weber, as cited by Malešević (2004).

3.   Per Siniša Malešević (2004), a sociologist interested in ethnicity and nationalism, who furthered the understanding of ethnicity presented by Max Weber.

4.   According to professor of law and political science, Donald Horowitz (1975).

5.   According to Kelley and Trebilcock's review (1998, 2010) of the major legislative immigration and citizenship acts in Canada.

6.   Approximately 6 USD at the time.

7.   Out of the first 1,700 admitted and checked, only one was Jewish, illustrating not only how selective the Canadian immigration policies were but also how few Jewish people served in the II Polish Army Corps since they were forbidden to leave the USSR.

8.   In a later analysis of the effectiveness of the Polish Resettlement Program from an economic perspective, Thornton (1989) confirmed the farm wages paid to the Polish soldiers in August 1946 were $30 below the average for farm workers at that time in Canada.

9.   Per Kelley and Trebilcock (1998, 2010).

5 Polish Veterans and Canadian Veterans

1. During an international meeting held May 5, 1944, Mackenzie King stated that Canada had an interest in Europe because of the population of Poles and Ukrainians. However, as Thornton (1989) notes, Canada was not going to "concern itself in depth with all Europe's problems...'In matters such as regional groupings, boundary disputes, dynastic successions or the form of government in a particular country, they might not be so primarily concerned.'"

2. Per Minister Fiederkiewicz, a former envoy in Canada, as quoted by Thornton (1989).

6 Interviewing the Veterans

1. A note regarding the language and translation: I made every effort to present the stories as they were shared with me and to preserve individual styles in a context and way they could be understood by readers in English. While translating the interview transcripts and other information acquired from various sources, I edited and sometimes paraphrased (when necessary) to create a chronological and logical storyline with minimal repetitions. The speakers sometimes used a different dialect or interwove Anglicized or Russified Polish words, or other languages into their everyday speech.

7 Anatol (Tony) Nieumierzycki (1923–2017)

1. *Żołnierze Polscy, Którzy Byli w Rosji w Walce o Wolność / The Poles Who Went To and Through Russia in Fight for Freedom / I Soldati Polacchi che Sono Stati in Russia in Lotta per la Liberta,* translated and edited by Lucjan Paff, 1945, Rome, Rererat (Referat) Kultury i Prasy Kresowej Dywizji Piechoty.

2. NKVD, or the People's Commissariat for Internal Affairs, was the interior ministry of the Soviet Union.

8 Władysław (Walter) Niewiński (1918–2012)

1. "The Red Poppies at Monte Casino"

Red poppies at Monte Cassino
Instead of dew, were drinking Polish blood
Through these poppies walked soldier and perished
But stronger than death was his wrath
Years go by and centuries will pass
The traces of old days will last
And all the poppies at Monte Cassino
Will be redder because from Polish gore they'll grow

Lyrics by Feliks Konarski, music by Alfred Longin Schutz.

Selected Reading

World War II

Władysław Anders narrated his interesting and invaluable perspective of the history of the II Polish Army Corps in his out-of-print book *An Army in Exile* (Macmillan, 1949). Regarding the British Eighth Army, of which the Anders Army was a part in the Italian Campaign, two books I consulted were: *The War: Fifth Year* by Edgar McInnis (Oxford University Press, 1945) and *Cassino, The Hollow Victory: The Battle for Rome January–June 1944* by J. Ellis (Andre Deutsch, 1984). The details of the movement of the German armies after the attack on the territory of Poland on September 1, 1939 were found in *World War II: The Definitive Encyclopedia and Document Collection, Vol. 1*, edited by Spencer Tucker (ABC-CLIO, 2016).

Media

To analyze the reaction to the events unfolding in Poland and in Europe, I examined both the headlines and the content of the news and editorials in available copies of the *Montreal Gazette*, *The Calgary Herald*, *Edmonton Journal*, *The Ottawa Citizen*, and *The Evening Citizen* (Ottawa) and in particular compared the content of the local newspapers in Alberta with that of Montreal and Ottawa—Canada's capital city. I also reviewed coverage I found of the Polish veterans in the other Canadian newspapers, such as *The Windsor Daily Star*, *Winnipeg Free Press* and *Toronto Daily Star*. The *Maple Leaf* newspaper published for the Canadian Armed Forces was helpful while I was exploring the portrayal of the II Polish Army Corp at the Battle of Monte Cassino. I also looked at articles in London's *Times* (regarding the Resettlement Act), the Soviet newspaper *Pravda* (for its lack of reporting on the deportation and the resettlement of the Polish population) and *Nowa Gazeta Tomaszowska* and *Dziennik Łódzki*, in Polish. *The Fog of War: Censorship of Canada's Media in World War Two* by Mark Bourrie (Douglas & McIntyre, 2011) informed my research about the Canadian media during WWII.

Historical Documents

The Avalon Project was my resource for essential documents in law, history and diplomacy (http://avalon.law.yale.edu). Examples included relevant documents on the Sikorski–Mayski Military Agreement, also known as Polish–Soviet Union Agreement, July 30, 1941; the 1943 Tehran, the 1945 Yalta, and the 1945 Potsdam WWII strategy conferences; and the Molotov–Ribbentrop Pact and its (secret additional) Protocol, German–Soviet Boundary and Friendship Treaty of September 28, 1939.

The British War Bluebook provided information on the Anglo-Polish Agreement of Mutual Assistance, London, August 25, 1939.

The text of the Kasprzycki–Gamelin Military Protocol was found on the website of Poland's Instytut Pamięci Narodowej (Institute of National Remembrance): https://ipn.gov.pl/.

Poland

The Institute of National Remembrance—Commission for the Prosecution of Crimes against the Polish Nation was established by the Polish Parliament in 1998 and proved especially useful for material in Polish, including information on the Second Polish Republic. The record of Poles arrested, imprisoned as POWs and sent to labour camps in various locations in the USSR was located in the institute's Index of Repressed at http://indeksrepresjonowanych.pl/int/ wyszukiwanie/94,Wyszukiwanie.html. The casualties of the Polish population were recorded in a book published in Polish in 2009 by this same institute: *Polska 1939–1945: Straty Osobowe i Ofiary Represji pod Dwiema Okupacjami* (Poland 1939–1945: Personal Losses and Victims of Repression under the Two Occupations) edited by Wojciech Materski and Tomasz Szarota. The website also provides an English version and some of the data.

Rzeczypospolita Londyńska: 1940–1990, on the website of the Polish Embassy UK, provided information about the activity of the exiled Polish authorities and the wider Polish émigré community in Britain both during WWII and in the postwar period up until the political breakthrough of 1989–1991: www.msz.gov. pl/en/p/rie_gb_en/republic_in_exile/.

Britain

Exploring the reaction of the British government to the events of the war in Poland, and later, the creation of the Resettlement Act, the records of the British House of Commons Hansard (among other sources) were useful. A general link to the Hansard, the official report of debates in parliament of Great Britain can be found at https://api.parliament.uk/historic-hansard/index.html. Two debates of particular interest regarding the situation in Poland occurred on September 20, 1939, and December 15, 1944.

United States

The Office of Historian provided information on foreign relations and diplomatic papers of the United States and, in particular, specific reaction to the events surrounding the conflicts between Poland and the Soviet Union during WWII (https://history.state.gov/about). Information on the transcript of the Lend-Lease Act (1941) was found via A National Initiative on American History, Civics, and Service at www.ourdocuments.gov/.

The USSR

For information on Joseph Stalin's correspondence with the Union of Polish Patriots, I examined the Josef Stalin Internet Archive located at www.marxists.org/reference/archive/stalin/index.htm.

Canada

Managing the Canadian Mosaic in Wartime: Shaping Citizenship Policy, 1939–1945, by Ivana Caccia (McGill-Queen's University Press, 2010) is an excellent read on Canada's immigration policies. Researching how Canadian immigration policies were shaped throughout the years, starting from the pre-Confederation time until the 1990s, I also consulted *The Making of the Mosaic: A History of Canadian Immigration Policy*, by Ninette Kelley and Michael J. Trebilcock (University of Toronto Press, 1998 and 2010). Settlement in this country over the centuries, and how immigration policies have helped to define the character of immigration in various periods, is covered in political and social historian Valerie Knowles' *Strangers at our Gates: Canadian Immigration and Immigration Policy, 1540–2006* (Dundurn Group, 1997). Also helpful was *The Shaping of Peace: Canada and the Search for World Order, 1943-1957, Vol. 1* (University of Toronto Press, 1979) written by influential essayist John W. Holmes, following his career in the Department of External Affairs. John Porter's classic text, *The Vertical Mosaic. An Analysis of Social Class and Power in Canada* (University of Toronto Press, 1965), offered background in his study of the relationship between social class and power in Canadian society.

For information on the Polish Resettlement Corps, I consulted several articles by Martin Thornton, a senior lecturer in International History and Politics at the Centre of Canadian Studies, at the University of Leeds, UK, who had looked into the decision making regarding the resettlement of Polish ex-servicemen after World War II, including "The Second Polish Corps, 1943-46: Were They a Functional Mixture of Soldiers, Refugees and Social Workers?" in the *Journal of Slavic Military Studies* (1997, vol. 10, no. 2), and "The Resettlement in Canada of 4,527 Polish Ex-servicemen, 1946-47" in *Immigrants & Minorities* (1989, vol.8, no. 3).

And for statistical data related to immigrants to Canada, such as the average wages of male farm help, and the numbers and circulations of daily and weekly foreign-language newspapers, I consulted Statistics Canada: *Immigrant arrivals in Canada, 1892 to 1946*; and *Canada Year Book 1942*; and *Canada Year Book, 1947.*

For information on the philosophy and program of the Veterans Charter with a focus on specific benefits of the charter, I referred to work of Don Ives, "The Veterans Charter: The Compensation Principle and the Principle of Recognition for Service." This chapter is part of *The Veterans Charter and Post-World War II Canada* edited by Peter Neary and J.L. Granatstein (McGill-Queen's University Press, 1998). In this same book, the work of Desmond Morton, "Canadian Veterans' Heritage from the Great War" provided information on compensation for the Canadian veterans from WWI. The website of The Loyal Edmonton Regiment Museum also provided information on veterans' rights.

Ethnicity

These sources in particular helped illuminate my understanding of ideas about ethnicity. *Ethnicity: Theory and Experience* (1975), edited by Nathan Glazer and Daniel Patrick Moynihan, contains two chapters that were especially useful: "Some Theoretical Considerations on the Nature and Trends of Change of Ethnicity" by Talcott Parsons, and "Ethnic Identity" by Donald L. Horowitz. Additionally, I referred to *The Sociology of Ethnicity* (2004) by Siniša Malešević, who, along with his own studies, cites important work done in the early twentieth century by German sociologist Max Weber.

Interviews

In addition to my interviews with Władysław Niewiński, Anatol Nieumierzycki and Zbigniew Rogowski, as well as Stefan Koselak's surviving family, Ewa Koselak and Chris Fisher, I also reviewed available interviews of Władysław Niewiński and Anatol Nieumierzycki posted on YouTube. Moreover, I examined memoirs written by Władysław Niewiński and Anatol Nieumierzycki.

Index

aftermath, *164*, 235
cemetery and burials, *236*, *240*,
    241, *242*, 264
Koselak's experience, 234, 242–43
Nieumierzycki's experience, 129
Niewiński's experience, 159–60,
    162–66
overview, 40–41, 42–44, 45–48,
    263
perception by soldiers, 101–02
Polish casualties, 48
"The Red Poppies at Monte
    Cassino" (song), 135, 290n1
Rogowski's experience, 193–202,
    218–19
stole taken by Niewiński, *165*, *166*,
    175
behavioural assimilation, 82
Berling, Zygmunt, 51, 52
Berling Army (1 Polish Army), 51–52,
    52–53, 54, 118, 135–36
Bevin, Ernest, 58, 61–62, 118
Białecki, Lieutenant, 241
Bohusz-Szyszko, Zygmunt, 25, 168
Bologna, Battle of, 49, 243, 246
Bonefox, George, 210–11
Bourrie, Mark, 66
Burns Ranch, 125–26

Caccia, Ivana, 67
The Calgary Herald
    on anti-Polish sentiment in
        England, 275
    on Canadian citizenship, 282–83
    on Canadian veterans, 92–94
    on German POWs, 282

impact on public perceptions, 15
on invasion of Poland, 6–9, 12–15
portrayals of Polish veterans in
    Alberta, 78, 84–85, 85–86, 120,
    271, 275–76, 280–81
Canada
    admittance of Polish refugees, 76
    admittance of Polish veterans,
        59, 77–78, 81, 87–88, 269–70,
        288n7
    assimilation expectations for
        immigrants, 68–69, 81–82
    Canadian citizenship, 79, 282–83
    civil liberty restrictions during
        WWII, 74
    concerns about immigrants, 82–83
    immigration policies and
        restrictions, 73–74, 75, 76–77,
        79–80, 88
    interest in European problems,
        289n1
    Montreal Gazette on Canadian
        entry in WWII, 10–11
    Polish veterans as "other," 67–68
    See also Polish Resettlement Corps
Canadian Citizenship Act (1947), 79
Canadian media
    impacts on public perceptions, 15
    on invasion of Poland, 4–12, 12–15
    on Polish government-in-exile,
        36–38
    portrayals of Polish veterans,
        63–68, 83–85, 85–86, 269, 271,
        275–76, 280–81
    reportage of military details, 6

Canadian Polish Congress, 277

Canadian veterans

    double standard in treatment, 94

    educational assistance, 92

    housing for, 93–94

    legislative supports, 90–91

    war brides, 92–93

Castle, J.P., 275

cemeteries

    significance for Polish people,
       261–62

Chamberlain, Neville, 18–19

chocolate rations, 198

Christianity, 152–53, 182, 183

Chuchla, Walter Frank, 122–23, 171,
    274

Churchill, Winston, 34, 41–42, 45,
    56, 102

citizenship

    Canadian citizenship, 79, 282–83

    eligibility for Polish Resettlement
       Corps members, 59

    Koselak's experience, 237, 238

    loss of Polish citizenship, 60,
       62–63, 118, 168

    Nieumierzycki's experience, 118,
       127

    Niewiński's experience, 136, 138

    Polish citizenship, 28

    refusal to accept Soviet citizenship,
       20, 145

    Rogowski's experience, 219

    Soviet view of Poles as Soviet
       citizens, 30–31, 36, 287n9

Civil Employment Acts, 91

collective farms, *see* kolkhoz
    (collective farms)

Curzon Line, 41, 52, 54, 102

Danzig, Free City of (Gdańsk), 3, 4–5,
    7, 21

deportation, to USSR

    Anders on, 287n7

    Nieumierzycki's experience, 20,
       22, 107–08, 110–12

    overview, 20–21, 22–23, 99

    Rogowski's experience, 20, 21, 180

diaspora, 72–73

discourse analysis, 287n3

dog tags, 129–30

Easter, 152–53. *See also* Christianity

EC&M Company, 123–24, 127

Edmonton Journal, 64–66, 270,
    272–73, 276

education

    Canadian veterans, 91, 92

    Polish veterans, 57, 81

    Rogowski's experience on
       collective farm, 182

English language, 68, 121, 239, 260,
    271, 277

entrance status, 81

ethnicity, 71–72. *See also* diaspora

The Evening Citizen (Ottawa
    newspaper), 11–12, 15, 36–38

Fairclough, Norman, 287n3

Fiedler, Arkady, 118, 130–31

Fish Creek Provincial Park, 126

Fisher, Chris (Stefan Koselak's
daughter)
author's introduction to, 221–22,
227
childhood, 253, 257
on father's illness, 237
reflections on father's life, 228,
256, 259–60
research on father's story, 246,
248, 258–59
visit to Poland, 259, 261, 265–66
See also Koselak, Stefan
Foch, Ferdinand, 128
food, military rations, 198

Gdańsk, *see* Danzig, Free City of
German POWs
Calgary Herald on, 282
perception of Polish veterans as
replacement for, 66–67, 73,
78–79, 120, 270, 282
Germany
Canadian media on invasion of
Poland, 4–9
invasion of Poland, 3–4
invasion of USSR, 23–24
partition of Poland with USSR, 12
Polish POWs captured by, 19
Gorzkowska, Barbara, 280–81
Great Britain
anti-Polish sentiment, 275
encouragement of Polish soldiers
to return to Poland, 57–58,
61–62, 106, 168
II Polish Army Corps and, 25, 28

Polish Resettlement Corps, 58,
77–78
grenades, 200, 201
Gurkha soldiers, 42, 197

Hardy, H.R., 64–67, 68–69
Harriman, W. Averell, 27, 52–53,
53–54
health care, assistance for new Polish
immigrants, 131–32, 277
Hitler, Adolf, 4–5
Holmes, John, 80
housing, for Canadian veterans,
93–94

Immigration Act (1952), 79, 80
immigration and immigrants
admittance of Polish refugees, 76
admittance of Polish veterans,
59, 77–78, 81, 87–88, 269–70,
288n7
Canadian policies and restrictions,
73–74, 75, 76–77, 79–80, 88,
288n7
concerns about immigrants, 82–83
expectations for immigrants,
68–69, 81–82
war brides, 92–93
Iran
military training in, 30
Niewiński's experience, 150–53,
151, 155
Polish army evacuation to, 27, 28,
29–30
Rogowski's experience, 191–92
Israel, *see* Palestine

NKVD, 113, 141, 156, 289n2

Ostkierko, Anna, 224

Palestine, 158, 159, 192–93
patriotism, 100–01, 136
Penski, Sergeant, 150
Persia, *see* Iran
Poland
    Berling on pro-Soviet government,
        52
    Big Three discussions on, 41–42,
        54–55, 55–56, 102
    border conflicts with USSR, 21–22
    Communist presentation of war
        history, 135–36, 139–40
    demographics pre-invasion, 17–18
    evacuation of displaced Poles from
        Russia, 155–56, 158–59
    overseas travel during Cold War,
        264–65
    Provisional Government of
        National Unity, 54–55, 57, 60,
        106, 285n4
    remembrance of ancestors, 261–62
    treatment of Poles as Soviet
        citizens, 30–31, 36, 287n9
    See also Poland, government-in-
        exile; Poland, invasion during
        WWII
Poland, government-in-exile
    awareness of by Poles in USSR, 113
    derecognition by Big Three, 55,
        102
    duration of, 287n2
    Evening Citizen on, 36–38

Polish army and, 24–25, 27, 28, 38,
    102
post-Communist Poland and, 174
relationship with USSR, 24–25,
    30–32, 33–36
Sikorski–Mayski Agreement (1941),
    24
Sikorski's death and, 39
Poland, invasion during WWII
    Canadian media on, 4–12, 12–15
    deportation of civilians to USSR,
        20–21, 22–23, 99
    evacuation of Polish government,
        19
    expectations for Western
        assistance, 4, 286n2
    by Germany, 3–4
    massacre of Polish officers by
        Soviets, 32–33, 34
    partition between Germany and
        USSR, 12
    Polish casualties, 17, 18, 286n1
    Polish POWs, 19–20, 28, 287n6
    by USSR, 4, 18–19
Polish Canadian Association of
    Calgary (Polish Alliance), 123,
    127, 276
Polish Canadian Cultural Centre, vii,
    173, 176, 277, 278
Polish Citizenship Act (1920), 28, 60
Polish Combatants' Association
    author's introduction to, 134
    Calgary branch, vii–viii, 173, 276,
    280
    Canadian branches, 172
    establishment, 168

reflections on life in Canada, 215–16

reflections on war experience, 101, 179, 216–18, 278–79, 280

Soviet invasion of Lvov, 179–80

suicidal thoughts, 199–200, 216

work experiences in Alberta, 212–15, 273

Rokita (barber), 274

Rola-Żymierski, Michał, 62

Roosevelt, Franklin D., 34, 35, 102

Royal Canadian Legion, 216, 277

Safran, William, 72–73

sappers, 243

Saskatchewan

Polish veterans' experiences, 88–89

Sikorski, Władysław

death, 39

diplomacy by, 24, 31, 32, 34, 56

Evening Citizen on, 36

II Polish Army Corps and, 25, 26, 27, 28, 38

Niewiński on, 174

Sikorski–Mayski Agreement (1941), 24, 31, 113

Skorpion tank regiment, *see* 4th Armoured Regiment (Skorpions), II Polish Army Corps

Sosnkowski, Kazimierz, 39, 44

Soviet army

Niewiński's experience, 141–43, 144, 145–46

Poles drafted by, 20, 23

See also 1 Polish Army (Berling Army); Union of Soviet Socialist Republics (USSR)

SS *Sea Snipe*, 118–19, 209–10, 248, 251

Stalin, Joseph, 28–29, 32–33, 34, 36, 54, 102, 156, 181

Stevens, Edmund, 37–38, 287n10

structural assimilation, 82

suicidal thoughts, 68, 199–200, 216

Swanson, Frank, 275

Szarota, Tomasz, 286n1

tanks, *see* 4th Armoured Regiment (Skorpions), II Polish Army Corps

Tehran Conference (1943), 55, 102

telecommunications, 124, 129

Thornton, Martin, 69–70, 87, 88, 90, 270, 272, 288n8, 289n1

The Times (London newspaper), 59, 60, 61, 62, 63

Toronto Daily Star, 63–64

Treaty of Riga (1921), 22

Trebilcock, Michael J., 74

Truman, Harry S., 55

Tworkowski, Dr., 153, 155

uniforms, military, 85, 121, 166, 175, 235, 258, 272

Union of Polish Patriots, 35, 36

Union of Soviet Socialist Republics (USSR)

1 Polish Army (Berling Army), 51–52, 52–53, 54, 118, 135–36

Churchill support for, 41–42

Other Titles from University of Alberta Press

The Little Third Reich on Lake Superior
A History of Canadian Internment Camp R

Ernest Robert Zimmermann

Michel S. Beaulieu & David K. Ratz, Editors

Accessible history of the controversial POW camp run during World War II in northern Ontario.

The Stories Were Not Told
Canada's First World War Internment Camps

Sandra Semchuk

Through oral history and photography, Semchuk examines the consequences of Canada's first internment camps.

Surviving the Gulag
A German Woman's Memoir

Ilse Johansen

Heather Marshall, Editor

Hans Rudolf Gahler, Translator

Personal narrative of a German woman surviving five years in Russian prison camps.

More information at www.uap.ualberta.ca